THE ILLIBERAL IMAGINATION

THE ILLIBERAL IMAGINATION

Class and the Rise of the U.S. Novel

Joe Shapiro

University of Virginia Press

Charlottesville and London

University of Virginia Press
© 2017 by the Rector and Visitors of the University of Virginia
All rights reserved
Printed in the United States of America on acid-free paper

First published 2017

9 8 7 6 5 4 3 2 1

Library of Congress Cataloging-in-Publication Data

Names: Shapiro, Joe 1981– author.
Title: The illiberal imagination : class and the rise of the U.S. novel / Joe Shapiro.
Description: Charlottesville : University of Virginia Press, 2017. | Includes
    bibliographical references and index.
Identifiers: LCCN 2017011674 | ISBN 9780813940502 (cloth : alk. paper) | ISBN
    9780813940519 (pbk. : alk. paper) | ISBN 9780813940526 (e-book)
Subjects: LCSH: American fiction—19th century—History and criticism. | Social
    classes in literature. | Social conflict in literature.
Classification: LCC PS374.S68 S53 2017 | DDC 813/.309355—dc23
LC record available at https://lccn.loc.gov/2017011674

Cover art: "The sight of this weapon secured the victory, the black faced villain
shrinking back into a corner begging piteously not to be shot," by Felix Octavius Carr
Darley for *The Redskins,* James Fenimore Cooper (New York: W. A. Townsend & Co.,
1860). (Courtesy of the American Antiquarian Society)

Contents

Acknowledgments

First, hearty thanks go to Angie Hogan at the University of Virginia Press, to the press readers, and to my copy editor, Ruth Melville.

This book began as a dissertation at Stanford University. I was fortunate to take courses there with John Bender, Terry Castle, Amir Eshel, Shelley Fisher Fishkin, Jay Fliegelman, Roland Greene, Seth Lerer, Hayden White, Alex Woloch, and Bryan Wolff. I owe the members of my dissertation committee—Franco Moretti, Gavin Jones, Ezra Tawil, and Nancy Ruttenburg—massive intellectual debts. I also benefited from the brilliance of my fellow students at Stanford: Sarah Allison, Mike Benveniste, Joel Burges, Nigel Hatton, Heather Houser, Ju Yon Kim, Kenny Ligda, David Marno, Christopher Phillips, Jayson Gonzales Sae-Saue, Nikil Saval, Claire Seiler, Nirvana Tanoukhi, and Jennifer Harford Vargas taught me heaps.

The path that led to this book began at Brown University. Nancy Armstrong and Leonard Tennenhouse first introduced me to the theory of the novel. Jim Egan and Philip Gould got me hooked on early and nineteenth-century American literature. I'm very pleased to have the opportunity here to thank these formative influences on me for their excellent teaching and for their guidance.

At Southern Illinois University, David Anthony and George Boulukos read drafts, helped me to see this book to completion, and steered me through "probation"; Ed Brunner, Anne Chandler, Betsy Dougherty, K. K. Collins, Dave Johnson, Elizabeth Klaver, Eric Lenz, Lisa McClure, Scott McEathron, Ryan Netzley, Rachel Stocking, Jonathan Wiesen, and Natasha Zaretsky have shared their professional wisdom with me; Scott

Blackwood, Laurel Fredrickson, and Jacob Haubenreich have been the best of comrades.

Harris Feinsod has been my most important interlocutor since long before I got started on the project that became *The Illiberal Imagination;* this book has been the beneficiary not only of Harris's generous feedback and sage counsel on it from its infancy to its final shape but also of his enduring friendship. Matt Garrett has permitted me to bounce this book off of him at least one time too many, but he has also helped me to think more carefully about the bigger picture.

Finally, I want to express my gratitude to my family—and to Haley Farthing. This book wouldn't be without her, but I owe her so much more than that.

A version of chapter 3 first appeared in *American Literary History* 27.2 (2015); it is reprinted with the permission of Oxford University Press. Under the title "White Slaves in the Late-Eighteenth- and Nineteenth-Century American Literary Imagination," portions of chapter 5 were published in *The Cambridge Companion to Slavery in American Literature,* ed. Ezra Tawil (New York: Cambridge University Press, 2016); they are reprinted here with the permission of Cambridge University Press.

THE ILLIBERAL IMAGINATION

INTRODUCTION

The title of this book, *The Illiberal Imagination*, is meant to evoke two much earlier books: Lionel Trilling's *The Liberal Imagination* (1950) and Louis Hartz's *The Liberal Tradition in America* (1955). And it is intended to emphasize that this book is in large part an argument with the understanding of U.S. literary history for which these earlier books laid the foundation.

In the United States, Trilling famously argued, "the real basis of the novel has never existed—that is, the tension between a middle class and an aristocracy which brings manners into observable relief as the living representation of ideals and the living comment on ideas. Our class structure has been extraordinarily fluid."[1] That class tensions do not shape nineteenth-century U.S. fiction, Trilling contends, is evident in what he calls the "great characters of American fiction, such, say, as Captain Ahab and Natty Bumppo": these characters "tend to be mythic," Trilling writes, "because of the rare fineness and abstractness of the ideas they represent; and their *very freedom from class* gives them a large and glowing generality."[2] Likewise, Hartz argued that U.S. political history is free from class conflict, insofar as the unfolding of U.S. political history is divorced from the eighteenth- and nineteenth-century conflicts between aristocracy and bourgeoisie that for Hartz sowed the seeds of later radicalism in Europe.[3] For these founding figures of American studies, the United States is exceptional not only because it lacks an aristocracy. Rather, the United States is exceptional because working-class radicalism is inorganic to it, or, in other words, fundamentally insignificant to its culture and politics. And working-class radicalism is inorganic to the United States, so the story goes, because in the United

States individuals do not think of themselves as members of classes or as shaped by class processes, but instead as self-possessing individuals in a society that is essentially fluid.[4] If individual aspirations are thwarted in the United States, this is understood to be an effect of identity categories such as race, gender, or ethnicity, and not class per se.[5] In this sense, the United States is liberal through and through.

Can we, though, really characterize the early U.S. bourgeoisie and its literature as "liberal"? Do we find an unambiguous celebration of possessive individualism—of "market society," of a socioeconomic order in which "market relations . . . shape or permeate all social relations"?[6] Not precisely. According to a number of recent studies, early and antebellum novels reveal members of the U.S. bourgeoisie to be in fact deeply anxious about their participation in market relations, and about the consequences for themselves of economic individualism and market-based competition. Moreover, scholars have found that the individualisms expressed by early and antebellum literature are far from patently liberal.[7] We can now say that the bourgeois self that is articulated by early and antebellum U.S. literature is internally divided—a bundle of tensions and contradictory attitudes—where the market is concerned.

Even so, the Cold War exceptionalism of Trilling and Hartz continues to haunt the study of pre–Civil War U.S. literature in general and the study of the pre–Civil War U.S. novel in particular. Granted, the novel is now often understood to function not as a reflection of a world in which class does not matter but as a discourse linked to a specific class, namely, "the middle class."[8] In other words, the novel and what are taken to be its core logics—its commitment to individual self-making, to social fluidity, and to the notion of middle-classness as widely or even universally attainable for white citizens in the United States—are understood to be central to *middle-class ideology* in the nineteenth-century United States.[9] Yet, theories of the early and antebellum U.S. novel, despite assuming a link between the novel and middle-class ideology, often tend to assume the total dominance of liberal individualism in U.S. culture. As Amy Schrager Lang argues, "The understanding of the middle class that predominates in scholarship on American literature posits a middle class so 'triumphant' that it not only '[takes] itself for granted' but frames and articulates a possessive individualism so widely embraced as to be the common property of Americans regardless of their place in the scheme of production or, indeed, of consumption."[10] If the novel articulates middle-class ideology, it could not have done anything but this: just as with Trilling and Hartz, the common sense behind much scholarship on nineteenth-century U.S. literature is that what has now come to be understood as *the* middle-class ideology is not merely dominant in the United States but always already universal.[11]

In contrast to the liberal consensus model of U.S. literary history, my argument in *The Illiberal Imagination* is that the consolidation of the early U.S. novel *includes* the representation of class inequality and class struggle, and that the early U.S. novel helps to consolidate the U.S. bourgeoisie precisely through its representations of class inequality and class struggle.[12] Here, protest against capitalist economic inequality is both organic to early U.S. social history and central to early U.S. literary history. In each of the chapters that follow, I call attention to the extent to which early and antebellum U.S. novels met the challenge of antiliberal, oppositional arguments "from below" to class inequality in the new nation. In so doing, I demonstrate that major novelists in the story of what we can call the rise of the U.S. novel—in particular, Charles Brockden Brown, Hugh Henry Brackenridge, Catharine Maria Sedgwick, James Fenimore Cooper, and Harriet Beecher Stowe—all in their respective fashions responded to varieties of radical political economy and to working-class class consciousness that protested capitalist economic inequality in the United States. *The Illiberal Imagination* is thus a fellow traveler with recent scholarship that brings working-class politics and protest front and center in the making of U.S. literature.[13] That said, the implication of major monographs on class and U.S. literature is that class—in the dual sense of economic inequality under capitalism and working-class class consciousness—becomes a part of the story of the U.S. novel only with George Lippard, for novelists that get their respective starts in the 1840s and 1850s, or for novelists who turned their attention to manifestly industrialized forms of production and labor.[14] By reaching back to the late eighteenth century and looking to novelists like Cooper and Stowe, novelists who have been associated largely with conflicts other than ones pertaining specifically to class division among whites, I hope to challenge the received wisdom about the arc of U.S. literature more broadly. Class, class struggle, and class consciousness were a part of the raw material U.S. fiction worked on long before what literary historical common sense would have us suppose.

Moreover, it is not merely that class and class struggle are themes that cut across and bind early U.S. fiction; rather, through the 1840s, a number of major U.S. novelists fashioned novels that, instead of skirting or dodging or veiling socioeconomic division in the United States, work to naturalize class inequality among whites. Which is to say, if literary historians have attended to how early and antebellum U.S. novels perform a denial of the reality of class by staging class mobility, I highlight the ways in which foundational early U.S. novelists in fact invest in, endorse, and ratify structures of economic inequality. The early U.S. novel was as committed to narrating and legitimating the relationship between the so-called middle class and the working class as it was in producing a middle-class evasion of class altogether—or, in producing what Stuart Blumin dubs "an ideology of social atomism."[15] So, while Lockean liberalism functioned in its own way to justify class inequality, because "liberal" in the context of American studies means something like the evasion of class, I instead characterize the early U.S. novel as "illiberal."[16]

I am not arguing that early U.S. novels entirely eschew representing the U.S. in terms of social fluidity and class mobility. Certainly, mobility is "in" the early U.S. novels on which I focus. Charles Brockden Brown's *Arthur Mervyn* is, crudely summarized, the story of a poor young man who becomes finally a member of the bourgeoisie. Hugh Henry Brackenridge's narrator in *Modern Chivalry* tells us that "the offspring of a plain farmer may be a philosopher; a lawyer; a judge."[17] A major character in Catharine Maria Sedgwick's *The Poor Rich Man, and the Rich Poor Man* insists that "the poor family of this generation is the rich family of the next."[18] And in James Fenimore Cooper's Littlepage trilogy, poor but virtuous heroines marry "up" into elite, landowning families.

I am arguing, though, that U.S. novelists through the 1840s work to construe the existence of class inequality as natural, right, and desirable. Indeed, for early U.S. novelists, white men and their families are not, will not, or—and this is crucial—should not become "middle class" or members of one economic class. Not for nothing, in novels published through the 1840s, characters that protest economic inequality, their subordinate positions within the economy, or private accumulation of great fortunes by elites are as a rule also villains—thieves, murderers, would-be dictators. For early U.S. novelists, collective movements to abolish class inequality and to produce a society free of class are to be thought of as supremely dangerous. Where class is concerned, the early U.S. novel is not as utopian as we might expect it to be. Recognizing as much enhances, I would suggest, our understanding both of the early U.S. novel and of the itinerary of bourgeois ideology in the United States.

We might say that the early U.S. novel, rather than denying or evading class through narratives of mobility, mythologizes class.[19] Writes Roland Barthes of myth: "Myth hides nothing and flaunts nothing: it distorts; myth is neither a lie nor a confession: it is an inflexion." For Barthes, myth "transforms history into nature."[20] Between constitutional ratification and the crisis over slavery, "the market revolution" (to use Charles Sellers's apt phrase) exacerbated disparities in wealth in the United States;[21] and, for their part, U.S. novelists through the 1840s offered narratives that teach us that the division of the United States into classes—into rich and poor, into those who own property and those who do not, into those who can buy labor power with accumulated wealth and those who must sell their labor power to survive—is, again, natural, just, and desirable.[22]

Though in conversation with intellectual and labor history, *The Illiberal Imagination* is, as I hope my gesture to Barthes above indicates, finally an inquiry into the *literary* representation of class in the early United States. My goal is to trace how a commitment to economic inequality manifests itself on the level of literary form. To that end, I track the representation of class across five different subgenres of the early U.S. novel: the bildungsroman, the episodic travel novel, the sentimental novel, the frontier romance, and the antislavery novel. Here, class is not the exclusive possession of patently industrial fiction, of fiction about factories and industrial work; instead, class ripples across a diverse array of subgenres of the early U.S. novel. By the same token, I also aim to demonstrate that these different subgenres are keyed to different ways in which class was realized—was manifested—in the early United States.[23] Charles Brockden Brown's bildungsromans *Ormond* and *Arthur Mervyn* deal with poverty and wage labor. Hugh Henry Brackenridge's episodic travel novel *Modern Chivalry* ruminates on radical plebeian notions of class and their political expression. Catharine Maria Sedgwick's sentimental novels of the 1830s, like Brown's bildungsromans, are about poverty and wage labor, and they explicitly address socialist and working-class polemics that construed Christianity and economic inequality as antithetical to one another. The frontier romances of James Fenimore Cooper's Anti-Rent trilogy turn on property rights in land, responding directly both to agrarian radicalism and to working-class land reformers who insisted that the unequal distribution of land was the source of economic inequality and exploitation in the United States. Harriet Beecher Stowe's antislavery novel *Dred* stands as a polemic about both slavery and white poverty, directly counters proslavery accounts of inequality and exploitation resulting from capitalism, and taps into white working-class arguments about the relationship between slavery and economic inequality in the United States. *The Illiberal Imagination* explores, then, how different subgenres of the early U.S. novel in their own particular ways mediated specific inflections of oppositional economic egalitarianism. In the final sections of this introduction and in the chapters that follow, I elaborate on precisely how—on the levels of both theme and structure—these different subgenres of the early U.S. novel mythologized class. Early U.S. novels "about" class are, I hope to show, explicitly—loudly and clearly—didactic and moralizing where matters of class are concerned. These novels are on the level of form anything but egalitarian. My contention is that early U.S. novels reproduce inequality—and thereby insist on its naturalness—on the very level of form.[24]

A Structural Definition of Class: Class as Process

But before plunging ahead into analysis proper of novels, a theoretical and historical excursus on "class" is in order.

"One thing," writes Karl Marx in *Capital*, "is clear: nature does not produce on the one hand owners of money or commodities, and on the other hand men possessing nothing but their own labour-power. This relation has no basis in natural history, nor does it have a social basis common to all periods of human history."[25] Marx's point is that capitalism is historical in nature. More specifically, the social relations of economic production that define capitalism are historical in nature. For Marx, capitalism is not merely the exchange of commodities for money on a market. Rather, capitalism is a form of economic production that properly "arises only when the owner of the means of production and subsistence finds the free worker available, on the market, as the seller of his own labour-power."[26] One side of the labor relationship that defines capitalism consists of those who must sell their labor power "in order to live," as Marx puts it in *Wage Labor and Capital*.[27] These "free workers" become available only when they are split off from possession of—dispossessed of—"the means of production and subsistence," when they are no longer themselves owners of productive property. This dispossession itself results from the violent, historical process that Marx dubs "primitive accumulation."[28] On the other side of the capitalist labor relationship are those who have come to possess wealth enough to purchase the labor power of others, and, in so doing, are able to amass even greater wealth. For Marx, the buying of labor power is the source of "profit-making" under capitalism.[29] Marx does not hold that there are not other positions to occupy within capitalism,[30] but he does argue that this relationship is the heart of exploitation under capitalism: it is the "specific economic form" under capitalism by which "unpaid surplus-labour is pumped out of the direct producers."[31]

Furthermore, in *The Communist Manifesto* (and elsewhere) Marx argues that while in previous modes of production "we find almost everywhere a complicated arrangement of society into various orders, a manifold gradation of social rank," capitalist society has "simplified class antagonisms" and is "more and more splitting up into two great hostile camps, into two great classes directly facing each other: Bourgeoisie and Proletariat."[32] Marx thus also proposes a narrative of inevitable class polarization, class struggle, and finally the transcendence of capitalist class relations via revolution.[33]

Varieties of post-Marxism have suggested that Marx's theory and narrative of class fail to capture the actual political identities of individual and collective subjects under capitalism and thus, too, the vectors of political struggle that we find—or might hope to find—under capitalism. According to Wai Chee Dimock and Michael T. Gilmore, "The boundaries of class are unstable, . . . the experience of it is uneven, . . . [class] is necessary but not sufficient for the constitution of human identities."[34] J. K. Gibson-Graham likewise encourages us to recognize that "individuals may participate in a variety of class processes at one moment and over time. Their class identities are therefore potentially multiple and shifting. Their class struggles (over exploitation, or over the distribution of its fruits) may be interpersonal and may not necessarily involve affiliation with a group."[35] Post-Marxism might thus be thought of as a call for a more finely grained class analysis—for an analysis that attends to the complexity and contradictions in class identities, to the intersections of class identity and class exploitation with racial, gendered, and national identities and hierarchies, and thus to the historical vagaries of class politics. As Richard Seymour puts its, "The unity of classes—in pursuit of political objectives or whatever—can no way be assumed."[36]

While we should not assume class to be the sole determinant of subjectivity (or presume class to be the sole category around which political struggles in the present should be organized), we should nonetheless continue to recognize that literature reflects on class in the structural sense of economic exploitation (that is, extraction of surplus value and thus the private, asymmetrical accumulation of wealth). According to Eric Schocket, an anti-essentialist concept of class understands class "apart from its various personifications, objectifications, and reifications."[37] In other words, an anti-essentialist concept of class defines class as a process of exploitation, rather than as a static (and always coherent) identity and location that an individual inhabits within an economic system.[38] As Julian Markels puts it, "To write about class is not necessarily to write about people belonging to a single class at its identity site."[39] An anti-essentialist concept of class-as-process thus "argues against the paradoxical commonplace that class mobility makes class irrelevant within the United States."[40] It likewise recognizes that class-as-process "must be understood to imbricate the [literary] text itself, to inhabit its structure, and to effect its trajectory as a symbolic act."[41]

An anti-essentialist, structural definition of class in which class is recognized as a process of exploitation, as opposed to Marx's theories about the inevitable tendencies of class struggle, is what I mean by *class* throughout *The Illiberal Imagination.*[42] I define class struggle as "the continual battle over the social surplus: how it is produced, how it is appropriated, how it is distributed."[43] I follow E. P. Thompson in defining class consciousness as "consciousness of the identity of the interests of the working class . . . *against* those of other classes" as well as "the claim for an alternative *system.*"[44] To write about class in the early U.S. novel is, I contend, to write about the ways in which early U.S. novelists represent economic exploitation and inequality—as well as opposition to it—under early U.S. capitalism. Indeed, from its beginning, the early U.S. novel was in conversation with writers and activists who protested surplus wealth being "pumped out of" and siphoned away from white workers.

Manifold Inequalities

My attention to the representation of class inequality among whites in the early U.S. novel is governed by the assumption that racism and sexism neither completely explain actual inequalities nor fully capture discourses of inequality in the early United States.[45] In other words, animating *The Illiberal Imagination* is the recognition that early U.S. economic inequality is neither fully subsumed under nor merely a symptom of racial and gender inequality.[46]

Of course, in the early and antebellum United States, racism and sexism were very much fulcrums of asymmetrical labor relations—of class relationships: racial slavery was a class relationship, and so too was the relationship predicated on ideologies of gender difference between women who performed unpaid domestic work and both their husbands and their husbands' employers.[47] The early and antebellum United States is evidence truly that racism and sexism were constitutive of— necessary ingredients in—capitalism's takeoff. Writes Silvia Federici: "Capitalism, as a social-economic system, is necessarily committed to racism and sexism."[48] According to Federici, the historical process of primitive accumulation "was not simply an accumulation and concentration of exploitable workers and capital. It was *also an accumulation of differences and divisions within the working class,* whereby hierarchies built upon gender, as well as 'race' and age, became constitutive of class rule and the formation of the modern proletariat."[49] While there is a long tradition, especially within Marxism, of drawing a line between capitalism and slavery (i.e., capitalism and slavery are different regimes of exploitation, because capitalism is the exploitation of "free" laborers via the wage relation and value form while slavery is exploitation of a different kind), capitalism and slavery in the Atlantic world were materially interrelated.[50] "American slavery," writes Cedric Robinson, "was a *subsystem* of world capitalism."[51] Moreover, capitalism and slavery were interrelated on the level of ideology. As I discuss at greater length in chapter 5, white wageworkers in the antebellum United States were able to conceive of themselves as "free" in large measure because of racial slavery, and the racism on which racial slavery was predicated helped to inhibit white worker solidarity with black workers (both "free" and slave).[52]

We thus need to be wary of that strain of current polemic for which historical inquiry and political organizing around racism and sexism spell the evasion of (and thus legitimation of) class inequality.[53] As Nancy Fraser tells us, "identity politics" does not "simply ignore maldistribution" of economic resources, recognizing as it does that "cultural injustices are often linked to economic ones."[54] "Identity politics" can entail both the politics of recognition *and* the politics of distribution (to use Fraser's terms). Likewise, Eric Lott persuasively argues that, contrary to those who tout "class-not-race" or "class-not-gender," "identity politics" (antiracism, antisexism, etc.) is the form that efficacious struggle against capitalist exploitation often takes today.[55] Yet, to rewrite struggles organized around race and gender as "really about class" is to risk a reactionary marginalization of—if not silencing of—these struggles, which is precisely what Lott cautions against.

The Illiberal Imagination does not argue that class is more important than race or gender in constituting the dynamics of identity and inequality in the early United States or in the terrain of early U.S. literature. *The Illiberal Imagination* should not be read as endorsing the project of privileging class over so-called identity politics. I do not mean to suggest that "identity politics" necessarily abjures a critique of capitalism, or that forms of antiracism and antisexism in the early and antebellum United States were not in their own ways critiques of class. Neither should this book be read, then, as an attempt to identify the white, male working class as "*the* revolutionary subject of history"; doing so would be to woefully misunderstand the history of class in the United States.[56] I accept as axiomatic that the history of both middle-class and working-class identity formation in the early and antebellum United States hinges largely on how members of these classes thought about not just economic disparities among whites but also about race and gender; below, I touch on the ways in which working-class politics in the early United States were shot through with and rendered problematic by ideologies of racial and sexual difference. Yet, I would argue that class is, finally, a different kind of thing than race or gender. To undo ideologies and structures of racism and sexism is not to abolish class.[57] The eradication of racism and sexism in the form of race- and gender-blind markets for labor need not produce economic equality.[58]

And class—economic inequality among whites—was both a historical fact and an aspect of the literary imagination in the early and antebellum United States. Which is to say, economic inequality among whites as well as protests against it were developments that early U.S. novelists anxiously explored. Moreover, early U.S. novelists did not always suggest that white men are, are to be thought of as, or should be members of one economic class. In chapters that follow on Brockden Brown, Brackenridge, and Sedgwick I demonstrate that through the 1830s U.S. novelists did not hide economic inequality behind race and gender: here, white society is itself construed as a class society. The same is true in the 1840s for James Fenimore Cooper, though in chapters on Cooper and Stowe I show how novels in the 1840s and 1850s narrated class in large measure by deploying languages of race and gender. *The Illiberal Imagination* thus continues the project of sussing out precisely the extent to which representations of class inequality are imbricated with discourses of race and gender in U.S. literary history.

Class in the Early United States?

But, really, class in the early U.S. novel? How could this be so, given "American economic exceptionalism," or the "faith in widespread access to abundant material opportunities" in the early United States?[59] Do not the most canonical of early U.S. texts tell us that class division should not be part of what goes into the making of early U.S. fiction? "Here are no aristocratical families," the invented Farmer James writes in the famous third letter of Crèvecoeur's 1782 *Letters from an American Farmer*, "no courts, no kings, no bishops, no ecclesiastical dominion, no invisible power giving to a few a very visible one, no great manufactures employing thousands, no great refinements of luxury. The rich and the poor are not so far removed from each other as they are in Europe." In contrast to Europe, Farmer James explains, the United States is defined by a "pleasing uniformity of decent competence." In the absence of Europe's political structures (i.e., aristocratic privileges) and the presence of America's natural abundance, the American becomes a "new man" that has escaped from "voluntary idleness, servile dependence, penury, and useless labor" and has been "rewarded by ample subsistence."[60]

According to Joyce Appleby, by the time of Jefferson's ascendance to the presidency, Americans had come to think of their polity as one defined by a lack of class privileges: Jeffersonianism was, Appleby argues, "a vision of classlessness."[61] A consonant notion of classlessness is on display in Abraham Lincoln's 1856 address in Kalamazoo, wherein Lincoln tells us that in the United States "the man who labored for another last year, this year labors for himself, and next year he will hire others to labor for him."[62] For Lincoln, no man need be stuck permanently in the position of having to sell his labor in the United States.

Mainstream early U.S. political economy also suggests that the United States is essentially free from class. For Marx, classical political economy posits "the sphere of circulation or commodity exchange, within whose boundaries the sale and purchase of labour-power goes on" as "a very Eden of the innate rights of man. It is the exclusive realm of Freedom, Equality, Property, and Bentham."[63] The same can be said of mainstream early U.S. political economy, but mainstream early U.S. political economy, in addition to construing the relation between capital and labor in terms not of exploitation but of fair exchange, insists that all workers in the United States could accumulate wealth and thereby "rise" in the socioeconomic order.[64]

Yet, the evidence offered by labor historians belies notions of early U.S. classlessness (i.e., equal access to productive property and widespread mobility), even for white men and women. Those who were forced to sell their labor power in order to survive in the early United States more often than not barely eked out their subsistence, and rarely did they accumulate wealth enough to become buyers of labor or to permit their children to become buyers of labor.[65] "Perhaps more than we care to admit," writes Seth Rockman, "early republic capitalism operated with a kind of contingency that meant some people could be rich and powerful because others could be rendered poor and powerless."[66] Moreover, while according to American exceptionalism the early United States was free from class privileges and entitlements, scholars of early U.S. law have shown something nearly the opposite. Law in the early United States, Karen Orren contends, prescribed "enforceable obligations upon employees as a status," and in so doing it "defied the principle of the sovereign individual. By reinforcing the subordination of servant to master, [the law] contradicted the plan of a fluid society."[67] Likewise, Christopher Tomlins has demonstrated that the law "played a major role in concretizing . . . asymmetries of power and exchange in the social relations of employer and employee and the organization of employment."[68] Employers in the early United States enjoyed legal privileges that employees did not.

Many early Americans considered class inequality to be constitutive of their polity. During the 1780s, "classes . . . began to emerge as subjects in and objects of American political discourse."[69] One need only recall *Federalist* No.10: "The most common and durable source of factions, has been the various and unequal distribution of property. Those who hold, and those who are without property, have ever formed distinct interests in society."[70] Moreover, as labor historians such as Sean Wilentz and Ronald Schultz have demonstrated, something on the order of working-class class consciousness—and with it, forms of class struggle—began to emerge in the United States as early as the 1790s.[71] A robust tradition of labor history has not only uncovered the divided class structure of the early United States but also traced the polyvalent, often contradictory but nonetheless oppositional articulations and movements of the early U.S. working class.[72]

Some of the earliest U.S. novels stage what we might call the fact of class in the early United States. The eponymous protagonist of Martha Meredith Read's 1802 *Monima; or, the Beggar Girl* is a poor young woman with an ill father to support. She begins her novel in "search of the acquisition of a decent maintenance," but lives on the edge of starvation—unable to find work amid "the habitations that wore opulence" in Boston.[73] As Cathy Davidson observes, according to *Monima* "the Revolution did not perform its office for all Americans equally; wealthy Americans as convinced of their own privilege as any European aristocrats rob Monima of her money in order to force her first into financial dependence and then into sexual submission, graphic metaphors for oppressions by class and gender."[74] *Monima* unleashes a gothic critique on the fact of class (again, that some must sell their labor power, while others are wealthy enough to buy it). Sarah Savage's 1814 *The Factory Girl* tells a different kind of story. The protagonist of this novel goes to work in a cotton factory because her father's "hard labour" did not leave her "very well in the world."[75] In contrast to *Monima, The Factory Girl* narrates the condition of having to sell one's labor power as a blessing to the seller: it is the stuff of moral and spiritual growth for this novel's protagonist.[76] Taken together, *Monima* and *The Factory Girl* indicate that early U.S. fiction did not deny the reality of class so much as debate its meaning.

"The Genuine System of Property"

In at least one instance, early U.S. fiction imagined an alternative to class. In 1802, *The Temple of Reason*—a deist Philadelphia magazine—published *Equality, A Political Romance* in eight installments.[77] *Equality*, Roland Schultz writes, was "the first socialist tract written in America."[78] The first half of *Equality* describes the imaginary island of Lithconia, which is located in "those seas where lie Utopia, Brobdignag [*sic*], Lilliput, &c.," and on which class division has been eradicated.[79] "[T]here is no money in the country," we are told of Lithconia: "the lands are in common" and "labour is the duty required of every citizen" until "a certain age" (4). Each individual works only "four hours each day" (4); "no man is permitted to do another's work"—to sell his labor power to someone else (5); there are no markets, only storehouses where the goods produced by the society are kept and distributed equally (8); "there is no seduction"—and so, by implication, no novels of seduction (13); there are no elections, because every man and woman will serve in government when they reach the appropriate age (17); Lithconia is industrialized, and has "the appearance of one vast manufactory, conducted by one mind" (19). "As there is no such thing as debtor and creditor," the narrator explains," and as "there is no property to contend for," there are "consequently, no lawyers" (21). Lithconia is truly equal: "poverty and riches," the narrator tells us, "are words not to be found in [Lithconia's] language" (28).

In the second half of *Equality*, we learn how Lithconia came to be. Lithconia emerges as the final stage in a stadialist history that reaches back to the beginning of time. *Equality*'s five stages of history are the age of innocence, the age of iron, the age of brass, the age of invention, and, finally, Lithconian equality—or, "the genuine system of property" (75). The "age of innocence" lasts "[t]en millions of years": "men contented themselves with fruits and herbs," "they lived in harmony with brute creation," "their lands were undivided, and the whole stock continued in common," and they lived in "peace and friendship with each other" (48). The "age of iron," which lasts "20 millions of years," commences when geological and climatological changes, coupled with a population explosion, force men to begin hunting; it is an age racked by "[f]amine, pestilence, and war" (50). The "age of brass" comes about when overhunting leads men to farming and the domestication of animals; it is in this age that a "division of land" occurs and what the narrator calls the "evils" of the "system of separate property" thus emerge (56). As a result of "separate private property," the narrator explains, "nine-tenths of mankind groaned under the most oppressive tyranny, labouring from morning till night for a poor and scanty diet . . . while the other tenth enjoyed every luxury, and rioted in waste and profusion" (62). The "age of invention" is marked by material and intellectual innovation, as well as revolutions against monarchical rule. But it is, like the "age of brass," plagued by class inequality.

The "age of invention" corresponds to *Equality*'s historical present, and in part it serves to satirize and critique this historical present. The "age of invention" perpetuates the "evils" of the "age of brass," marked as it by laws that authorize "murder, robbery, larceny, swindling, cheating, extortioning and idleness" for the wealthy "classes" (70). And the wealthy "classes" of "the age of invention" establish strict barriers against the "free use of reason and investigation," which would otherwise reveal the illegitimacy of then-current social relations (72). Yet, on the other hand, the "age of invention" incubates Lithconia's material and philosophical preconditions. During the "age of invention," "genius and the powers of mind were displayed more than in any other" age—including in Lithconia (67). In fact, according to the narrator, the Lithconians are "indebted to" "the age of invention" for "the principal parts of their enjoyments" (68). This is because the "age of invention" is the age during which what *Equality* calls the "intelligent class" comes into its own—becoming, in a word, "formidable" (76). The "intelligent class" leads a charge against monarchy, bringing constitutional government into being. Having witnessed, however, the failure of constitutional government to eradicate "public plunder" and the existence of "idlers" and "swindlers," the "intelligent class" begins to speak of a "genuine system of property" as "no visionary phantom, but as a good, which might be realized" (86). The "age of invention" is marked by a "very stormy and factious" conflict between "separate property-men" and "the equal right men," a conflict that leads ultimately to the "revolution" spawning Lithconia's economic and political system (84).

Given its limited circulation, it is easy to neglect *Equality*. It is just as easy to dismiss it as a contribution to radical thought: in *Equality*, the idea of a "genuine system of property" does not emerge from below but instead from above as the gradual effect of programs carried out by the "intelligent class" (76). The "intelligent class" insists that "society" is "bound to relieve every kind of distress, brought on by the operations of nature" (82). This class thus enacts a law that transfers heirless estates to an "aggregate fund" for individuals born into a "miserable and scanty subsistence," creating a welfare state of sorts (83). The "natural operation" of this law is twofold. First, it makes "an ample provision for those who had before been the outcasts of society" (83). Second, it paves the way for collective ownership. The beneficiaries of the fund begin en masse to leave whatever wealth they accumulate to the fund. At the same time, the possessors of "separate property" realize that while they are "subjected to a thousand cares and anxieties," the beneficiaries of the fund are not (84). Those of "great fortune" eventually realize that it is to their advantage and the advantage of their children to "sink" their fortunes in the "aggregate fund" (84). Here, then, the road to revolution and the "genuine system of property" begins with reform by educated elites and ends with the choices of the wealthy. Moreover, while *Equality* insists that the "genuine system of property" is the endpoint of human civilization, it defers the "genuine system of property" to a far-off future: the "age of invention" lasts "thousands of years" (75).

Despite all this, *Equality* reveals that as early as 1802 certain Americans were dubious that laissez-faire capitalism would produce economic equality. *Equality* might be read as a prescient critique of the role that legal apparatuses and lawyers in the early United States played in abetting unequal access to productive property and wealth.[80] In *Equality*'s "age of brass," when property was made "separate," "a new order of beings sprung up, who, under the pretense of explaining their rights, acquired an authority over the lives and property of their fellow men, which nearly deprived them of all right" (62). This "order of beings" survives into the "age of invention," and is only abolished once a "genuine system of property" finally prevails. *Equality* is also prescient of a way of thinking about historical conflict that emerged in the early nineteenth-century United States. Like early nineteenth-century labor activists, who prefigured the Preamble of Marx's *The Communist Manifesto* in their notions of history-as-class conflict, *Equality* suggests that history is defined by—given shape by—the conflict between those who stand for economic equality and those who do not. Finally, then, *Equality* indexes the desire for something other than the existing politico-economic regime of its present, for a world where access to wealth is truly the right of all individuals—for a world in which no one is faced with the prospect of scraping by at the whims of the market and in which no individual can amass wealth from others' labors.

An Oppositional Political Economy

I hope that *Equality* and the following examples make clear that I am not importing Marx to, or imposing Marx onto, the early United States; instead, I am suggesting that we bring ideas and ways of writing about class already present in the early United States—ideas that resonate with, if not prefigure, Marxian ones—to bear on the early U.S. novel. From the late eighteenth to the mid-nineteenth century, what we find in the annals of labor and intellectual history is protest against class exploitation in the United States as well as proposals—from legal reform to more radical interventions into the way productive property is distributed—about how to overcome this exploitation.

William Manning's *The Key of Liberty* (1799), although never published in Manning's day, affords access to turn-of-the-century radical plebeian ideas about class in the United States. For Manning, the United States is plagued by "the great scuffle between the Few and the Many."[81] The "Few" "live without labor"; the "Many," in turn, are "conscious that it is labor that supports the whole, and that the more there are who live without labor—and the higher they live or the greater their salaries and fees are—so much the harder must [the laborer] work, or the shorter must [the laborer] live" (136). According to Manning, "no person can possess property without laboring, unless he get it by force or craft, fraud or fortune, out of the earnings of others" (136). Now, Manning and turn-of-the-century plebeian racialism were not precisely anticapitalist, insofar as wage labor itself was not the focus of their critique of economic inequality and exploitation in the early United States. Yet, for Manning and other radical plebeians of his moment, there can be no "liberty" in the United States so long as certain individuals are able to appropriate wealth produced by "the Many." Thus Manning articulates an oppositional political economy: he inveighs against the private accumulation of wealth through the exploitation of labor. As early as the late eighteenth century, then, forms of economically egalitarian class consciousness began to take shape in the United States. Moreover, the terms that Manning used—"the Few" and "the Many"—continued to populate radical working-class political economy in the decades to follow. In his 1833 *Address to the Working Men of New England*, Seth Luther suggests that capitalists "have destroyed the happiness of the MANY, that the FEW may roll and riot in splendid luxury."[82]

By the 1820s, capitalist labor relations themselves were very much an object of critique in the United States. According to Thomas Skidmore's 1829 *The Rights of Man to Property!*, no individual should have to sell his labor power to another:

> *title* to property exists for all; and for all alike; not because others have been; nor because they have *not* been; not because they had a certain being for a parent, rather than another being; not because they appear later, or earlier, on the stage of life, than others; not because of purchase, of conquest, of preocuppancy, or what not; but BECAUSE THEY ARE: BECAUSE THEY EXIST. I AM; THEREFORE IS PROPERTY MINE. . . . Such is the language of nature; such is the language of right; and such are the principles which will justify any people in pulling down any government; which denies, even to a *single* individual of the human race, his possession, his real tangible possession, of this unalienable nature; or its unquestionable equivalent.[83]

Skidmore's call for individual, albeit universal, possession of property may appear consistent with Lockean possessive individualism, linking as it does "personhood and proprietorship."[84] Yet, as Locke argues in *The Second Treatise of Government* (1690), "it is plain"—and right—"that men have agreed to disproportionate and *unequal possession of the earth*."[85] Even though Skidmore does insist upon the right to private ownership of land, he nonetheless parts ways with Locke's naturalization of "unequal possession," of asymmetrical labor markets, and of boundless individual accumulation. Skidmore, like Marx after him, distinguishes between two kinds of private property. For Marx, "the "private property of the worker in his means of production" is not to be confused with "capitalist private property, which rests on the exploitation of alien, but formally free labour."[86] Skidmore contends that every adult individual—*regardless of sex or race*—in the United States should by right possess private productive property precisely so that no one must labor for someone else's private profit. What's more, a line can be drawn from Skidmore to Marx himself and to Marxian socialism: according to Lewis Feuer, "the embryonic socialist consciousness and the vision of a workingmen's state" that influenced the young Marx "was first born among Skidmore and his fellow 'worker-intellectuals.'"[87] In his 1844 *Economic and Philosophic Manuscripts,* Marx writes that "*communism* is the *positive* expression of annulled private property—at first as *universal* private property."[88] Here, Marx imagines demands for "*universal* private property" as the first expression of the movement toward the abolition of capitalist labor relations.

Skidmore was not alone in critiquing U.S. capitalism in proto-Marxian terms. In his 1831 *The Working Man's Manual,* Stephen Simpson argues that the "revolution of 1776, is . . . not yet fully accomplished."[89] This is because "the fruit of every man's labour, instead of going to enrich himself, contributes to swell the hoard of accumulating capital" (45–46). In the United States, according to Simpson, workers "produce all the wealth of society without sharing a thousandth part of it" (29). Deploying a labor theory of wealth, Simpson argues that "CAPITAL is the super-abundant aggregate stock of labour, in the hands of individuals, government, and nation. . . . All capital, therefore, is *produced* by the working men of a nation, although they seldom attain to, or possess it, owing to a wrong principle, regulating the distribution of wealth, by which capital is almost solely acquired by the idle speculator, the wary monopolist, or the sordid accumulator" (64).

For Simpson, the United States is "daily approximating to the same horrible inequality" of Britain, "owing to that tendency in capital to attract, extort, and accumulate from the wages of labour; besides legalized monopolies—grinding down industry to the scanty pittance necessary to sustain life" (66).[90] Despite his criticisms of capitalism, Simpson was not exactly a socialist. At the outset of *The Working Man's Manual,* he writes: "It is a perversion of the aims of the enlightened advocates of labour, to represent that they are contending for an *equality of wealth,* or a *community of property*" (27).[91] Yet, Simpson nonetheless articulates anticapitalist notions, railing against the exploitation of laborers by capitalists: "Capitalists live and grow rich by the labour of others. The laboring man lives by his own industry, enriches others by his own industry, but very seldom grows rich himself. Is this just?" (70). According to Simpson, "capital is naturally a tyrant; always standing on the alert to grind down the mere operative, who lives from hand to mouth, and who must sell, because he must eat" (70). Simpson articulates a desire for an economic system without such tyranny, without "a monied aristocracy" that "intercepts the just wages of labour" (76).

By the 1840s, some writers construed wage laborers as slaves to capitalists. In *The Communist Manifesto,* Marx writes that wageworkers must "sell themselves piece-meal, are commodity like every other article of commerce"; industrial workers for Marx are thus "slaves of the bourgeois class," "of the bourgeois State," and they are "enslaved by the machine, by the over-looker, and, above all, by the individual bourgeois manufacturer himself."[92] John Pickering's 1847 *The Working Man's Political Economy* deploys the same figure of worker-as-slave:

> Everywhere we see toiling millions the slaves of the capitalist; consequently we find unconsumable wealth in the possession of a few, while poverty, discomfort and wretchedness is the lot of the great mass of the people. . . . The rich few overburthened with wealth; the poor suffering with want. The history of the world shows us this fact, that in all civilized countries, as the rich become richer, the poor become poorer; the greater the amount of wealth in a country, the less is the poor man's share, and the harder he has to work for a bare subsistence, and as the capitalist rises in riches, power and splendor, so in proportion the working man sinks into poverty, want and wretchedness.[93]

Like other working-class radicals in the United States and abroad, Pickering construes the wageworker as slave in order to protest the division of society into those who must sell their labor power to survive and those who accumulate private wealth by exploiting labor.[94]

It bears acknowledging again here that working-class identity—and working-class politics—in the early United States were, just as they were later, in many respects overdetermined "by deep-seated ethnic, religious, racial and sexual antagonisms within the [U.S.] working class."[95] As W. E. B. DuBois, Alexander Saxton, David Roediger, and Lott have demonstrated, white worker solidarity with black workers (both "free" and slave) was fundamentally impeded by the racial ideologies embraced by substantial numbers of the white working class, with "whiteness" itself helping to secure white workers' consent to their own forms of subordination.[96] Writes Roediger (summarizing DuBois): "The pleasures of whiteness could function as a 'wage' for white workers. That is, status and privilege conferred by race could be used to make up for alienating and exploitative class relationships, North and South. White workers could, and did, define and accept their class positions by fashioning identities as 'not slaves' and as 'not Blacks.'"[97]

Likewise, antebellum workingmen embraced ideologies of sexual inequality. It is now widely accepted that middle-class identity formation and the ideology of separate spheres—the notion that men are by nature designed for competition in the world of the market as "breadwinners," women in contrast for the intimate space of the home as caretakers and mothers—were two sides of the same coin.[98] Especially for working-class Americans, the ideology of separate spheres was a mystification of social reality, precisely because, as Amy Dru Stanley reminds us, "the deepening intrusion of market relations into family economies involved all sorts of different women in selling commodities, making commodities, buying commodities, turning parts of their homes into commodities, disposing of their time and skill as commodities."[99] Yet, as Jeanne Boydston points out, working-class activists often themselves subscribed to the ideology of separate spheres:

> The speeches of early [male] labor activists . . . frequently invoked both the rhetoric of the ideology of spheres and specifically pastoral images of the household, implying a sharp contrast between "the odious, cruel, unjust and tyrannical system" of the factory, which "compels the operative Mechanic to exhaust his physical and mental powers," and the presumably rejuvenating powers of the home. Discouraging women from carrying their labor "beyond the home," working men called upon women to devote themselves to improving the quality of life within their families. When the men described that undertaking, however, they focused, not on the myriad ways wives contributed daily to the material welfare of their households, but on a mission of passive benevolence.[100]

Adopting an ideology of separate spheres, male workers complained that "wage-earning women"—women who went "beyond the home"—were "taking jobs, and thus the proper masculine role, away from men" (155). Thus, working-class men "organized to call for 'the family wage,' a wage packet for the male 'breadwinner' high enough to permit his wife and children to withdraw from paid work" (156). The demand for the family wage itself can be read as an insistence upon economic prerogatives of men over women (135).[101]

Rather than focusing on the contradictions plaguing working-class political self-expression or exploring how the white, male working class was co-opted by ideologies of race and gender, in *The Illiberal Imagination* I concentrate on the ways in which the novel from its beginning in the United States responded to the challenge of varieties of radical political economy (despite their many shortcomings), and how the early U.S. novel naturalized class relations among whites. Yet, by attending to how early U.S novelists responded to protests against class exploitation, I hope to offer here something other than literary historical antiquarianism. "Why," asks Christopher Tomlins, "study class and class struggle? First, because these convulsive phenomena offer more than a stage for the production of historical complexity: rather, they structure the universe of time under discussion. Second, because as such, class and class struggle remain a route to an absolutely distinct understanding of history. Third, because only through that distinct understanding can one begin to grasp what, as historians, we owe the past."[102] To study the early U.S. novel in terms of class and class struggle is to make the case for a distinct understanding of history. To study class in the early U.S. novel is to link the early U.S. novel to what Fredric Jameson calls "a single great collective story" of "the collective struggle to wrest a realm of Freedom from a realm of Necessity"—to the "single vast unfinished plot" that is class struggle.[103]

READING CLASS IN THE EARLY U.S. NOVEL

While the novels I treat take up different facets of class and are in many respects formally dissimilar, they nonetheless share some basic formal— and, I contend, ideologically overdetermined—principles. Over the next few pages, I aim to underscore how early U.S. novels—how their representational strategies—are, on the level of form, *inside* class. A commitment to economic inequality manifests itself in the class-charged and asymmetrical distribution of speech-space.[104] Inequality also manifests itself in the didacticism of early U.S. novels. The intrusive narrators of early U.S. novels are baldly didactic on matters of poverty, economic inequality, and working-class radicalism: they emphatically instruct their readers how to think about class. And the effectual subordination of story to polemicizing bourgeois discourse in early U.S. novels rehearses on the level of form the unequal economic relationships on behalf of which the dominant, didactic bourgeois voices in early U.S. novels speak. My argument, then, is that *on the level of form* early U.S. novels do not invite their readers to be dubious of economic inequality, but in fact instruct their readers to see it as natural.

First, speech-space. One way of theorizing the novel in general as a particular kind of literary structure—as a form—has been to focus à la M. M. Bakhtin on its inclusion and orchestration of competing "speech types," of voices. "The novel," writes Bakhtin in "Discourse in the Novel," "can be defined as a diversity of social speech types (sometimes even diversity of languages) and diversity of individual voices, artistically organized."[105] Bakhtin lists five "basic types of compositional-stylistic unities into which the novelistic whole usually breaks down":

(1) Direct authorial-literary artistic narration (in all its diverse variants);

(2) Stylization of the various forms of oral everyday narration (*skaz*);

(3) Stylization of the various forms of semiliterary (written) everyday narration (the letter, the diary, etc.);

(4) Various forms of literary but extra-artistic authorial speech (moral, philosophical or scientific statements, oratory, ethnographic descriptions, memoranda and so forth);

(5) The stylistically individualized speech of characters. (262)

According to Bakhtin, these "heterogeneous stylistic unities, upon entering the novel, combine to form a structured artistic system, and are subordinated to the higher stylistic unity of the work as a whole, a unity that cannot be identified with any single one of the unities subordinated to it. The stylistic uniqueness of the novel as a genre consists precisely in the combination of these subordinated, yet still relatively autonomous unities . . . into the higher unity of the work as a whole" (262). Moreover, for Bakhtin, the "stylistic unities" combined into "a structured artistic system" by a novel are "ideologically saturated": each expresses a "worldview" potentially antagonistic to the "worldview" expressed by the other "stylistic unties" with which it shares space in a given novel (271).[106] "Every language in the novel," writes Bakhtin, "is a point of view, a socio-ideological conceptual system of real social groups and their embodied representatives" (411). It is not my goal to defend the accuracy of Bakhtin's five "basic types" for analyzing early U.S. novels (or, to put it differently, to suggest that these five types represent an exhaustive catalogue of the "compositional-stylistic unities" to be discovered in early U.S. novels); rather, I invoke this list and Bakhtin's claim that novels subordinate heterogeneous, "ideologically saturated" "speech types" into "higher stylistic unities" in order to lay a conceptual groundwork for thinking about how early U.S. novels work as ideological performances. Key here is the relationship between the "individualized speech of characters" and "extra-artistic authorial speech," or the relationships between the voices of characters and the voice of the narrator.

There is a lot of talk about class within the novels I treat. And there are in early U.S. novels voices of working-class disaffection with economic inequality. A host of characters in early U.S. novels vent their frustration with—their dismay and anger about—economic inequality in the United States. I go to lengths in the chapters that follow to link voices of working-class protest inside early U.S. novels to critiques of inequality and working-class movements outside of early U.S. novels; doing so is to locate early U.S. novels against a particular historical horizon, situating them within what Jameson calls "the antagonistic dialogue of class voices."[107] Just like many historical, actual voices of working-class protest outside of early U.S. novels, fictional voices of working-class protest in early U.S. novels are supremely rhetorical: they evaluate the U.S. socioeconomic order, aiming to persuade other characters in their respective novels that the U.S. socioeconomic order is deficient and should be transformed.[108] Yet, voices of working-class protest against economic inequality in U.S. novels are indeed inside of novels—and thus parts of larger literary structures.

Crucially, early U.S. novels do not throw their weight behind voices of working-class protest. Voices of working-class protest in early U.S. novels are decidedly circumscribed, minor: they are the voices of minor characters. While what characterizes the novel as a form for Bakhtin is its inclusion of multiple, antagonistic, ideologically saturated voices, he does not argue that the novel as a form is necessarily, or prone to be, open or subversive or egalitarian.[109] And in early U.S. novels, voices of working-class protest are structurally subordinate to equally rhetorical opposing voices—especially to the intrusive voices of narrators, which perform plenty of cultural work where class is concerned.

It is now a truth universally acknowledged that early U.S. novels were largely written by and for the bourgeoisie. I want to emphasize here, though, that the plane of discourse in early U.S. novels is indeed largely—and loudly—bourgeois. By "plane of discourse," I am invoking the narratological distinction between story (or, "the sequence of actions or events" related by a narrative) and discourse (or, "the discursive presentation or narration of events").[110] Every narrative," writes Seymour Chatman, "is a structure with a content plane (called 'story') and an expression plane (called 'discourse')." [111] While narratorial speechifying might be thought of as an event within a novel (as something that "happens" in a novel), for Chatman and the narratological tradition he draws on, narratorial speech is to be conceived of as separate from story and as existing on the plane of discourse.[112] And early U.S. novels are shot through with narratorial speechifying about the "benefits" of economic inequality and about what are construed to be inescapable and intolerable outcomes were working-class desires to eradicate it actualized. Novels by Brown, Brackenridge, Sedgwick, and Cooper that turn on class have narrators that speak up on behalf of economic inequality and speak up against working-class disaffection with economic inequality. In Brown's novels, narrators extol the virtues of poverty for individual intellectual development. In Brackenridge's *Modern Chivalry,* the narrator insists that plebeian political desires would spell the end of "liberty" in the United States. In Sedgwick's novels, narrators sermonize on the mutuality of economic inequality and Christian virtue. The narrators of Cooper's Anti-Rent trilogy inveigh against agrarian radicalism, casting it, again, as an assault on "liberty." Moreover, it is not just that the narratorial voice of early U.S. novels is bourgeois, but that bourgeois voices dominate the space of these novels: they are afforded massively more space to talk—more speech-space—about class than those voices that critique economic inequality. In early U.S. novels, it is predominantly bourgeois voices that speak, and these voices are categorically moralizing and didactic where matters of class are concerned.

Granting that the audience for early U.S. novels was predominantly bourgeois, we can imagine bourgeois readers nodding in assent to the "lessons" they would find, but perhaps already embraced, about class offered to them by dominant voices in early U.S. novels.[113] Moreover, it is now customary to think of the early and antebellum U.S. novel as bound up with pedagogy, as performing a pedagogic function.[114] And, like the 1850s sentimental novel, the early U.S. novel "about" class can be read "not as an artifice of eternity answerable to certain formal criteria and to certain psychological and philosophical concerns, but as a political enterprise, halfway between sermon and social theory, that codifies and attempts to mold the values of its time."[115] My point is that in early U.S. novels "about" class, a particularly loud inflection of the pedagogic, moralizing impulse is especially apparent.

Now, there are early U.S. novels where not-exactly-bourgeois characters are apportioned plenty of space to talk. The eponymous protagonist of Brown's *Arthur Mervyn* is also this novel's primary narrator, and he is for much of the novel poor. Likewise, the dialogue of—the speech of—poor characters in Sedgwick's *The Poor Rich Man, and the Rich Poor Man* and *Live and Let Live* occupies ample space in these novels. Yet, poor characters in these novels give voice to bourgeois bromides about class. Again, in *Arthur Mervyn* it is the poor Arthur Mervyn who extols the virtues of poverty for individual intellectual development. The poor protagonists of Sedgwick's fiction in fact echo their respective novels' narrators' pronouncements about economic inequality as the very precondition of Christian virtue. In early U.S. novels, the poor who are given ample space to speak do so on behalf of the bourgeois order of things and in a way consonant with bourgeois speech about class.

In chapter 5 I argue that Harriet Beecher Stowe's *Dred* marks a departure from earlier novels, insofar as it, unlike earlier U.S. novels "about" class, is explicitly opposed to economic inequality among whites in the United States. Nonetheless, in *Dred* bourgeois voices dominate: the protagonists of this novel are wealthy, white abolitionists. These protagonists—along with the narrator—lament economic inequality among whites in the U.S. South. Yet, these protagonists and the narrator monopolize the novel's discussion, as it were, about the causes and remedies for economic inequality. For these protagonists and for the narrator, racial slavery is the sole cause of economic inequality in the United States, and thus racial slavery's abolition will spell the end of class inequality among whites in the United States. For the protagonists and narrator of *Dred*, northern capitalism is not itself guilty of producing class division. The dominant voices of Stowe's novel are thus too in their own ways bourgeois: as much as they may speak to white working-class antagonism toward racial slavery, they do not channel white working-class antagonism toward capitalism.

To generalize, then: early U.S. novels are not democratically pluralistic, but are instead fundamentally asymmetrical on one level of form—on the distribution of what I am calling speech-space when it comes to speech about the structure of the U.S. economy. And this asymmetry on the level of form, I would like to suggest, refracts and normalizes the socioeconomic asymmetries protested by working-class characters both inside and outside of early U.S. novels. Didactic, moralizing bourgeois voices are in control of—in possession of—the vast majority of these novels' material realities, and this formal principle is itself a mode of normalizing economic inequality.

This is not to say that novels like Brown's *Arthur Mervyn* or Brackenridge's *Modern Chivalry* or even Cooper's *The Chainbearer* and *The Redskins* are not in certain respects messy, that they are not host to interpretative cruxes that render their politics at least partially ambiguous. What the eponymous protagonist-narrator of *Arthur Mervyn* represents is for many critics an open riddle: is Mervyn a disinterested republican citizen (and at times innocent victim of con artists), or is he a self-interested man on the make (who has been in league with criminals and a con artist himself)? And, what is Brown's novel saying to us if Meryvn is one or the other?[116] All we have to go on are the assumptions of minor characters in the novel and Mervyn's testimony about himself. The protagonist of *Modern Chivalry,* Farrago, rails against plebeian radicals as incapable of the disinterested deliberation political office requires, yet the novel exposes Farrago to be not exactly disinterested—and instead self-serving and manipulative in addition to elitist: can *Modern Chivalry* really be patently, unambiguously "for" the rentier class to which Farrago belongs? Likewise, the protagonist-narrators of *The Chainbearer* and *The Redskins* reveal themselves to be less than heroic by the standards of masculine heroism Cooper lays out in other novels: can Cooper's novels really be "for" the landlords in the Anti-Rent War, or are these novels—perhaps inadvertently—satirizing the landlords as much as defending them?

Yet, *pace* critics who see *Arthur Mervyn* or *Modern Chivalry* or even *The Chainbearer* as self-deconstructing texts, the dominant, organizing voices of early U.S. novels about class never leave implicit—never equivocate about—what they think of economic inequality or working-class radicalism, never leave implicit the "lessons" readers are meant to take away with them on these matters. Arthur Mervyn tells us a number of times that his fall into poverty, which in a world without class division is unthinkable, was fortunate. Even if Mervyn says as much to ingratiate himself with his auditor (Dr. Stevens), we have to take his lesson as "true" for *Arthur Mervyn:* characters in the novel who believe otherwise—who believe that it is unfair, or irrational, that they are subject to poverty— are unquestionably villainous. While Farrago may be a manipulative elitist, Brackenridge's narrator makes clear that Farrago should be seen as a necessary evil: for Brackenridge's narrator, the radical political aims of plebeians portend disasters for U.S. civil society. And Cooper's virtuous heroines and the "good" Indians he trots out, as much as his narrators, make sure to tell us that agrarian radicals' beliefs and actions are immoral.

Of course, novels in general—and early U.S. novels in particular— are not merely bundles of voices. Novels are narratives. Novels may have intrusive, speechifying, didactic narrators, but they also relate stories. And, in general, the plane of story and the plane of discourse in a novel need not always agree with one another. We can imagine an intrusive narrator suggesting an interpretation of events or of a social relation staged in a novel for which the story plane itself implies a different, contrary interpretation. Yet, in early U.S. novels "about" class, story very much serves discourse: story in early U.S. novels occasions but also confirms the "truth" of didactic pronouncements from narrators (and major characters) about class. Again, the narrators of Brown's *Ormond* and *Arthur Mervyn* insist that the fall into poverty makes possible forms of individual intellectual development—and the stories these novels relate bear this out. In Brackenridge's *Modern Chivalry,* episodes in the novel that turn on plebeian political self-expression occasion—but also function as the confirmation for—the protagonist's (Farrago's) and the narrator's arguments against plebeian political radicalism. In Sedgwick's 1830s fiction, narrators and, often, working-class characters sermonize on economic inequality as the precondition of Christian virtue—and the stories in these novels function as evidence of these sermons. In Cooper's Anti-Rent trilogy, first-person narrators and their allies pontificate against agrarian radicalism, and the stories these narrators tell about the behaviors of agrarian radicals serve as validation of the argument that agrarian radicalism jeopardizes personal "liberty" in the United States. Even in *Dred*, story confirms discourse: the narrator (and major characters) insist that abolition is what will liberate poor whites from poverty, and the framing subplot of the novel about a poor, white girl named Fanny Cripps shows this to be "true": Fanny is indeed rescued from poverty by wealthy abolitionists.

I would thus like to suggest that the complementariness of—the harmony between—story and dominant discourse in these novels stands as another way in which on the level of form they argue, as it were, for socioeconomic inequality. Just as dominant voices in early U.S. novels about class insist that workers should be obedient (or, in Stowe's case, need to be rescued by wealthy whites), the tendency to make the "lesson" about class clear via stories that complement didactic narratorial intrusions and vice versa betrays a desire to summon not an active, suspicious interpretative attitude but rather an attitude of obedient "listening."[117] A pedagogical impulse is apparent in early U.S. novels about class, I wrote earlier. We can add now that early U.S. novels instantiate a version of one-way pedagogy. Your job as a reader of these novels is in large measure to have "lessons" about class spelled out for you, and not to figure out your own view on whether class is "good" or "bad." Early U.S. novels "about" class can be described as what Roland Barthes names the readerly (*lisible*): the readerly text makes its reader not a "producer" but a "consumer" of it, and it is "characterized by the pitiless divorce . . . between the producer of the text and of its user, between its owner and its customer, between its author and its reader."[118] Again, the commitment to socioeconomic inequality in early U.S. novels is a property of their form, though here this commitment is located additionally in the asymmetric relationship between text and reader invited by these novels.

"Narrative," writes Terry Eagleton, "far from constituting some ruling-class conspiracy, is a valid and ineradicable mode of all human experience. More precisely, it is the very form of the ideological." All ideologies are narratives, Eagleton contends, because subjects "cannot think, act, or desire except in narrative; it is by narrative that the subject constructs that 'sutured' chain of signifiers which grants its true condition of division sufficient 'imaginary' coherence to enable it to act."[119] Which is to say, it is narratives—stories the subject is told, that the subject tells itself—that allow the subject to think of itself as a subject in the first place as well as to consent to a less than ideal existence.[120] Yet, ideology is narrative in another sense: ideologies can be thought of as stories about where a community is and where community is—should be—heading.[121] Moving, then, back to what might properly be called the level of "content" in early U.S. novels "about" class, let me reiterate that through the 1840s, early U.S. novelists tendered narratives according to which the United States is a class society but need not—should not—become otherwise.

THE STRUCTURE OF THIS BOOK

Chapter 1 considers Charles Brockden Brown's *Ormond; or, The Secret Witness* (1799) and *Arthur Mervyn; or, Memoirs of the Years 1793* (1799, 1800) as responses both to the socioeconomic realities of late eighteenth-century Philadelphia and to early forms of economic egalitarianism. It situates these novels within the polarities of wealth that defined 1790s Philadelphia. And it reads these novels against a tradition of Enlightenment political economy (which subtended both the Godwinian socialism Brown knew and early artisan class consciousness in 1790s Philadelphia) according to which propertylessness and the attendant need to work for others are antithetical to an individual's autonomy. Most scholarship interested in Brown's stance on questions pertaining to the economy departs from the historical transition from republican to liberal values, investigating whether Brown's fictional portrayals of commercial selfhood endorse liberal self-interestedness. In contrast, my approach to these novels foregrounds Brown's obsession with economic subalternity and his use of the emerging conventions and themes of the bildungsroman. I thus emphasize how Brown's novels legitimate proletarianization in the new nation: the protagonists of these novels spend significant time poor, but the narrators of these novels insist—and the stories they tell confirm—that poverty should be considered as facilitating personal and social growth for individuals subjected to it. Ratifying poverty, even temporary poverty, Brown's novels ratify the class processes of which it is a symptom.

Chapter 2 examines how Hugh Henry Brackenridge's sprawling episodic travel novel *Modern Chivalry* (1792–1815) responds to plebeian radicalism and this radicalism's particular protest of class in the first decades of the nineteenth century. According to the now dominant reading of this novel, *Modern Chivalry* reflects the transition from Federalism to Jeffersonian democracy, working to satirize and deconstruct both political positions. I argue, in contrast, that by defining "democracy" as "an equal right of suffrage, and an equal right of office," *Modern Chivalry* functions as retort to the threat of a then emerging plebeian definition of "democracy" (what some scholars have called "artisan republicanism"), according to which "free government" requires fundamental economic equality. According to plebeian radicals both outside and inside Brackenridge's novel, leisured gentleman and members of the legal profession—what William Manning called "The Few"—perpetuate economic exploitation; moreover, for plebeian radicals (again, both outside and inside Brackenridge's novel), the achievement of actual democracy requires fundamental political reform. Yet, Brackenridge's voluble narrator argues against plebeian notions of class and plebeian political desires: he insists that "the Few" are not in fact the enemies of plebeians, that the United States has already achieved "democracy," and that the political reforms desired by plebeians are antithetical to "liberty." Thus, the narrator defends in his own way the attempts by Farrago, the novel's not-uncomplicated protagonist and a member of the rentier class, to curtail plebeian radicalism. According to the dominant voice of *Modern Chivalry*, "democracy" needs a politically conservative rentier class. And it needs this class to talk. If a number of critics have argued that *Modern Chivalry* is exemplary of the polyphonic novel and thus radically democratic, I argue instead that the novel's polyphony works to disrupt radical plebeian political desire. *Modern Chivalry* does not suggest that only elites should hold office, but the novel's particular ideal of polyphony, in which elite voices are necessary to "democracy," refuses to allow what we might call a plebeian future—a United States composed entirely of plebeians and plebeian voices—from coming into being.

Chapter 3 argues that 1830s sentimental fiction can be read as a response to early U.S. Christian socialism. Accounts of U.S. sentimentalism, focused as they are on the 1850s, often overlook the contributions of Catharine Maria Sedgwick, well known for her historical romance *Hope Leslie*, but who in the 1830s also penned a series of popular sentimental novels. Studies of 1850s sentimentalism also argue that sentimental fiction promotes a notion of classlessness in the United States through protagonists that exist somehow outside of class. Yet, the intrusive narrators, the main working-class protagonists, and the stories of Sedgwick's *The Poor Rich Man, and the Rich Poor Man* (1836) and *Live and Let Live* (1837) insist that there will always be—and should always be—individuals and families in the United States who are "poor" and others who are "rich." In so doing, Sedgwick's novels self-consciously counteracted the challenge posed by Christian economic egalitarianism in the 1830s. This variety of egalitarianism, prevalent among working-class activists, held that economic inequality was at odds with God's plan and a direct impediment to Christian behavior; Christian laborites argued for economic redistribution and, at times, for forms of socialism. Sedgwick's domestic novels, structured as comparative portraits of the ways in which the "good" and "bad" rich treat the poor and workers, disseminate the notion that since the rich can behave as good Christians toward those they employ, class inequality is providential. (In a coda to this chapter, I connect Sedgwick's 1830s novels to Rebecca Harding Davis's much better know 1855 *Life in the Iron-Mills,* arguing that Sedgwick's novels foreshadow Davis's response to the specter of Christian socialism.)

Chapter 4 argues for the cultural significance of James Fenimore Cooper's oft-overlooked Littlepage trilogy (1845–46), which Cooper wrote in response to the Anti-Rent War then taking place in the Hudson Valley. In the 1840s, labor activists focused their energies on land reform. Radicalizing the Lockean notion of the natural rights of each individual to the full fruits of his labor, these activists insisted that property in land must be equally distributed. In *The Chainbearer* (1845) and *The Redskins* (1846), Cooper's narrators—themselves landlords—denounce agrarian radicals and the principles of land reform. Moreover, the stories these narrators tell mobilize the conventions of frontier romance against land reform, casting those who hold egalitarian beliefs about land ownership as villains who threaten the fulfillment of love plots based in mutual attraction and affection. Economic egalitarianism becomes in these novels the enemy of individual sexual autonomy. These novels put working-class rebels in the position of "bad Indians," suggesting that they have degenerated racially and relegating them to justifiable annihilation. In so doing, these novels suggest that "white" civilization is by definition economically stratified.

Taken together, chapters 1 through 4 reveal that through the mid-1840s novelists did not always suggest that whites in United States are to be considered—or should in reality be—economic equals.[122] In other words, through the 1840s novelists writing about the North did not always imaginatively make class go away. Disavowing class inequalities

among whites would become a project for the novel in the 1850s, especially when southern apologists for slavery began to launch a rhetorical assault on northern capitalism. According to the proslavery writer
George Fitzhugh's 1854 *Sociology for the South, or the Failure of Free
Society,* under the *"laissez-faire* system" "a few individuals possessed of
capital and cunning acquire a power to employ the laboring class on
such terms as they please, and they seldom fail to use that power. Hence,
the numbers and destitution of the poor in free society are daily increasing, the numbers of the middle or independent class diminishing, and
the few rich men growing hourly richer."[123] Here is a strident version of
anticapitalism. Capitalism is for Fitzhugh a system "that places all mankind in antagonistic positions, and puts all society at war" (23). And
capitalism is "especially injurious to the poorer class," he writes: "besides
the labor necessary to support the family, the poor man is burdened with
the care of finding a home, and procuring employment, and attending to
all domestic wants and concerns" (27). For Fitzhugh, capitalism is anything but Christian. Slavery, on the other hand, according to Fitzhugh, is
a boon to the slave: "Slavery relieves our slaves of these cares altogether,
and slavery is a form, and the very best form, of socialism" (28). Slavery
would "relieve the laborer of many of the cares of household affairs, and
protect and support him in sickness and old age" (28). Like Fitzhugh,
proslavery anti-Tom novels such as Charles Peterson's *The Cabin and
the Parlor; or, Slaves and Masters* (1852), Caroline Hentz's *The Planter's
Northern Bride* (1854), and Caroline Rush's *The North and the South; or,
Slavery and its Contrasts* (1854)—novels that were direct responses to
Stowe's *Uncle Tom's Cabin*—painted white workers in the North as subject to damaging forms of exploitation.

According to pro-abolition Henry C. Carey, in contrast, the North is
already a classless society. As Jeffery Sklansky explains, for Carey, whose
writing spanned the 1830s, 1840s, and 1850s, "a fully free market would
bring emancipation from the bonds of property and class." U.S. capitalism according to Carey was tending toward "a single-class society of
self-employed, independent proprietors."[124] To the extent that the esca-
lation of the conflict between North and South redounded by the 1850s
to a dismissal of permanent economic inequality and to an insistence on
individual mobility within northern capitalism by the most prominent
antislavery political economists, what a northern, middle-class, antislavery novelist might say about economic inequality in the North was

by the 1850s circumscribed. Put differently, by the 1850s a novelist in the North had new reasons not to make the case for the existence of class in the North.

Chapter 5 situates Harriet Beecher Stowe's 1856 novel *Dred: Tale of the Great Dismal Swamp* in this context. *Dred*'s cultural work is in part, I argue, to construe abolition as a desire for economic equality rather than a commitment to the unbridled acquisitiveness that defines capitalism according to anti-Tom novels. At key moments, *Dred* stages southern plantation owners as opposed both to economic equality among whites in the South and to workers' rights in the North. Stowe thus draws on one strain of white working-class abolitionism—namely, what Bernard Mandel long ago described as working-class suspicions about "the slave-power conspiracy." Moreover, abolitionist characters in *Dred* desire a world without class inequalities among whites. Stowe thus piggybacks on the attempt by a number of prominent abolitionists—for instance, Frederick Douglass—to invite white workers in the North to be in solidarity with the cause of abolition. Stowe is in *Dred,* though, no anticapitalist: *Dred* tells us—*Dred*'s narrator and its protagonists tell us, its subplots tell us—that the only thing standing in the way of a classless United States are chattel slavery and the ideologies of plantation owners. For *Dred,* the capitalist U.S. North is free from significant class divisions among whites. *Dred* quite literally has no space for white working-class critiques of class relations in the U.S. North. Even so, because in *Dred* bourgeois activists who desire a world free from class division among whites are protagonists—are heroes, are the novel's dominant voices—*Dred* departs from the cultural logic of earlier U.S. novels, and thus marks the end, in this study, of what I am calling the illiberal imagination.

The conclusion revisits and expands upon *The Illiberal Imagination*'s historiographical and methodological contributions, meditating upon how the arguments of this book speak, on the one hand, to foundational accounts of the early nineteenth-century European novel's class politics and, on the other, to recent reappraisals of "symptomatic reading" and "critique" more broadly.

1   CHARLES BROCKDEN BROWN, POVERTY, AND THE BILDUNGSROMAN

> Of native *novels* we have no great stock, and none good; our democratic institutions placing all the people on a dead level of political equality; and the pretty equal diffusion of property throughout the country affords but little room for varieties, and contrasts of character.
> —John Bristed, *The Resources of the United States of America* (1818)

> [Bristed] should have excepted from this censure the Wieland, Ormond, and Arthur Mervyn of C. B. Brown, which combine grandeur and simplicity in an extraordinary degree.
> —"Bristed's America and her Resources," *Edinburgh Monthly Review* (1819)

> I am poor.
> —Arthur Mervyn

In *Ormond; or, The Secret Witness* (1799) and *Arthur Mervyn; or, Memoirs of the Year 1793* (1799, 1800), Charles Brockden Brown— the late eighteenth-century U.S. novelist most celebrated by early nineteenth-century American writers and most studied by twentieth- and twenty-first-century critics—tells the same story twice. At the outset of both novels, Brown's protagonists—Constantia Dudley and Arthur Mervyn, respectively—fall into "poverty." Having become "poor," these protagonists must sell their labor to others in order to acquire "subsistence." They become, then, members of late eighteenth-century Philadelphia's "lower sort." While Constantia and Arthur eventually—and fortuitously—ascend to property at the close of their respective novels, both *Ormond* and *Arthur Mervyn* are predominantly dedicated to narrating what "poverty" entails for their protagonists. To what end, this chapter asks, did Brown—a man who never wanted for money and was "entirely supported by his parents or extended family until he was thirty years old"[1]—write novels about young people who must negotiate material deprivation and economic precariousness in late eighteenth-century Philadelphia? And, moreover, to what end do Brown's Philadelphia novels construe the fall into poverty as a "fortunate" one?

To ask these questions, and thus to focus on Brown's representation of economic subalternity, is to reveal a facet of his writing that has yet to be fully appreciated. Of course, that Brown's novels, especially *Arthur Mervyn*, are "about" early U.S. capitalism is widely acknowledged among scholars of early U.S. literature. As James Justus observes of *Arthur Mervyn*, in "no other novel before the Civil War are we so assaulted by the immediacy and pervasiveness of a commercial society."[2] The typical line of inquiry into Brown's representation of capitalism in *Arthur Mervyn* situates Brown within the historical friction between a residual republicanism and an emergent liberalism. According to the republicanism-liberalism paradigm, late eighteenth-century economic transformations and the expansion of the market unleashed a conflict between a new culture of private economic ambition and an older ideal of "civic virtue" that celebrated self-sacrifice on behalf of the polity and for which "commerce" necessarily augured "corruption." "America in the 1790s," Teresa Goddu writes, "was both buoyed by a liberal ideology that believed in the benefits of commerce and troubled by the vestiges of a civic republicanism that feared commerce was an infection."[3] Which is to say, late eighteenth-century U.S. writing about "commerce" registers a deep ambivalence, marked at turns both by liberal celebrations of making one's living by buying and selling goods and by republican critiques of the selfish dispositions that such livelihoods might foster. On the one hand, the market could be seen as a "civilizing" force.[4] On the other hand, the market could be seen as the dissolvent of civic-mindedness.[5] Thus the typical question put to Brown's representation of capitalism is this: do his novels authorize commerce by extolling liberal individualism, or do they critique commerce by depicting liberal individualism as corrupt and corrupting—as incompatible with civic virtue?[6]

Yet, to ask whether *Arthur Mervyn* endorses liberal individualism or instead critiques it from the vantage of residual republicanism is to read *Arthur Mervyn* primarily as a meditation on economic activities that were largely the province of the property-owning class in the early United States—rather than as a meditation on the condition of economic subalternity itself. Which is to say, though a number of scholars have explored what *Arthur Mervyn* might say about greed and financial speculation, we have not yet sufficiently attended to the significance of the fact that the protagonist of *Arthur Mervyn* must sell his labor and is thus not in fact a capitalist—not a merchant or speculator. Certainly, the world that Arthur inhabits is a capitalist one, but, as I will argue below, Arthur's story is not a story of speculation or capitalist accumulation or even of an emergent capitalist ethos of acquisitive individualism rendered in biographical form. Rather, it is largely a story about being poor in a massively unequal society, just as Constantia's is.

What I seek to theorize, then, is how Brown's Philadelphia novels, in narrating stories about the "poor," are weighing in on economic inequality and asymmetric labor relations in the early United States.[7] Indeed, to examine how Brown's Philadelphia novels—*Arthur Mervyn,* but also *Ormond*—represent poverty in the early United States is, I would submit, to better understand precisely how an approval of economic inequality manifests itself in the novels of this unquestionably foundational early U.S. novelist. So, while a number of critics have argued that *Arthur Mervyn* links the commercial ethos of liberalism to fraud and deception and thereby tenders "a bitter, somber critique of late-eighteenth-century capitalism,"[8] I want to argue nearly the opposite: that *Arthur Mervyn,* but also *Ormond,* represent poverty as potentially beneficial to individuals subjected to it and, by extension, work to ratify the inequality of which this poverty is a symptom.[9]

A focus on Brown's representation of poverty, in addition to shedding new light on his literary practice in particular, also revises literary historical common sense about the kinds of narratives Americans told themselves in the early republic. While it is a commonplace that the late eighteenth- and early nineteenth-century discourse of American exceptionalism insisted that the United States had already escaped—or was destined imminently to escape—the poverty endemic to Europe, novels such as *Ormond* and *Arthur Mervyn* counter this exceptionalism with a deliberate celebration of class inequality in the United States. In *Ormond* and *Arthur Mervyn,* poverty exists in the United States—and it is good that it does.[10]

Brown was familiar, through his reading of William Godwin, with a strain of philosophy for which poverty was, to use Gavin Jones's apt words, "an ethical dilemma" that "provokes questions of distributive justice."[11] Yet, while characters in *Ormond* and *Arthur Mervyn* at times broach questions of distributive justice, these novels do not finally lament economic inequality or demand its end. An indicator of the class politics of Brown's Philadelphia novels is to be found in the fates of those characters that refuse to learn to submit to their own economic subalternity: these characters are villains—and are punished, usually with death. In contrast to those characters that refuse to submit to economic subalternity, poor characters in Brown's novels who do signal their consent to the unequal distribution of wealth in the United States are rewarded—and not just with wealth—in their respective stories.

These poor characters become protagonists in versions of the bildungsroman. Brown is usually understood as a writer of gothic fiction, but in Constantia and Arthur "one finds a dynamic unity in the hero's image," as Bakhtin writes of the protagonist of the bildungsroman; here, "changes in the hero . . . acquire *plot* significance."[12] Yet, the bildungsroman is more than a novel in which "changes in the hero . . . acquire *plot* significance"; rather, it is a form that works to reconcile "the conflict between the ideal of *self-determination* and the equally imperious demands of *socialization*" through a narrative of a young person's "maturation."[13] In *Ormond* and *Arthur Mervyn,* Brown reconciles an ideal of self-determination with socialization by inviting his readers to imagine subjection to poverty and free-subjectivity as, paradoxically enough, one and the same.[14] For the narrators and the plots of these novels, poverty need not spell exploitation and oppression, but instead entails freedom and individual intellectual expansion. In *Ormond* and *Arthur Mervyn,* poverty itself provides the occasion for Constantia Dudley's and Arthur Mervyn's "intellectual improvement" (since it increases their knowledge of the world and themselves); it allows these characters to practice "benevolence" and heroism; and, it allows them to encounter extraordinary personages and expand their circles of friends.

By rewriting "poverty" as "freedom," Brown's Philadelphia novels revise their moment's governing discursive formations. Early Americans thought of poverty and freedom as fundamentally antithetical.[15] Both republicanism and emergent liberalism equated personal autonomy with property ownership.[16] "It was an axiom of Enlightenment political thought," writes Amy Dru Stanley, "that persons who sold their labor—however voluntarily—were dependent, and therefore not fully autonomous or capable of exercising the virtue required of citizens."[17]

Because Constantia and Arthur do "rise" out of poverty, we might read *Ormond* and *Arthur Mervyn* as early instantiations of a nationalist ideology of class mobility. As Karen Sánchez-Eppler contends, "National ideologies of class promise that in the United States poverty, like childhood, is merely a stage to be outgrown."[18] Yet, because Brown's Philadelphia novels invest in poverty as an *essential* stage of their protagonists' developments, they do not insist that the United States should one day outgrow poverty as a feature of its economic life. Alternatively, because of whom they permit to "rise" out of poverty, we might read Brown's novels as primarily working to imagine a wealthy class that deserves to be wealthy. This is the argument that Matthew Pethers has put forward about *Ormond*. For Pethers, *Ormond* is exemplary of what he names the "parabolic social mobility narrative." In *Ormond* and a host of other novels published in the first decade of the nineteenth century, Pethers discovers a narrative form in which the ascent from poverty to wealth is, first, limited to characters who were initially wealthy, and, second, a matter not of a character accumulating wealth via work but instead a matter of Providence's recognition that this character has responded "virtuously" to poverty.[19] Like Pethers, I also observe that the ascent from poverty to wealth in *Ormond*—but also *Arthur Mervyn*—is not about accumulating wealth via work so much as it is about an individual being bequeathed wealth: Brown does not tell stories of economic "bootstrapping." Additionally, I also investigate the extent to which Brown's fiction works to portray members of the propertied class as "moral." Yet, in contrast to Pethers's account of the "parabolic social mobility narrative," I am arguing that Brown's Philadelphia novels primarily work not to link wealth with virtue but instead to legitimate the very existence of poverty by, again, aligning poverty with freedom and intellectual expansion.

Moreover, I want to suggest that Brown's Philadelphia novels turn the representation of poverty into a source of pleasure for those who have not experienced poverty but instead read about it in the pages of his novels. Insofar as *Ormond* and *Arthur Mervyn* construct poverty as the precondition of positive, noneconomic transformation for their protagonists, poverty itself becomes the price of admission for narrative pleasure—for captivating stories.

To exploit poverty on behalf of narrative pleasure in this fashion is a quintessentially anti-utopian gesture. Indeed, in the utopian world of Reynolds's *Equality, A Political Romance* (1802), the kind of stories that Brown offers in *Ormond* and *Arthur Mervyn* are ruled out from the start. The first half of *Equality*, as I explained in the introduction, paints a portrait of Lithconia, a society in which class inequality has been overcome. Yet, equality in Lithconia functions as an impediment to the production of stories. As Louis Marin has pointed out, "utopia knows nothing of time. . . . Utopia knows nothing of change."[20] In Lithconia, equality means an absence of conflict, and the absence of change is expressed as absolute social integration and normality. "The period of the life of *one* man is employed nearly in the same manner as any other," the narrator explains: "To give the history, then, of one Lithconian, is to describe the manners of the nation" (23). There are no adventures—no trials and tribulations—in Lithconia. The only "plot" deserving of the name in Lithconia is the arrival of an outsider, the text's narrator. For Charles Brockden Brown the novelist, this political dream—where not even the young can drop into poverty—would make two of his novels essentially impossible. There has to be poverty for Brown's young protagonists to fall into; there must be economic inequality to tell the stories that he does.

"The Absurd and Unequal Distribution of Wealth and Power"

According to the exceptionalist imagination, the European who comes to America leaves behind an exquisitely detailed variety of rank, along with the extreme divergence of wealth and poverty. This exceptionalism finds its most cogent expression in Letter 3 of Crèvecoeur's 1782 *Letters from an American Farmer,* the salient moment for my purposes here which I want to quote once more. "Here are no aristocratical families," the invented Farmer James writes, "no courts, no kings, no bishops, no ecclesiastical dominion, no invisible power giving to a few a very visible one, no great manufactures employing thousands, no great refinements of luxury. The rich and the poor are not so far removed from each other as they are in Europe" (67). In contrast to Europe, Farmer James explains, the United States is defined by a "pleasing uniformity of decent competence" (67). In the absence of Europe's political structures and the presence of America's natural abundance, the American becomes a "new man" that has escaped from "voluntary idleness, servile dependence, penury, and useless labor" and has been "rewarded by ample subsistence" (70).

But by the end of the eighteenth century, this promise of "competence" and "ample subsistence" for individuals of European ancestry was already being undercut by the paradoxes of capitalist accumulation, especially in mid-Atlantic cities like Philadelphia. As Billy G. Smith has documented, "One group of Philadelphians became rich as their neighbors grew poor during much of the second half of the century."[21]

"The vast majority of laboring people were without property," Smith explains, and their "positions at the bottom" of the economic ladder "more permanent" than just-so stories of mobility suggest (133, 149). Wealth did not "trickle down" to workers, who led precarious and anxiety-wracked lives (149). "Competence" and "ample subsistence" were anything but guaranteed in Philadelphia at the end of the eighteenth century.

For some late eighteenth-century political economists and philosophers, moreover, economic inequality was at odds with Enlightenment—or with what Immanuel Kant called the ability "to use one's understanding without guidance from another."[22] None other than Adam Smith suggested that "the progress of the division of labour," by reducing "those who labour" to "a few very simple operations," creates a kind of worker who "has no occasion to exert his understanding."[23] Thus excluded from "the habit of" intellectual "exertion," Smith continues, this worker "becomes as stupid and ignorant as it is possible for a human creature to become" (2:784). This worker, "not only incapable of relishing or bearing a part in any rational conversation, but of conceiving any general, noble, or tender sentiment," is, in a word, dehumanized (2:784). Such a "stupid" worker is, Smith suspects, the necessary flipside of economic development: "[I]n every improved and civilized society this is the state into which the labouring poor, that is, the great body of the people, must necessarily fall" (2:782).

In his *Enquiry Concerning Political Justice,* William Godwin—who, of course, made a deep impression on Brown's intellectual formation and his approach to literary experimentation—radicalizes Smith's thoughts on the perils of economic inequality, suggesting that "human society" predicated on the unequal distribution of property is fundamentally inhospitable to ethical action. Because of the unequal distribution of property, Godwin argues, "the whole structure of human society, is made a system of the narrowest selfishness."[24] For Godwin, economic inequality leads to a series of vices: the "spirit of oppression, the spirit of servility, and the spirit of fraud." These vices are, Godwin continues, "*alike hostile to intellectual and moral improvement*" (294). Economic inequality is thus antithetical to both individual and collective development—to individual and collective *Bildung.* Godwin concludes that "equality of conditions" is synonymous with "justice": "Equality of conditions . . . is a law rigorously enjoined upon mankind by the voice of justice. All other changes in society are good, only as they are fragments of this, or steps to its attainment. All other existing abuses are to be deprecated, only as they serve to increase and perpetuate the inequality of conditions" (295).

Yet, Brown was skeptical of the desire for an egalitarian distribution of economic resources. "Walstein's School of History," for example, often read as a plan for *Arthur Mervyn,* exhibits Godwinian overtones, but it is neither as stringent nor as demanding in its calls for social reform as *Political Justice.*[25] Where Godwin emphasizes the "evils" that emerge from "inequality of conditions," Brown points out in "Walstein's School of History" that "benefits" can "be conferred in spite of poverty."[26] "In spite of poverty": this very formulation encapsulates Brown's response to those late eighteenth-century writers who critiqued economic inequality. In *Memoirs of Carwin the Biloquist,* to give another example, Brown invokes Godwin's 1793 arguments about economic inequality through the figure of Ludloe. According to Ludloe, as Carwin explains, "The absurd and unequal distribution of power and property gave birth to poverty and riches, and these were the sources of luxury and crimes."[27] Like Godwin—or like the Godwin Brown knew—Ludloe identifies economic inequality as the source of social and political "ills," and believes that economic inequality is not caused by "natural necessity," and hence can be overcome.[28] From his belief in human perfectibility to his proto-anarchism, Ludloe is a caricature of the early Godwin. It is therefore telling that Ludloe is also a quintessential Brown villain: he manipulates others through deception in order to achieve his goals. At the very least, it is curious that, in Ludloe, Brown associates an activist commitment to economic equality with villainy. Like "Walstein's School of History" and *Memoirs of Carwin the Biloquist,* Brown's Philadelphia novels invite their readers to temper any disaffection they might harbor toward economic inequality by making the desire for equality a characteristic of villains.

The Spirit of Capitalism: Morphology of the Villain

What is a villain? In the Russian folktale, Vladímir Propp explains, "the villain, first of all, assumes a disguise."[29] But "villain" also carries with it meanings charged by class. "The original social meaning of the word 'villain,'" writes Lionel Trilling, "bears decisively upon its later moral meaning. The opprobrious term referred to the man who stood lowest in the scale of feudal society; the villain of plays and novels is characteristically a person who seeks to rise above the station to which he was born. He is not what he is: this can be said of him both because by his intention he denies and violates his social identity and because he can achieve his unnatural purpose only by covert acts, by guile."[30] In Brown's Philadelphia novels, the disguise—guile—is the signifier of villainy; moreover, characters in these novels that commit acts of "guile" often do so because they, like Trilling's villains, are disaffected with the socioeconomic order in which they find themselves.

Indeed, a morphological analysis of Brown's Philadelphia novels reveals two kinds of villains. First, Ormond in *Ormond* is, like Ludloe in *Memoirs of Carwin the Biloquist,* a European radical who believes that the world-as-it-is is fundamentally flawed and thus that only a profound revolution can bring about an ethical world; this kind of villain will use any means necessary—from disguises to murder—to accomplish the social, political, and economic transformations he deems necessary. Second, characters like Craig in *Ormond* or Welbeck in *Arthur Mervyn* steal wealth from others through deception, fraud, and forgery. These villains commit acts of "guile" in order to transcend their respective economic subalternity.

For many critics, Craig and Welbeck are evidence of Brown's indictment of early U.S. "commerce." Critics often read Craig and Welbeck as personifications of the liberal-capitalist ethos of unbridled greed, identifying the fraud perpetrated by these characters as Brown's way of critiquing capitalism.[31] But one complicating factor in such readings is that these characters, putative personifications of liberal capitalism in America, are explicitly foreigners who in fact refuse "free labor"—or, more precisely, refuse to inhabit subordinate positions within the labor market as sellers of their labor power.[32]

Capitalism, Max Weber famously argued, is not synonymous with "absolute unscrupulousness in the pursuit of selfish interests by the making of money."[33] According to Weber, capitalism is not defined by greed or acquisition so much as it is by an ethos with respect to work. Under capitalism, Weber writes, "labour must . . . be performed as if it were an absolute end in itself" (63). If capitalism endows work and acquisition through work with ethical value, Craig and Welbeck in contrast find no ethical value in work for work's sake. Craig enters *Ormond* as the apprentice to Stephen Dudley (who is the father of the novel's protagonist, Constantia Dudley); Craig's labor eventually liberates Stephen Dudley from work altogether, providing Dudley with "constantly accumulating" wealth.[34] Yet, Craig embezzles Stephen Dudley's savings because, we eventually learn, what he is doing is trying to escape from his captivity in the labor market and his position in an asymmetric economic relationship.[35] Welbeck, too, commits his crimes so as to escape from the class position into which he has fallen: he tells Arthur that, upon his arrival in the United States, "I possessed no means of subsistence. . . . I was unqualified for manual labour by all the habits of my life; but there was no choice between penury and diligence—between honest labour and criminal inactivity. . . . The perverseness of my nature led me on from one guilty thought to another. I took refuge in my customary sophistries, and reconciled myself at length to a scheme of—*forgery!*"[36] Welbeck suggests that, given his lack of resources, he can either be a member of the working poor or a thief— but he finds no value in being a member of the working poor. Like Craig, Welbeck engages in fraudulent representations in order to avoid having to sell his labor. We would be remiss to attribute a fully formed, radical class consciousness to Craig and Welbeck: they never express concern for social transformations that would elevate workers or ensure workers a greater share of the collective social wealth they produce. It would be fair to say, however, that they are insubordinate vis-à-vis what Weber defines as the specific "spirit of capitalism," insofar as they refuse to be workers. In the words of Clithero in Brown's *Edgar Huntly,* they are defined by "an impatience of subjection and poverty."[37] They are "bad subjects" *par excellence,* individuals who "take the ideology of free subjectivity too much to heart and do not freely consent to their subjection."[38]

Just as capitalism requires a labor force willing to work, it also requires a capitalist class—or at least the image of a capitalist class—for whom acquisition appears as a "virtuous" activity. The "ideal type of capitalistic entrepreneur," Weber explains, "avoids ostentation and unnecessary expenditure" while conceiving of "money-making as an end itself to which people [are] bound, as a calling" (71, 73). *Ormond*'s Balfour corresponds to this "ideal type": he is "governed by the principles of mercantile integrity in all his dealings"; in "all his transactions" he is "sedate and considerate" (81). With Balfour, who is neither fraudulent nor criminal, Brown suggests that "commerce" need not be synonymous with villainy.

In the cases of Craig and Welbeck, then, Brown's narratives of fraud do not signify an indictment of "commerce" so much as they forge a link between plebeian insubordination and treachery, falsehood—"evil." In other words, you are destined to become a villain in Brown's Philadelphia novels when you allow yourself to become disaffected with your economic subalternity and the working for others' profits that it demands. Consenting to poverty, on the other hand, guarantees you a different story.

"WHATEVER WERE ITS EVILS": THE "FORTUNATE" FALL INTO POVERTY

Ormond can be read as a subversive novel that criticizes early U.S. patriarchy, reveals how early U.S. citizenship is predicated on white male privilege and the exclusions of women and nonwhites, and imagines the progressive possibilities of female community.[39] This may all be true; nonetheless, left out of this picture is the fact that *Ormond*'s narrative of an empowered poor woman legitimates class inequality in the early United States.

It may seem absurd to argue that *Ormond* celebrates poverty, given that the first third of the novel details the hardships and anxieties Constantia Dudley encounters as a member of the Philadelphia poor while she struggles to support herself and her father after her mother's death and the onset of her father's blindness. In the novel's language, she is "[i]mmersed in poverty, friendless, burdened with the maintenance and nurture of her father" (72). The precariousness of her situation, the difficulty Constantia has finding work, the pressure she faces trying to make rent payments, and the looming danger of the yellow fever provoke a self-critical response from the novel's narrator, Sophia Courtland: "O my friend! Methinks I now see thee, encountering the sneers and obstinacy of the meanest of mankind, subjecting that frame of thine, so exquisitely delicate, and therefore so feeble, to the vilest drudgery. . . . Why was I not partaker of thy cares and labours?" (31–32). Without question, *Ormond* begins as an exposé of poverty in Philadelphia, and here Sophia offers a sentimental protest against poverty. Why should a "good person" like

Constantia—a virtuous, hardworking, inquisitive, and intelligent person—be forced to experience poverty's deprivations and its angsts?

For her part, Constantia does not complain about her situation. When
her family is reduced to poverty and she is forced to become a "work-
woman" (a member of Philadelphia's working class), she "indulged herself in no fits of exclamation or moodiness" (25, 23). In fact, her "new
situation" provides "motives to courage and activity" (23). Unlike her
father and unlike Welbeck in *Arthur Mervyn,* Constantia takes to her
"new situation" with "grace and cheerfulness" (25). *Ormond* rewards
Constantia's acceptance of her poverty, turning it into a boon for her
despite Sophia's early lamentations.

As a member of the working poor, Constantia discovers leisure for
intellectual pursuits despite her poverty, especially during the yellow
fever. The yellow fever might stand symbolically in Brown's Philadelphia
novels for the "infection" of the French Revolution and the "unhealthi-
ness" of "commerce,"[40] but it also compounds the struggles of Philadelphia's working poor, Constantia included, in Brown's novels: "The
labours of the artizan and the speculations of the merchant were suspended. All shops, but those of the apothecaries were shut. . . . The customary sources of subsistence were cut off. . . . Those who lived by the
fruits of their daily labour were subjected, in this total inactivity, to the
alternative of starving, or of subsisting upon public charity" (55). Yet,
Constantia and her father are able to transcend this predicament by subsisting on a diet of polenta. (Eating only polenta, "three persons" can
survive "during four months, at the trivial expense of three dollars" [57].)
Unemployment itself has its rewards: Constantia's "hands were unemployed, but her mind was kept in continual activity. . . . Her father's in-
structions were sufficient to give her a competent acquaintance with the
Italian and French languages" (57). As Sophia encapsulates the matter,
"the yellow fever, by affording" Constantia "respite from toil, supplying
leisure for acquisition of a useful branch of knowledge, and leading her
to the discovery of a cheaper, more simple, and more wholesome method
of subsistence, had been friendly, instead of adverse, to her happiness"
(73). If unemployment caused by the yellow fever should only amplify
Constantia's hardships as a member of Philadelphia's working poor, it is
instead liberating: Constantia's "situation, which, whatever were its evils,
gave her as much freedom from restraint as is consistent with the state
of human affairs" (83).

"Whatever were its evils": the syntax is telling. In such phrasings, Brown develops a style for writing about the experience of poverty that trades in qualification and compromise (as opposed to protest). Sophia time and again qualifies her reproofs of the poverty Constantia endures, and she suggests that poverty is—despite its "evils"—also synonymous with female empowerment. Early in the novel Sophia explains that in Constantia the "infirmities of sex and age vanished before the motives to courage and activity flowing from her new situation" (23). Poverty is likewise "fortunate," according to Sophia, for Constantia's father: "Perhaps in a rational estimate," Sophia opines, "one of the most fortunate events that could have befallen those persons, was that period of adversity through which they had been doomed to pass. Most of the defects that adhered to the character of Mr. Dudley, had, by this means, been exterminated. He was now cured of those prejudices which his early prosperity had instilled, and which flowed from luxurious indulgences. He had learned to estimate himself at true value, and to sympathize with the sufferings which he himself had partaken" (174). This is an exemplary instance of Sophia's qualifying style: though Dudley's life as a wageworker after Craig robs him of his wealth and livelihood is represented earlier as a nearly unbearable state of exploitation and indignity, Sophia here redeems Dudley's "adversity." Poverty, Sophia explains, reforms Dudley, eradicating his pride and activating what might be called his moral sentiments. Indeed, *Ormond* ultimately romances Stephen Dudley's poverty, suggesting that it is better for him than the intellectual stagnation of his earlier petit bourgeois life.

Moreover, poverty becomes the soil in which a peaceful revolution in filial relations can grow. As it reforms Dudley and liberates Constantia, poverty renders more equal the relationship between daughter and father. Poverty has made Dudley dependent on his daughter—on "the wisdom of her measures" and "her fortitude and skill in every emergency" (174). Yet, as Sophia explains, Dudley "resigned himself with pleasure to [Constantia's] guidance. The chain of subordination and duties was reversed" (174). In *Ormond,* poverty can lead to the subversion of patriarchy within the family, because it launches daughters into new roles and because it creates fathers who can appreciate reversals of filial power as much as their daughters might.

Just as poverty occasions a revolution in father-daughter power relations, so too does poverty stand as a state of relative freedom for the novel's female protagonist vis-à-vis the institution of bourgeois marriage. In chapter 9, Balfour, the virtuous merchant, proposes marriage to Constantia. Constantia rejects him for two reasons. Her first reason has to do with what she perceives to be their intellectual inequality: in part, she rejects Balfour because of the "poverty of his discourse and ideas" (83). Her second reason turns on the nature of bourgeois marriage as an asymmetrical economic relationship: though marriage to Balfour would rescue Constantia from her precarious economic situation, "so far from possessing property, she herself would become the property of another" (84). Yet, the critique of bourgeois marriage to which the novel gives voice as Sophia imagines Constantia's thought processes, despite being prescient of critiques such as Engels's *The Origins of the Family* and Perkins Gilman's *Women and Economics,* is wonky.[41] This is because the novel suggests that Constantia is *freer*—intellectually and economically—*in poverty,* despite the precariousness of her economic situation: "Now she was at least mistress of the product of her own labour. . . . Marriage would annihilate this power. Henceforth she would be bereft even of personal freedom" (84). The novel asks its readers to entertain the thought that poverty is synonymous with female freedom even though, as Pattie Cowell duly points out, "when it becomes necessary for" Constantia "to work outside the home, she must accept gender-specific (i.e., low-paying) jobs, and as an unescorted woman, she is repeatedly exposed to verbal abuse on the streets."[42] Yet, the novel does not suggest that poverty and marriage are *both* disempowering to women, but instead insists that poverty is better than a less than ideal bourgeois marriage. "Homely liberty," Constantia thinks, is "better than splendid servitude" (85).

"It is one of the most typical elements in Brown's narrative design," Wil Verhoeven observes, "that many of his heroes and hero-villains are continuously being maneuvered into positions where they are forced to make choices."[43] Constantia's choice between Balfour and continued poverty is exemplary of one of these imposed choices. The conclusion of the Balfour episode is also a decisive moment in *Ormond.* It is a moment when Brown opens up a choice for himself. He has the option of sending Constantia into absolute economic subjection. By rejecting Balfour she exposes herself to the possibility of intensifying debasement in poverty: "As her means of subsistence began to decay, she reflected on the change of employment that might become necessary. She was mistress of no lucrative art, but that which now threatened to be useless. There was but one avenue through which she could hope to escape the pressure of absolute want. This, she regarded with an aversion, that nothing but extreme necessity, and the failure of every other expedient, would be able to subdue. This was hiring herself as a servant" (87). At this juncture, the novel could have become a story about the lives of serving girls in 1790s Philadelphia. But, and this point is crucial to my reading of *Ormond,* Constantia is rewarded—and *Ormond*'s readers are rewarded—by her choice to remain in poverty. The novel does not take her finally down the path of deepening subjection to poverty. Constantia's choice to remain in poverty makes possible the novel's introduction of Ormond and Martinette, characters that serve to bring wide-ranging historical and philosophical discussions into the novel at the same time that they increase Constantia's knowledge of history and philosophy. "To what entire and incredible reverses is the tenor of human life subject," Brown writes (108). By meeting Ormond, Constantia gains immense wealth. And Ormond's attempt to rape her at the end of the novel makes possible her final act of gender-norm subversion. Constantia's interactions with Ormond certainly have their costs: her father is murdered and Helen commits suicide. Yet, because of Ormond, Constantia ends the novel intellectually and materially enriched as well as independent. It is good that Constantia chooses poverty. It is good that there is poverty for her to choose. In *Ormond,* poverty never really becomes poverty.

That Constantia's choice of poverty opens new narrative opportunities is precisely how the metonymic logic of *Ormond's story* grafts freedom onto poverty. Indeed, Constantia meets Ormond when she is seeking charity from one of her father's former associates (Mr. Melbourne) and runs into Craig. Of the conversations that Constantia has with Ormond, Sophia has this to report: "By the variety of topics and the excitement to reflection it supplied, a more plenteous influx of knowledge was produced, than could have flowed from any other source. There was no end to the detailing of facts, and the canvassing of theories" (177). Constantia likewise meets Martinette—aptly described by Paul Lewis as "a trans-Atlantic, cross-dressing revolutionary who provides a model of the woman warrior"—on a journey to the Melbournes', this time to visit Melbourne's daughter, with whom Constantia has become friends.[44] Constantia meets Martinette when, hearing the lute she had previously pawned to meet a rent payment being played in a neighboring house, she inquires after its owner. Of Constantia's experience of Martinette's stories, Sophia reports:

> Each incident fastened on the memory of Constance, and gave birth to numberless reflections. Her prospect of mankind seemed to be enlarged, on a sudden, to double its ancient dimensions. Ormond's narratives had carried her beyond the Mississippi, and into the deserts of Siberia. He had recounted the perils of a Russian war, and painted the manners of Mongals and Naudowessies. Her new friend pourtrayed the other half of the species. Men, in their two forms, of savage and refined, had been scrutinized by these observers, and what was wanting in the delineations of one, was liberally supplied by the other. (205)

From Adam Smith to William Godwin, late eighteenth-century thinkers assailed economic inequality because they thought it led to the existence of a class of people for whom, according to these writers, "intellectual improvement" was nearly impossible. But in *Ormond,* poverty sets in motion a series of events that lead to the incredible expansion of its protagonist's mind.

As I pointed out at the beginning of this section, critics have argued that *Ormond* tenders a feminist revision of eighteenth-century sentimental fiction by imagining a boldly independent and empowered female protagonist who defies late eighteenth-century novelistic stereotypes of women.[45] For example, Paul Lewis characterizes *Ormond* as an early "female bildungsroman" that "pushed beyond familiar questions about woman's place to boldly feminist positions."[46] Lewis aptly summarizes the novel's plot: "*Ormond* follows the eventful maturation and testing of Constantia Dudley, a young woman given a man's education and then compelled by extreme adversity to support her father, manage a household, deal with various dangers, make crucial life decisions, and, finally and most remarkably, defend herself from physical attack."[47] I have sought to emphasize the importance of poverty to Constantia's *Bildung.* According to *Ormond*'s narrator and *Ormond*'s narrative logic (the novel's sequence of cause and effect), poverty makes Constantia's *Bildung* possible: poverty "improves" Constantia, it paves her way to expansive intellectual vistas, and it puts her in a position to triumph over one of early American literature's most nefarious villains. "Poverty, disease, servile labour, a criminal and hapless parent, have been evils which thou hast not ungracefully sustained," Ormond tells Constantia (258). Though Ormond is certain that his attempted rape is categorically different from any of the "evils" Constantia has faced, he is mistaken to think that "drudgery," "sickness," and "privation of friends"—all symptoms of poverty—have not prepared Constantia to repel his assault (259). She has not "studied so long in the school of adversity" to no purpose (145).

Arthur Mervyn's Apprenticeship

Scholars interested in how Brown dramatizes economic matters have typically focused their attention on his other Philadelphia novel, *Arthur Mervyn*. Yet, critical preoccupation with Arthur's moral ambiguity (is he just Welbeck's accomplice?), as well as with the question of whether he represents republican civic-mindedness or liberal self-interestedness, tends to obscure *Arthur Mervyn*'s fundamental interest in relative economic lack as a material state of selfhood and social being.[48] If anything, *Arthur Mervyn* accentuates *Ormond*'s paradoxical celebration of poverty, as if Brown were making sure that *Ormond*'s message on poverty did not go unrecognized.[49]

Like Constantia does in her novel, Arthur opens his novel by falling from economic security into poverty. When Dr. Stevens (the first narrator of *Arthur Mervyn*) introduces us to Arthur, we learn that he is poor, unskilled, and unemployed: "He was unqualified, by his education, for any liberal profession. His poverty was likewise an insuperable impediment. He could afford to spend no time in the acquisition of a trade. He must labour not for future emolument but for immediate subsistence" (9). Because Arthur must work for someone else in order to "maintain himself" (23), he thus begins the novel in a position of economic dependence.

What's more, this position provokes anxiety in Arthur, as Dr. Stevens explains: "He must not sacrifice the end for the means. . . . If his tasks should enable him to live, but at the same time, bereave him of all satisfaction, they inflicted injury and were to be shunned as evils worse that death. . . . He knew how to value the thoughts of other people, but he could not part with the privilege of observing and thinking for himself. He wanted business which would suffer at least nine tenths of his attention to go free" (10).

In chapter 2, as Arthur begins to relate his story directly, the novel re-iterates these notions about the potential conflict between economic dependence and personal autonomy. It is in this chapter that we learn that Arthur's economic subalternity is a new circumstance for him. Living on his father's farm as a boy, Arthur "long enjoyed the pleasures of independence"; now that his father's farm has passed into the hands of his father's new wife (and former servant), Arthur heads to Philadelphia— thinking at first that he must "[b]ecome a day-labourer in the service of strangers," though he soon decides "to apprentice [himself] to some mechanical trade" (21). In any case, Arthur tells Dr. Stevens, he "hoped to procure an immediate subsistence without forfeiting [his] liberty" (23). "My poverty, but not my will consents," Arthur says to Welbeck— quoting Shakespeare—when he first signs on as Welbeck's amanuensis (50). When Arthur reflects that his "poverty" and working for an "immediate subsistence" threaten the "privilege of observing and thinking for himself"—when he leans on Shakespeare to draw a line between "poverty" and "will"—we should hear echoes of the late eighteenth-century critique of inequality according to which the "poor" and "workers" are by virtue of their economic position excluded from "intellectual improvement" and freedom. Arthur, at the beginning of his novel, goes so far as to utter a sentimental protest against economic inequality: "My heart dictated the comparison between my own condition and that of the proprietors of this domain. How wide and impassible was the gulf by which they were separated! This fair inheritance had fallen to one who, perhaps, would only abuse it to the purposes of luxury, while I, with intentions worthy of the friend of mankind, was doomed to wield the flail and the mattock" (47). As he says shortly after, "Wealth has ever been capriciously distributed. The mere physical relation of birth is all that intitles us to manors and thrones" (57). Arthur—at the beginning of his plot—suggests that economic inequality is illogical, having neither a moral nor a utilitarian foundation.

Yet, Arthur ultimately overcomes and puts to rest his anxieties about poverty and the inequality of which it is an expression. Roughly two-thirds into *Arthur Mervyn,* he formulates a plan for his ideal "apprenticeship":

Competence, fixed property and a settled abode, rural occupations and conjugal pleasures, were justly to be prized; but their value could be known, and their benefits fully enjoyed only by those who have tried all scenes; who have mixed with all classes and ranks; who have partaken of all conditions; and who have visited different hemispheres and climates and nations. The next five or eight years of my life, should be devoted to activity and change: it should be a period of hardship, danger, and privation: it should be my apprenticeship to fortitude and wisdom, and be employed to fit me for the tranquil pleasures and steadfast exertions of the remainder of my life. (293)

Within the motivation of *Arthur Mervyn*'s plot, Arthur formulates this plan to justify not marrying Eliza Hadwin and assuming ownership of her father's farm (when owning the farm is still an option). To marry Eliza is, for Arthur, to escape economic subalternity, but it is also to sacrifice a kind of private, sexual autonomy. Yet, just as *Ormond* suggests that it is better for Constantia to be poor than to be Balfour's wife, Arthur suggests that it is better to remain a worker than to marry Eliza and become the owner of Hadwin's farm. The apprenticeship plan reflects, then, *Arthur Mervyn*'s change in tone on poverty.

The plan can also be read as the novel commenting self-reflexively on the shape of its protagonist's story. While Arthur's plan for himself never perfectly materializes within the novel (which ends in the space of months), Arthur's apprenticeship plan points up how *Arthur Mervyn* works as a whole: the novel follows Arthur through "a period of hardship, danger and privation" and concludes just as he is about to marry the wealthy Achsa Fielding. The plan—and the novel more broadly—both correspond to the basic narrative architecture of the nineteenth-century bildungsroman, which relies on a developmental plot that is equally committed to youth and maturity as it is to self-determination and social normality.[50] "In a special instance of embedding," notes George Spangler, Arthur "envisions his future as if he wanted to be the protagonist of a *Bildungsroman*."[51] My point is that he is precisely this, but moreover, that the apprenticeship plan and the novel more broadly offer a narrative that figures potentially antagonistic class positions as stages of personal growth: this is a version of the bildungsroman that is also equally committed to poverty and to wealth.

Pace critics who see Arthur as a personification of capitalist acquisitiveness, in his plan Arthur is neither a Robinson Crusoe nor a Horatio Alger protagonist: the "five to eight years" are not the means to wealth through work, or a period devoted either to speculation or accumulation, but instead stand as an escape from a bourgeois existence of "tranquil pleasures and steadfast exertions."[52] Likewise, Arthur's eventual "rise" into the bourgeoisie at the end of the novel is not a story either of bootstrapping or of financial investments rewarded, even though many critics like to see his ability at the end of the novel to move into the bourgeois world as a kind of metaphoric speculation rewarded.[53] Though early in his youth (when the son of a landowner), he benefited from the labor of others, at no point in the novel does he make money from land, or from money invested, or most importantly from others' labors. Arthur does not imagine himself as a merchant; instead, the plan—like the novel itself—romances the selling of labor.[54] The "five to eight years" of the "apprenticeship" plan are about becoming ready to enter bourgeois life, but not about gathering the material resources to do so; these resources, in the magic of the apprenticeship plan and the novel itself, appear when the subject is ready for them. And though Arthur may not be disinterested, his self-interest exceeds mere economic calculations.

The plan and novel rewrite the precariousness experienced by so many early Americans as an ideal of subject formation. Capital is, by nature, mobile; capital chases opportunities for profit around the globe. In the late eighteenth century, labor—capital's opposite—was forced to be mobile, too. According to Marcus Rediker, the life of eighteenth-century plebeians in seaboard American cities was one of *forced* mobility: "The cultural world of free wage labour was essentially picaresque," Rediker writes, and workers were "pushed or pulled according to the vagaries of the economy."[55] Arthur's plan is reminiscent of Sarsefield's international journeys in *Edgar Huntly,* journeys defined by "vicissitude and hardship," by "poverty" and becoming "mendicant" (61). In the apprenticeship plan, it is as if Brown comments on this kind of subaltern mobility, acknowledging that the condition of propertylessness is one of endless migration. The plan mutes, however, the ways in which this mobility is in fact forced (a matter of being "pushed" and "pulled"). The plan's period of "hardship, danger and privation" is imagined to be finite, limited, giving way to social integration; in this way, in its finitude, this period is at odds with the logic of "commerce," which is defined by endless movement.[56] If the ideological logic of upward mobility entails the mystification of class via stories of class permeability, the logic of Arthur's plan affirms class division by locating in it a fantasy of a certain kind of subaltern geographic mobility.[57] The "five to eight years" of the "apprenticeship" plan retroactively figure Arthur's experiences of domination (his encounters with Welbeck and the yellow fever), as well as establish Arthur's later conflicts (with Philip Hadwin and the Maurices), as beneficial experiences of "activity and change" and "hardship, danger, and privation" that "improve" him and make him "fit" for society—as, in a word, *Bildung*.

Despite lamenting his poverty early in the novel, then, Arthur ultimately invites us to extol economic subalternity. When his former love interest (and now friend) Eliza Hadwin loses her father's property to her less than savory uncle in a subplot that mirrors Arthur's own downward mobility, Arthur explains that Eliza now "must find subsistence in tending the big-wheel or the milk-pail." Though this work is "but little different" from what she did "in her father's house," there "these employments were dignified by being, in some degree, voluntary, and relieved by frequent intervals of recreation of leisure" (311). Now that Eliza must work for someone else, "these employments" "were likely to prove irksome and servile, in consequence of being performed for hire, and imposed by necessity. Equality, parental solicitude, and sisterly endearments would be wanting to lighten the yoke" (311). But if Eliza's propertylessness entails a kind of servitude, for Arthur it should be imagined as a windfall. Strain and indignity are but "inconveniences," Arthur reflects, and "imaginary." Economic dependence represents a new opportunity for Eliza's personal growth, according to Arthur: "This was the school in which fortitude and independence were to be learned. . . . The affections of parent and sister would be supplied by the fonder and more rational attachments of friendship" (311). Eliza's imposed farmwork may have the "tendency to quench the spirit of liberal curiosity" and might "habituate" her "to bodily, rather than intellectual, exertions." No matter: Eliza can develop "studious habits" in the interim before her employment starts, and these "habits" can survive—even flourish—in her new situation (312). Yet, Arthur, by figuring propertylessness and the attendant need to work for someone else as "school," dismantles the opposition between economic dependence and free subjectivity.[58] Eliza could be another Constantia Dudley. But whereas Sophia Courtland instructs *Ormond's* readers on how to read Constantia's poverty, in *Arthur Mervyn*, the defense of poverty comes from someone who has, at least in the world of the novel, a claim to firsthand knowledge of poverty and wage labor.

Arthur is a poor character who nonetheless speaks on behalf of capitalist labor relations and the inequalities they entail.

Arthur's apprenticeship plan and his endorsement of propertyless-ness for Eliza reverberate in his later evaluation of his own time with Welbeck. Arthur explains to Mrs. Wentworth that his "connection" with Welbeck should not be seen as "unfortunate": "It has done away a part of my ignorance of the world in which I live. It has led me to the situa-tion in which I am now placed. It has introduced me to the knowledge of many good people. It has made me the witness of and the subject of acts of beneficence and generosity. My knowledge of Welbeck has been useful to me. It has enabled me to be useful to others. I look back upon that allotment of my destiny which first led me to his door, with grati-tude and pleasure" (357–58). Arthur is grateful for the poverty that put him at Welbeck's mercy. Like Sophia Courtland, he imagines poverty as "fortunate." To become an economic subaltern is on Arthur's account, paradoxically enough, to have the opportunity to increase one's knowl-edge of the world; it is to be in a position of increased social agency ("the subject of acts of beneficence and generosity"); it is to have the opportu-nity to meet interesting people and to expand one's social circle. In his response to Mrs. Wentworth, Arthur offers a causal chain according to which his poverty enlarges his world, and so he offers a narrative logic that allows readers to appreciate poverty as the gateway to interesting stories and not mindless repetition, torpor, and fatigue.

That Arthur defends his time with Welbeck might appear strange to some readers of the novel. While employed by Welbeck early in the novel, Arthur's autonomy would seem to be all but obliterated. For example, he figures himself as an automaton under Welbeck's control: "I was driven, by a sort of mechanical impulse, in his footsteps" (113). But Welbeck's power over Arthur is ultimately partial and delimited. Each time Wel-beck makes Arthur feel like he has no agency, Arthur revolts. For in-stance, "I had acted long enough a servile and mechanical part; and been guided by blind and foreign impulses," he admits, but "it was time to lay aside my fetters, and demand to know whither the path tended" (114). And because Arthur knows about Welbeck's crimes, he can effectively end Welbeck's life—if only he would publicize these crimes. In their final encounter together in the debtors' prison (after Welbeck has been nabbed in Baltimore), Arthur has the lion's share of power. Welbeck has become "a monument of ruin" (335).[59] Arthur, though partially sympathetic to the plight of his former employer, does not worry about what his knowledge of Welbeck's crimes and his disclosure of them to Dr. Stevens might mean: "But why," he ponders, "should I ruminate, with anguish and doubt, upon the past?" (338). In *Arthur Mervyn,* would-be exploiters die; their employees, in contrast, can have futures. Seth Rockman contends that "the disparity in power between those buying labor and those performing it" was part of "the very foundations of capitalism in the early republic."[60] The sensational conflict between Welbeck-the-employer and Arthur-the-employee, however, serves in *Arthur Mervyn* to reverse this disparity.

Arthur's first-person narration itself mirrors Arthur's relationship to Welbeck: it allows him to be both the object of Welbeck's scheming and a self-reflexive subject. It is a mode of narration that calls attention as much to what Arthur thinks as to what he does. "Mervyn's labor-power," Stephen Shapiro contends, "is rarely commodified as something exchangeable, in protoproletarianizing conditions of wage labor. Instead his body as commodity, rather than the body's quantified labor, is transferred from place to place in conditions akin to slavery."[61] But Arthur is not reduced to his body (even though he contracts the yellow fever). Arthur explains: "My existence is a series of thoughts rather than of motions. Ratiocination and deduction leave my senses unemployed" (265). Arthur's story turns on a series of mental events, and the novel's first-person narration projects an expansive mental life for its protagonist during his time as an economic subaltern. Never does Welbeck truly turn Arthur into merely a mindless functionary.

Indeed, though Adam Smith suggested that workers are "reduced to a few simple operations," Arthur's economic subalternity—his being cut off from the means of production and thus forced to work for others—does not deprive him of intellectual autonomy. "My occupations," Arthur says of his time as a worker on Hadwin's farm, "are salutary and meritorious; I am a stranger to cares as well as to the enjoyment of riches; abundant means of knowledge are possessed by me as long as I have eyes to gaze at man and at nature, as they are exhibited in their original forms or in books" (128). Arthur's "labours" are so "light" that he has time to embark on a translation of the Italian Lodi manuscript, which he took from Welbeck's quarters during his escape. Though translating this manuscript might seem "phantastic and impracticable," it proves an "experiment" "within the compass" of Arthur's "powers" (126). This "experiment" demonstrates, Arthur insists, how "human ingenuity and patience are able to surmount" daunting "impediments"; it shows how the "mind, unassisted" can discover the principles of linguistic "similitude" and thus also "unspeakable pleasure" along the way (126). Arthur finds time, in other words, for gratifying intellectual endeavors. As a boy on his father's farm, Arthur hated school: he "hated to be classed, cribbed, rebuked, and feruled"; instead, he "preferred to ramble in the forest and loiter on the hill" while pursuing "those trains of thought which" nature provokes (341). But his experiences as a result of his poverty set his mind on fire. He has plenty of opportunity, in other words, for what he calls "mental exercise" (342). Arthur's "attention" in the novel seems always to go "free"—at least from work itself. If poverty does not become poverty for Constantia, neither does poverty become poverty for Arthur.

"These Modern Knights"

While some scholars have pointed to Arthur as a literary embodiment of the ideal of republican disinterestedness, his failed attempts as a crusader against economic injustice work hand in glove with, on the one hand, Brown's punishment of Craig and Welbeck and, on the other, Brown's celebration of poverty.[62] This is because Arthur's adventures always conclude with Arthur reconciling himself to economic inequality.

Arthur tries, for example, to rescue Wallace from the yellow fever, which shatters the pastoral peace Arthur experiences on Hadwin's farm when it infects Wallace. This "youth," Wallace, "had made himself clerk to a merchant" in order to make enough money "to support a family" and wed Susan Hadwin (131). "Wallace was without kindred, and probably without friends, in the city"; to compound this helplessness, "the merchant, in whose service he had placed himself, was connected with him by no consideration but that of interest" (133). Arthur has reason to identity with Wallace, and identify he does. Learning that Wallace may be less than savory in his own right, though, Arthur reconciles himself to Wallace's death: "Honest purposes, though they may not bestow happiness on others, will, at least, secure it to him who fosters them. . . . I prepared to rejoice alike, whether Wallace should be found to have escaped or perished" (270). The Wallace episode is paradigmatic: Arthur time and again figures out a way to live with the failure of a crusade for social justice.

When Arthur travels to Philadelphia to rescue Wallace, he brings the money he has discovered in the Lodi manuscript, intending to return it to Clemenza (from whom Welbeck has, in essence, stolen it): Clemenza is, on Arthur's account, "desolate and indigent" and so his "duty" to her "cannot be mistaken. The lady must be sought and the money restored to her" (128). When Arthur contracts the fever and thinks he is about to die, believing Clemenza is dead, he decides the money can best be used to aid Philadelphia's poor, who were especially affected by the fever: "I could not conceive any more beneficial application of this property," he explains, "than to the service of the indigent, at this season of multiplied distress" (183). Yet, Arthur has no regrets about torching the money and thus forfeiting this "beneficial application" when he is lead to believe, wrongly, that the money is forged. When Eliza loses her land to her greedy uncle, Arthur tries to convince the uncle that he is robbing his niece of her patrimony; failing to convince this uncle of Eliza's claim and realizing that the law is on the uncle's side, Arthur submits and accommodates himself to Eliza's fate as a laborer (as we have seen).

In each of these episodes, Arthur does not accomplish what he sets out to do, which is, in each case, to undo fraud and help the poor. While we might read Arthur's failures in these episodes as evidence of his metaphoric infection by Welbeck's destructiveness (as Goddu does, for example),[63] to do so is to overlook how they allow Arthur to project a sense of agency despite failing to intervene in the distribution of resources: "I was conscious," Arthur says, "that my happiness depended not on the revolutions of nature and the caprice of man. All without was, indeed, vicissitude and uncertainty; but within my bosom was a centre not to be shaken or removed" (312). Arthur's sense of individual agency corresponds, I would argue, to what Marx in the *Grundrisse* calls the "illusion" of "naturally independent, autonomous subjects" presumed by both social contract theory and classical political economy.[64]

Arthur can ultimately remain satisfied with his failed combat against economic injustice because it gives him occasion to interact with "virtuous" bourgeois individuals. A final example of failed heroism occurs when he travels to Baltimore to restore to the Maurices the money Welbeck has grifted from them. Arthur expects "to find virtuous indigence and sorrow lifted, by [his] means, to affluence and exultation" (382). He expects, in other words, to lift the deserving poor out of their unjust poverty. Instead, he finds "nothing but sordidness, stupidity, and illiberal suspicion." Mrs. Maurice, Williams (Mrs. Maurice's brother) later informs Arthur, is "narrow, ignorant, bigoted, avaricious"; her eldest daughter, in turn, "resembles the old lady in many things" and "pride and ill-humor are her chief characteristics" (382). When Arthur asks Williams if "good has been done . . . by restoring this money," Williams responds in the negative: "If pleasure be good, you must have conferred a great deal on the Maurices; upon the mother and the two of the daughters, at least. The only pleasure, indeed, which their natures can receive. It is less than if you had raised them from absolute indigence, which has not been the case, since they had wherewithal to live upon beside their Jamaica property" (386). The Maurices own slaves at their home in Baltimore, and they have interests in a Jamaican plantation and its slavery-generated wealth.[65]

Because he winds up returning a fortune to individuals who are marked by "sordidness, stupidity, and illiberal suspicion," this episode could have reanimated Arthur's earlier dissatisfaction with the unequal distribution of resources. But the encounter with the Maurices does not become a conflict over the unequal distribution of resources. On some level, the Maurices purchase Arthur's consent by giving him a one thousand dollar reward: "In coming hither," Arthur explains to Hemmings, "I expected only an increase of my debts, to sink still deeper into poverty; but happily the issue has made me rich. This hour has given me competence, at least" (387). For some critics, Arthur's acceptance of the reward reveals that he is indeed more self-interested speculator than disinterested citizen; in other words, because Arthur acquires some wealth in this episode he represents a capitalist of sorts.[66] Against this reading, I would argue that Arthur here represents not a capitalist so much as a well-disciplined worker. Importantly, Arthur does not follow the suggestion of the Maurices' own attorney to demand more money from the Maurices, for whom twenty thousand dollars looks like a pittance. Though the encounter with the Maurices occasions an indictment of the "sordidness" of the wealthy, it does not ultimately lead Arthur to desire *a greater share of the wealth* at stake or to question the fundamental economic asymmetries that the wealth of the unsavory Maurices once again puts before him. Instead of this episode becoming a conflict about the unequal (and irrational) distribution of resources, it becomes an opportunity for Arthur to socialize with Mrs. Watson and Miss Maurice. Arthur is rewarded for his restraint. The youngest Maurice daughter is nothing like her mother and older sister: "The youngest daughter," Williams explains, "has nothing in mind or person in common with her family. Where they are irascible, she is patient; where they are imperious, she is humble; where they are covetous, she is liberal; where they are ignorant and indolent, she is studious and skillful" (385). When the Maurices do experience their share of economic hardship, this hardship only "afforded new opportunities for her most shining virtues—fortitude and charity" (386). Fanny Maurice is a second Constantia Dudley. With Fanny Maurice, Brown suggests that the bourgeoisie is not as a class entirely destitute of either morality or intelligence. Arthur describes the effect of talking with Fanny: "This intercourse was strangely fascinating. . . . I now found myself exalted to a genial element, and began to taste the delights of existence. In the intercourse of ingenious and sympathetic minds, I found a pleasure I had not previously conceived" (391). "Mervyn should have known his interest better," Hemmings suggest, when he learns that Arthur did not know about the full amount of the promised reward (or of the reward in the first place) (388). But Arthur (and Brown's novel) tell us otherwise, precisely because through the episode Arthur learns that, first, the bourgeoisie does have interesting, ethical, intelligent members and, second, he prefers conversation with such people to the solitary ramblings and reflections of his boyhood. Just as the metonymic sequence of events in *Ormond* leads Constantia to the expansive vistas provided through conversations with Ormond and Martinette, so too does Arthur's poverty pave the way to "ingenious and sympathetic minds" in domestic spaces.

Though Mrs. Maurice may represent the ethical inadequacies of the early U.S. bourgeoisie, she does not give Arthur reason to rethink his earlier defense of the asymmetric distribution of wealth, the logic of which is counterintuitive, if not fundamentally paradoxical: "I perceive the value of that wealth which I have accustomed to despise. Our corporeal, and intellectual wants are supplied at little expence; but our own wants are the wants of others, and that which remains, after our own necessities are obviated, it is always easy and just to employ in relieving the necessities of others" (267). Arthur further explains that it is not in his "power to supply" Clemenza "with decent raiment and honest bread" (267). Paradoxical logic, indeed: for Arthur, it is good that some people do have more wealth than others—that some people have wealth in excess of their needs—so that they can help those who do not have as much (or enough) wealth. Arthur does not suggest that it would be better if everyone had enough wealth in the first place.[67]

By the end of *Arthur Mervyn,* Brown has counterbalanced the fraud and deception of the novel's merchants with the charity of other bourgeois figures: Dr. Stevens, in addition to rescuing and defending Arthur from his accusers, helps Carlton rescue himself from debtors' prison, and he shelters Clemenza Lodi; later, after Arthur marries Achsa, Arthur becomes Eliza Hadwin's benefactor. Though Arthur is never able to rescue fellow—and, importantly, "deserving"—economic subalterns during his poverty, bourgeois figures altruistically do. In these solutions, Brown's novel vindicates Arthur's sanguine view of wealth's asymmetric distribution.[68] Just as Arthur learns that the Wallaces of the world might deserve their tragic ends, so too does he learn that the bourgeoisie may have something to offer. Crucially, it is precisely because of his experiences as an economic subaltern—experiences that include his failed attempts to rectify instances of fraud and perceived economic injustice, and his consequent dependence on bourgeois figures—that Arthur learns to accept his world as it is, and invites us to do the same.

Arthur's failed combat against economic injustice ultimately prepares him for entry into bourgeois life. Whereas the young Stephen Dudley wanted to be free from work so as to paint and Welbeck views bourgeois life as distasteful, Arthur is, at novel's end, proud to be a member of the working bourgeoisie. Arthur on his medical studies: "My mind gladly expanded itself, as it were, for the reception of new ideas. My curiosity grew more eager, in proportion as it was supplied with food, and every day added strength to the assurance that I was no insignificant and worthless being; that I was destined to be *something* in this scene of existence, and might sometime lay claim to the gratitude and homage of my fellow-man" (396). Arthur finds satisfaction and sense of self in his new work, because this work helps him to improve himself and it allows him to imagine that he contributes to a larger social good. He has no qualms about the privileges he now has as a bourgeois in training. His work, though, does not monopolize him: "I was far from being, however, monopolized by these pursuits. I was formed on purpose for the gratification of social intercourse. To love and be loved; to exchange hearts, and mingle sentiments with all the virtuous and amiable, whom good fortune had placed within the circuit of my knowledge, I always esteemed my highest enjoyment and my chief duty" (396). Participating in a bourgeois community of fellow feeling and conversation with the free time his new profession affords him can now become Arthur's self-professed ethical obligation. Arthur should be counted as one of Hegel's "modern knights":

> Young people especially are these modern knights. . . . Now the thing is to breach this order of things, to change the world, to improve it. . . . But in the modern world these fights are nothing more than "apprenticeship," the education of the individual into the realities of the present, and thereby they acquire their true significance. For the end of such apprenticeship consists in this, that the subject sows his wild oats, builds himself with his wishes and opinions into harmony with subsisting relationships and their rationality, enters the concatenation of the world, and acquires for himself an appropriate attitude to it.[69]

This former economic subaltern does not carry with him any resentment toward or derision for the class to which he can now by virtue of luck claim membership. Nor should we expect that he would. His earlier experiences as an economic subaltern have accommodated him to the unequal distribution of wealth.

"An Uncomfortable Conclusion"?

Many readers of *Arthur Mervyn,* including some of its earliest readers (for instance, P. B. Shelley), have been disappointed by the novel's conclusion.[70] A number of critics see *Arthur Mervyn*'s ending as a capitulation to domesticity and thus as a change of course in what is otherwise an oppositional novel; others see the ending as continuation of the novel's antagonistic relationship to then-dominant ideologies of self and society.[71] In contrast to both of these assessments, I want to argue that the novel's final page is neither a regression from nor an extension of an earlier subversive posture.

Arthur describes how he and Achsa will set up their home: "Our household, while we staid in America—in a year or two we hie to Europe—should be *thus* composed. Fidelity and skill and pure morals, should be sought out, and enticed, by generous recompenses, into our domestic service. Duties should be light and regular.—Such and such should be our amusements and employments abroad and at home, and would not this be true happiness?" (445). Here, Arthur imagines himself and Achsa as employers of domestic servants. That some are employers and others are employees is not, for Arthur at the end of the novel, the sign of an arbitrary and thus unjustifiable organization of economic life. Arthur and Achsa have money, which means that they can enjoy a life of leisure; because their employees do not have money, they become subordinated to the production of Arthur and Achsa's leisure. Yet, even though these employees are subordinate to the desires of Arthur and Achsa because of the unequal distribution of economic resources, by figuring his household as a space of "good" employment, Arthur celebrates the asymmetrical labor relationship—the fact of employers and employees—that economic inequality creates (and reproduces), just as he earlier in this novel (like Sophia Courtland in *Ormond*) celebrates the opportunities of poverty for both men and women. Contrary to one reading of the novel's ending, the model of bourgeois domestic life Arthur offers here is not a retreat from the world of the market, because the home Arthur imagines participates in the market for labor. And so neither, as should be clear, is this home at odds—as other critics have recently suggested—with the bourgeois order of things. If something has changed, it is the class accent of the novel: Arthur no longer defends economic inequality from the position of the economic subaltern.

Of course, because both Constantia and Arthur "rise" out of poverty at the end of their respective novels, we might be tempted to conclude that *Ormond* and *Arthur Mervyn* are committed to a vision of classlessness in the United States. In these novels, the poor in the early United States need not forever be poor.

Yet, we need to heed Schocket's cogent formulation: "Mobility changes the experience of class, but it does not make [class] go away."[72] That workers experience mobility, in other words, does not nullify the existence of capitalist exploitation. In the classless, socialist society imagined by *Equality*, mobility itself does not exist, cannot exist—no individual can fall into poverty or emerge from it. Again, as I pointed out in the introduction, in the ideal society imagined by *Equality*, each individual works only "four hours each day" (4) and "no man is permitted to do another's work"—to sell his labor power to someone else (5). Lithconia is truly equal: "poverty and riches," the narrator tells us, "are words not to be found in [Lithconia's] language" (28). There is no mobility in Lithconia—no one moves up or down the socioeconomic ladder, precisely because there is no socioeconomic ladder to move up or down. All citizens of Lithconia equally contribute to and share in the common stock of wealth. The society that the stories of *Ormond* and *Arthur Mervyn* legitimate is certainly quite far from this. Had Constantia and Arthur been born into Lithconia, they could never have been—even temporarily—poor; they could not have experienced their respective fortunate falls.

From another point of view, though, Brown's novels and *Equality* perform similar cultural work. *Equality*'s "age of invention," I argued, functions as a satire and critique of the historical present. The "age of invention" stands for the present but is an age of intense class inequality, marked by laws that legitimate "murder, robbery, larceny, swindling, cheating, extortioning and idleness" for the privileged "classes" (70). Yet, the "age of invention" incubates Lithconia's material and philosophical preconditions. During the "age of invention," "genius and the powers of mind were displayed more than in any other" age—including in Lithconia (67). In fact, according to *Equality*'s narrator, the Lithconians are "indebted to" "the age of invention" for "the principal part of their enjoyments" (68). While the description of the average life of a Lithconian can be recorded in a few pages, "it would fill a volume itself," our narrator tells us, "to describe the various means by which men of genius [in the age of invention] converted everything to their use" (67–68). *Equality* would seem to ask, its celebration of a world without class to the contrary, whether we really want to leave behind a world of class inequality. Good thing, then, that the age of invention lasts, the narrator points out, "thousands of years" (75). If *Equality* finds a way to defer desire for a world different from the one its readers inhabit—to defer desire for a world where economic mobility has become a thing of the past—*Ormond* and *Arthur Mervyn* do the same.

2   *Modern Chivalry*'s Defense of "the Few"
Class, Politics, and the Early U.S. Episodic Novel

66 **T**he imagination that has produced much of the best and most characteristic American fiction," writes Richard Chase at the outset of *The American Novel and Its Tradition* (1957), "has been shaped by the contradictions and not by the unities and harmonies of our culture."[1] Though absent from *The American Novel and Its Tradition,* Hugh Henry Brackenridge's *Modern Chivalry*—a sprawling episodic travel novel published in seven volumes over the course of twenty-three years (1792, 1792, 1793, 1797, 1804, 1805, 1815)—has been described in terms that recall Chase's account of how the American novel supposedly diverges from the European (and, especially, the British) novel.[2] For Joseph Ellis, *Modern Chivalry* is "the first American novel to describe American culture as a bundle of polarities, a set of irreconcilable contradictions and tensions."[3] Ellis explicitly cites Chase's dictum about what is "most characteristic" in American fiction, concluding that *Modern Chivalry* "qualifies as the first distinctively American novel."[4] While other critics have resisted the temptation to cast *Modern Chivalry* as more American than contemporaneous novels, they have nonetheless celebrated its commitment to representing conflict within early U.S. culture. Indeed, a number of critics have drawn on Bakhtinian concepts to argue that *Modern Chivalry*—in and through its form—discloses the early United States to be not politically homogenous but rather defined by conflicting "voices": this novel has been hailed as "the American dialogic novel par excellence,"[5] "defiantly polyphonic,"[6] and an "early attempt to represent the heterogeneous polyphony that America already was in 1790."[7]

Modern Chivalry's formal polyphony is subsequently often glossed in terms of the conflict between residual Federalism and emergent liberalism in the early United States (just as *Arthur Mervyn* is often situated along this axis), with the novel's two protagonists representing these competing ideologies. Captain John Farrago is a "man of about fifty-three years of age, of good natural sense, and considerable reading"; "he had the advantage of having in early life, an academic education; but having never applied himself to any of the learned professions, he had lived the greater part of his life on a small farm, which he cultivated with servants or hired hands" (3). Teague O'Regan, an illiterate Irish immigrant, is Farrago's servant (at least through volumes 1, 2, and part of 3). Farrago, writes Ellis, "is the decent, gentlemanly past; Teague is the ill-mannered, popular, democratic future."[8] Farrago "represents," according to Christopher Looby, "the outmoded pretense of rationality and reactionary attachment to deferential social protocol, while Teague represents emergent democracy."[9] If in the late eighteenth century Anti-Federalists argued that "American society could no longer be thought of as either a hierarchy of ranks or a homogeneous republican whole," if Anti-Federalists saw American society as "more pluralistic, more diverse, and more fragmented with interests than even someone as hard-headed and realistic as James Madison had," if they believed that "there was no possibility of a liberal enlightened elite speaking for the whole,"[10] then perhaps *Modern Chivalry*'s formal commitment to vocal pluralism expresses an anti-Federalist, democratic political content?

For two groundbreaking, influential studies of early U.S. literary culture, the answer to this question about the politics of *Modern Chivalry* as a form is "yes." In *Revolution and the Word: The Rise of the Novel in America,* Cathy Davidson argues that *Modern Chivalry* is exemplary of the early U.S. novel's resistance to the "repressive political agenda" of Federalism, standing as a refusal "to homogenize the *polis* with a rambunctious heterogeneity."[11] *Modern Chivalry* encourages its readers, Davidson suggests, to "sympathize with the prankster protagonist"—that is, with Teague—over against "his privileged antagonists and the immoral legalities whereby they hope to keep [Teague] in his place" (174). *Modern Chivalry* is thus, on Davidson's reading, "populist by design." Likewise, in *Voicing America: Language, Literary Form, and the Origins of the United States,* Looby argues that "it is evident that, in the manner of the novelistic heteroglossia so sympathetically traced by Bakhtin . . . , [Brackenridge's] deepest investment is in the subversive, transgressive, energizing agency of the rogue, the knave, and the fool"—and, thus, that

Modern Chivalry should be read finally as a satire of Farrago's "nostalgia" for Federalist notions of a ruling elite.[12]

In part, my goal here it to put pressure on the notion that the choice *Modern Chivalry* must make is between Federalism and liberalism. Especially in part 2, the conflict that *Modern Chivalry* stages is not so much Farrago versus Teague and his ambitions of upward mobility as it is Farrago versus a host of other plebeian characters that are far more politically conscious than Teague. Which is to say, especially in *Modern Chivalry*'s later volumes, Farrago engages in verbal battles against a brand of economic egalitarianism given voice by plebeian figures other than Teague.

This brand of economic egalitarianism, if overlooked by critics of *Modern Chivalry,* is one that has typically also been omitted from histories of the early republic. "Until recently," Seth Cotlar points outs, "historians' analyses of popular economic ideology in the early republic have revolved around the stark question of whether ordinary Americans were modern entrepreneurial capitalists in embryo or backward-looking agrarians who resisted the economic transformations of the late eighteenth century."[13] What this opposition of entrepreneurial capitalists and agrarians leaves out, Cotlar contends, is those politico-economic thinkers of the 1790s that conceived of "democratic politics as a tool that could both dismantle old and entrenched forms of economic inequality and push against the more inegalitarian dynamics of the modern commercial society they saw emerging around them" (158). Indeed, the 1790s witnessed the emergence of "a democratic theory of political economy that existed in critical tension with an emerging capitalist order" (120).

According to this "democratic theory of political economy"—a theory espoused by Atlantic radicals such as Thomas Paine, Mary Wollstonecraft, and William Godwin, but also by democratic American newspapers in the 1790s—"great concentrations of wealth" were to be understood as "a threat to the cherished ideal of popular sovereignty" (133). In late eighteenth-century democratic U.S. newspapers we find "pieces calling for a resurgence of popular action that would secure economic justice for ordinary citizens . . . side by side with fearful stories documenting the emergence of a new nobility of speculators and financiers that threatened the survival of the republic" (132). What Cotlar thus unearths is form of radicalism in the late eighteenth century that sought "to imagine what steps the new nation could take to encourage a more equitable distribution of property" (135). This radicalism "was not social-ism," Cotlar explains, "but neither was it simply a 'bourgeois' defense of laissez-faire capitalism": instead, it constituted "some of the first explor-atory steps toward a democratic theory of political economy where the central question was no longer how to protect existing property holdings against the encroachments of the people, but rather how the peoples' government could effectively oversee, regulate, and potentially restruc-ture economic arrangements to serve the interests of all, equally" (135). Moreover, in the years before and after 1800, plebeian radicals framed leisured landowners like Farrago and members of what *Modern Chiv-alry* calls the "the learned professions" (3), namely lawyers and judges, as enemies of economic justice—as economic parasites who live off of (who steal) wealth produced by others' labors, and who thus also seek to maintain legal apparatuses that serve only the interests of the wealthy "few." Plebeian radicals considered the existence of such a class and such theft inimical to their interests, to economic equality, and to what they understood by "democracy" (or "free government").

If prominent readings of *Modern Chivalry* have cast Brackenridge's novel as rambunctiously pluralist and thus populist and democratic, I in-stead want to call attention to *Modern Chivalry*'s very explicit antipathy toward late eighteenth- and early nineteenth-century plebeian economic egalitarianism—toward a form of politico-economic thought that does not fit easily within the category of "liberal democracy." By "very ex-plicit antipathy" I mean to highlight the *frame* by which *Modern Chiv-alry* organizes the conflict between plebeian and elite voices that plays out over and over again on the level of the novel's episodic story. This frame is the novel's narrator, who repeatedly intrudes into (in fact, takes over) the novel from its beginning to its end. Lest we have any doubt about this narrator's ideological commitments, it is worth observing that he tells us that "to propose agrarian laws, or an equality of goods and chattles" is "licentiousness" (371). Certainly, *Modern Chivalry* can be read as dialogic—as recording social conflict via novelistic heteroglossia. The story it tells is very much about the battle of different voices, voices that in turn index antagonistic sociopolitical worldviews tied to economic class positions. Yet, the novel's massively voluble narrator—who lives on the level of discourse rather than story (to invoke this narratological distinction once more)—puts his weight behind Farrago and rationalizes Farrago's attempts to dissuade plebeian radicals of their political desires, especially their desires to reform state and federal constitutions, insofar as he goes to great lengths to argue against the way radical plebeians think about class and against the particular reforms desired by the novel's plebeians but opposed by Farrago.

According to some critics, I should note, *Modern Chivalry*'s narrator is not to be read as authoritative, or reliable, or trustworthy—but, rather, as self-ironizing.[14] Yet, when the narrator speechifies on the role of educated elites in the United States and matters of constitutional reform (or, on precisely those issues that animate plebeian politics in the novel), his style is anything but self-undercutting: the narrator speaks, as it were, on these issues to the novel's imagined reader in what I would call a deliberative style. Moreover, when the narrator deliberates on plebeian ideas about class and plebeian political desires, he addresses his imagined reader as someone who can and should think about these ideas and desires from an abstract vantage point, as someone who can and should think about these ideas and desires in terms of what is "good" for U.S. society in general—not for plebeians in particular. In fact, the narrator—and I will highlight this below—entreats *Modern Chivalry*'s readers to understand radical plebeian political desires (the desire to abolish the independent judiciary, to delimit the power and influence of the legal profession, to revise state and federal constitutions) as fundamentally inimical to political "liberty" as well as to intellectual and economic progress in the United States. In the narrator's logic, it is plebeian radicals—and not elites like Farrago—who threaten "democracy." It is not quite right, I am thus proposing, to read *Modern Chivalry* ultimately as a satire of Farrago and the elite class from which he springs. Rather, the novel's narrator—who dominates the discussion of class in *Modern Chivalry*—invites *Modern Chivalry*'s readers to root for Farrago's voice, however duplicitous or manipulative Farrago is, and even though Farrago often comes off as, in Cynthia Jordan's apt phrase, an "officious interloper."[15] Which is to say, the narrator teaches *Modern Chivalry*'s readers to desire Farrago's success in his attempts to talk the novel's plebeians out of—to obstruct by way of speechifying—their radical political desires and actions.[16] Farrago and a character called "the blind lawyer" censure the most radical of plebeian desires in the novel, and the narrator of *Modern Chivalry* buttresses this censure through his deliberations on the dangers—to liberty, to the functioning of the economy—of the reforms that plebeian characters desire. And if for *Modern Chivalry*'s narrator plebeian political desires are the enemy of liberty, so too is this the case according to many of the novel's episodes. According to a host of episodes in *Modern Chivalry's* story, were plebeians to have their way, there would be no "learning" or "letters" in the United States; and without "learning," according to the dominant voices of *Modern Chivalry* (Farrago, but also the narrator) as well as the way events play out in the novel's episodes, the United States would descend into either tyranny or anarchy. *Modern Chivalry* insists that the United States needs a class that radical plebeians, plebeians both inside and outside the novel, thought should be abolished. Farrago and the class position he occupies are for the narrator a necessary evil.

What I am after, then, is how the very form of *Modern Chivalry*— the recurrence of and pride of place afforded to antiplebeian voices in *Modern Chivalry*—is anything but the novelistic equivalent of what Cotlar calls "a democratic theory of political economy." In fact, *Modern Chivalry* represents something quite the contrary. In one of *Modern Chivalry's* many metafictional moments, Brackenridge comments on "the vehicle" he has chosen "of supposed travels" and "conversations": "[T]he characters which we have introduced," he writes, "are many of them low" (410). The narrator continues: "Shakespeare had his Bardolph, Nym and Pistol, and the dialogue of these is a relief to the drama of the principal personages. It is so in nature; and why should it not be so represented in the images of her works. We have the sage and the fool, interspersed in society, and the fool gives occasion for the wise man to make his reflections. So in our book" (411). Brackenridge admits that his novel needs its "low" characters. It is predicated on the "work" they do as characters, which is not to create commodities but to talk and act. Brackenridge also cops to a kind of formalism. Despite arguing that his novel is an "image" of nature, in dividing his characters into "fools" and "sages," he makes explicit his rejection of mimesis. Yet, by deploying an established literary figuration of the social, the novel casts individuals as literary types with predetermined functions in an uneven novelistic division of labor.

Alex Woloch has identified "two pervasive extremes of minorness within the nineteenth-century novel," which he calls "the worker " and "the eccentric." "The worker," he suggests, "is reduced to a single functional use within the narrative"; "the eccentric" is "the fragmentary character who plays a disruptive, oppositional role within the plot." These figures, he argues, "are flip sides of the same coin," for in both the "free relationship between surface and depth is negated" and "the actualization of a human being is denied."[17] *Modern Chivalry*'s "low" characters are always either "workers" or "eccentrics," or a combination of the two principles. Teague drives the narrative forward, allowing Farrago and the narrator new opportunities for reflection. The other "low" figures are engines of disruption and opposition, thwarting Farrago's movement or dispatching him to new scenes, forcing responses from him and the narrator. While elites can at times occupy the role of "fool," "low" figures can never occupy the role of "sage." In *Modern Chivalry*, "low" characters are not also—and cannot also be—"men of letters," or thinkers.

Take the character dubbed "young man Valentine": Valentine aspires to Congress, but he does not possess "the advantage of mental recommendation" and is "not at all comprehending the necessity, or at least usefulness, of a knowledge of the geography of the world in commercial questions; or of history in political" (207, 208). Valentine relies entirely on physical power: "This young man Valentine had been accustomed to run a foot race with a wood-ranger; to lift a piece of timber at a house building, or log-rolling; or to wrestle at Cornish-hug with the young men of the village; and had imagined that the same degree of strength and dexterity, which had given him a superiority, or at least made him respectable in these, would raise him to reputation in the efforts of the human mind" (208). The novel may satirize Federalism's elitism, but it will not produce a dialectical opposition to that elitism in the form of a "low" character who is also a thinker. We cannot imagine Valentine in the position of the narrator, himself a "man of letters," who parades his learning at every opportunity. Plebeian figures like Valentine respond and act, often irrationally and violently. They are always characters of delimited knowledge, suspicious and prone to conspiratorial denunciations. They seek not to appropriate what Brackenridge calls "legal knowledge" and "political learning," but instead to do away with them altogether. They want to rule by force. "Learning" is the lynchpin of "democracy" for Brackenridge's narrator, but *Modern Chivalry* suggests that "learning" is only attainable by—and only desired by—a distinguished minority. *Modern Chivalry*'s representation of plebeian political self-expression thus rules out an aspiration of plebeian radicalism as it developed at the turn of the nineteenth century: the egalitarian distribution of intellectual resources (what Brackenridge calls "legal knowledge" and "political learning"), and thus the coming into being of the plebeian-intellectual. In *Modern Chivalry,* the social division of plebeians and thinkers is insurmountable, inscribed into the novel's formal organization.

My reading of *Modern Chivalry* thus questions the critical predilection to read the novel's polyphony as symptomatic of—as an expression of—egalitarianism. Critics are right to describe *Modern Chivalry* as enacting vocal polyphony and committed to political pluralism. Yet, according to Brackenridge's novel, the United States needs an elite class, and it needs this class to "talk": while *Modern Chivalry*'s plebeians frequently lament that they are forced to listen to Farrago and to lawyers, the novel makes us listen to these figures nonetheless, and its narrator explains that their voices need to be heard. *Modern Chivalry* does not suggest that plebeians should have no right to participate in government, or that only elites should vote or be elected to office: "There are but two characters that be respectable," the narrator says, "as representatives of the people. A plain man of good sense, whether farmer, mechanic, or merchant; or a man of education and literary talents" (209). But *Modern Chivalry*'s particular polyphony and its version of pluralism should be read, I am arguing, as a commitment to what plebeians would have considered class itself. That *Modern Chivalry* insists that the voice of economic elites is necessary to the political and economic health of the United States is how, to repeat what I said earlier, the novel intervenes in history: it is as if the novel's particular version of polyphony refuses to imagine what we might call a plebeian future—a United States made up entirely of plebeians—as worthy of coming into being.

Indeed, to understand the political significance of *Modern Chivalry*'s polyphony, we need to recognize that this polyphony is implicated in a fundamentally undialectical kind of story. *Modern Chivalry* is a travel narrative; its protagonist traverses a rather expansive geographical terrain, moving through a number of different imagined settlements dotting the Pennsylvanian frontier. Yet, the type of travel narrative we get in *Modern Chivalry* can be thought of as operating along the lines of what Bakhtin calls "adventure-time." In "adventure-time," writes Bakhtin, "nothing changes."[18] In *Modern Chivalry,* despite Farrago's travels—his adventures—nothing changes. While the protagonist of *Modern Chivalry* moves all over the place, *Modern Chivalry* itself goes nowhere. This is because each time Farrago moves, we get another version of the same thing: a conflict between elites and plebeians, between "the Few" and "the Many." Indeed, this conflict is never overcome—nor, I argue, does the novel suggest that the social division on which it is predicated should ever be overcome. In and through Farrago's adventures, *Modern Chivalry* narrates an endless repetition of this conflict in the early United States, but thereby also endorses the very existence of "the Few." Each iteration of the conflict between the elite Farrago and plebeians occasions another argument from the narrator on the dangers of plebeian political desires and on the necessity of elites in the United States. So, though *Modern Chivalry* turns on a protagonist moving through space, it is nonetheless *formally* committed to stasis. And thus it registers, again on the level of its story as much as in its narrator's explicit pronouncements, a bourgeois commitment not to transformation and change but instead to the immutability of class. What Lukács says of bourgeois thought is equally apropos of Brackenridge's novel: bourgeois thought's "starting-point and its goals are always, if not consciously," he writes in *History and Class Consciousness,* "an apologia for the existing order of things or at least proof of their immutability."[19] Against plebeians, *Modern Chivalry*'s form insists that the United States should not become anything other than what it already is. For *Modern Chivalry,* in which polyphony is implicated in a version of "adventure-time," the United States should remain polyphonic in the way that it already is: "the Few" should always exist, if only to speak up against the political desires of "the Many."[20]

Having suggested that *Modern Chivalry* apprehends class in and through a version of "adventure-time," I am now finally in a position to spell out the formal and ideological relationship between *Modern Chivalry* and Brown's Philadelphia novels. Though Brown's Philadelphia novels and *Modern Chivalry* were essentially contemporaneous, they respectively instantiate what for Bakhtin are opposing "chronotopes." As I argued in chapter 1, Brown's *Ormond* and *Arthur Mervyn* are to be read as versions of the bildungsroman. As I also noted in chapter 1, Bakhtin teaches us that in the bildungsroman "changes in the hero . . . acquire *plot* significance."[21] The bildungsroman, writes Bakhtin, "can be designated in the most general sense as the novel of human *emergence*" (22). In contrast, in "pure adventure time . . . man's emergence is impossible" (21). In "adventure-time," "the image of man" is "quite static, as static as the world that surrounds him." "Adventure-time," writes Bakhtin, "does not recognize human emergence and development" (11). *Modern*

Chivalry is, as should be clear by now, no bildungsroman. Of course, we might explain the chronotopic divergence of Brackenridge's *Modern Chivalry* from Brown's Philadelphia novels by pointing to the fact that Brackenridge and Brown set their novels in different social spaces: Brackenridge's novel "takes place" (again) on the Pennsylvanian frontier, while Brown's novel "takes place" in urban space. Yet, we might also account for this formal divergence by recognizing that Brockden Brown's bildungsromans and Brackenridge's *Modern Chivalry* represent different sides of the same ideological coin with respect to class. In other words, it is as if these novels have been assigned (or, as if their respective authors have assigned themselves) different—but complementary—ideological work with respect to class. Though they are bildungsromans, Brown's novels do not (I have argued) make the case for socioeconomic transformation. Rather, while these novels take up the subjective experience of the economic subaltern, they do so in such a fashion as to construe economic subalternity as "beneficial" to the individual subjected to it. This is how Brown's novels ratify economic inequality. *Modern Chivalry*, in contrast, does not narrate its protagonist's "development," but instead moves its protagonist through space in order to pronounce on class, not as a subjective experience, but as an abstraction—as a political relation. What *Modern Chivalry* purports to make sense of is the confrontation between classes in the early United States (as opposed to the experience of economic subalternity), but it also frames this confrontation in such a way as to ratify the very existence of elites in the early United States. Yes, different but complementary: if Brockden Brown's novels function as apprenticeships to "poverty," *Modern Chivalry* conversely stands as a defense of "the Few."

THE LEXICON OF CLASS CIRCA 1800: "THE MANY" AND "THE FEW"

In the late eighteenth century, a discourse of class emerged in the United States that divided the polity into those who produce wealth through labor and those who live off of the wealth produced by the labor of others. To some extent, this discourse echoed Adam Smith's distinction between productive labor, "which produces a value," and unproductive labor, which does not.[22] According to Smith, "[T]he labour of a manufacturer adds, generally, to the value of the material he works upon, that of his own maintenance, and of his master's profit." In contrast, the "labour of a menial servant . . . adds to the value of nothing." In distinguishing between productive and unproductive labor, Smith thus first contrasts two kinds of subordinate labor. Yet, he quickly likens the "labour of some of the most respectable orders of society" to that of "menial servants" (1:330). For Smith, the "class" of unproductive laborers also includes "some of the of the gravest and most important, and some of the most frivolous professions: churchmen, lawyers, physicians, men of letters of all kinds; players, buffons, musicians, opera-singers, opera-dancers, &c." (1:331).

Radical late eighteenth-century plebeian political economy had little use for the category of unproductive labor. For the self-professed "laborers" who assessed the socioeconomic order of the early United States, there are only two classes of people: those who labor and those who do not. Yet, they agree with Smith, insofar as they insist that "churchmen, lawyers, physicians, and men of letters of all kinds" belong to a category other than productive laborers. Indeed, U.S. plebeian writers construed such figures as exploiters of genuinely industrious laborers. Take, for example, the vision of class division, exploitation, and antagonism offered by "To Farmers, Mechanics, and other Industrious Citizens" (published in *The New York Time Piece* in 1798):

> There exists in all civilized nations two classes or descriptions of men. One are laborers, men who produce by their own industry something to the common stock of commodity. This class is made up of farmers, mechanics, etc. The second are such as live on the stock of the community, already produced, not by their labor, but obtained by their art and cunning. . . . These are . . . merchants, speculators, priests, lawyers, and men employed in the various departments of government. All this class get their living by thinking, not by their labor.[23]

The polity is here boiled down to independent producers, who create wealth, and educated professionals, who do not—and who thus essentially steal wealth from those who do produce it.

Like "To Farmers, Mechanics, and other Industrious Citizens," William Manning's 1799 *The Key of Liberty* designates its audience as "Republicans, Farmers, Mechanics, and Laborers in America."[24] Though it was not published in Manning's day, *The Key of Liberty* offers insight on how early U.S. plebeians may have thought about class. *The Key* puts forward a fundamental antagonism between nonlaborers and laborers. Manning calls this antagonism "the great scuffle between the Few and the Many" (137).[25] Whereas "the Many" must work, "the Few" do not. Manning adopts his notion of class, "his dividing line between the Few and the Many," from "A Free Republican," "a writer who wrote ten long numbers in the Chronicle in December 1785 and January 1786": Among the Few "A Free Republican" "reckons the merchant and physician; the lawyer and the divine; all in literary walks of life; the judicial and executive officers; and all the rich who could live on their income without bodily labor—so that the whole contention lies between those who labor for a living and those who do not" (127).[26] Yet, while "A Free Republican" draws his "dividing line" to determine that the Few should rule the American polity, Manning appropriates the language of the Few and the Many in order to identify what might be impediments to democracy's realization in the United States as well as to critique the way exploitation reproduces itself in the early United States: there can be no "liberty" for Manning so long as certain individuals are able to privately appropriate wealth produced by the Many.

Might we thus have, in the late eighteenth-century United States, the stirrings of a proto-Marxian class consciousness? Not exactly. The idea of class exploitation in "To Farmers" and *The Key of Liberty* does not turn on the extraction of surplus value via wage labor: the class spoken for here is largely self-employed—or, "independent"—farmers, mechanics, and so on. Indeed, "To Farmers" and *The Key of Liberty* both sidestep the potential conflicts between, on the on hand, "independent" laborers and, on the other, both wageworkers and laborers who also employ laborers. In other words, members of the Many could also be exploiters of labor.[27] Antagonism within the category of the Many manifested itself concretely, to give but one example, in 1806 when journeymen cordwainers in Philadelphia went on strike, demanding higher wages from master cordwainers. This conflict, which resulted in the journeymen being tried and convicted for conspiracy, indexes, first, how early U.S. law curtailed workers' rights and, second, the shortcomings of the notion of class found in "To Farmers" and *The Key of Liberty*.[28] Moreover, in their introduction to *The Key of Liberty*, Michael Merrill and Sean Wilentz observe that Manning "forthrightly stated that because people were born with a wide variety of capacities, there would always be a very unequal distribution of property, even under the best governments. Nor did Manning condemn commercial markets—or their supporting cast of bankers, merchants, and professionals—as preternaturally evil."[29] For Gordon Wood, Manning is best characterized as a member of the "the middling sort—an improver and a small-time entrepreneurial hustler, or what later would be called a petty businessman."[30] For Marcus Rediker, Manning is a "conservative plebeian democrat . . . committed to electoral politics"; Rediker points out that Manning "raised a hue and cry against historically revolutionary extralegal forms of struggle such as mobs, popular committees, and self-organized actions."[31] Petit bourgeois critique, then?

Indeed, according to Lukács, we would be in error to attribute class consciousness (and thus world-historical significance) to the late eighteenth-century petit bourgeois political economy of "To Farmers" and *The Key of Liberty*. This is because "To Farmers" and Manning do not perceive history from the standpoint of a proletariat that has acknowledged the abolition of capitalism as its historical mission. A class that "fails to strike at the heart of that totality," Lukács argues, ". . . can never influence the course of history in either a conservative or progressive direction."[32] Marx himself dismissed the petit bourgeoisie: "The lower middle class," he argues in *The Communist Manifesto*, "the small manufacturer, the shopkeeper, the artisan, the peasant, all these fight against the bourgeoisie, to save from extinction their existence as fractions of the middle class. They are therefore not revolutionary, but conservative. Nay more. They are reactionary. They try to roll back the wheel of history."[33] For one strain of Marxism, late eighteenth-century U.S. plebeian protest would appear as merely an attempt to arrest capitalist development and thus the proletarianization of the petit bourgeoisie.

Yet, late eighteenth-century and early nineteenth-century U.S. plebeian protest represents, I want to suggest, something akin to class consciousness. According to Manning, "[N]o person can possess property without laboring, unless he get it by force or craft, fraud or fortune, out of the earnings of others" (136). His argument presupposes a labor theory of property: "[L]abor is the sole parent of all property. The land yieldeth nothing without it, and there is no food, clothing, shelter, vessel, or any necessary of life but what costs labor and is generally estimated valuable according to what labor it costs" (135–36). For Manning, the Few exist only to the extent that they "steal" wealth from the Many, who produce it. The accumulation of private wealth is thus inextricable from the exploitation of labor. And Manning insists that something like class consciousness already exists among laborers in the early United States. "The laborer is conscious," he writes, "that it is labor that supports the whole, and that the more there are that live without labor—and the higher they live or the greater their salaries and fees are—so much the harder must he work, the shorter must he live" (136). As I pointed out earlier, according to E. P. Thompson's notion of class consciousness, class consciousness exists when "some men, as a result of common experiences (inherited or shared), feel and articulate the identity of their interests as between themselves, and as against other men whose interests are different from (and usually opposed to) theirs."[34] True to Thompson's definition of class consciousness, Manning posits that the laborer senses that he is exploited and that his interests are opposed to those of the Few, who exploit him and other laborers.

The Key of Liberty also looks forward to materialist explanations of educational institutions. For Manning, education in the early United States reproduces relationships of economic inequality. The Few are able to perpetuate their exploitation of labor by perpetuating a monopoly on intellectual resources. "As learning and knowledge among the Many is the only support of liberty," Manning writes, "so no pain is spared by the few to suppress it" (139–40). "Instead of promoting cheap schools," he continues, the Few "are continually crying up the great advantage of costly colleges, national academies, and grammar schools." For Manning, "[N]o care, pains, or precautions ought to be spared to the make [the laws] as few, plain, comprehensive, and easy to understand as possible," but "the Few spare no pains nor arts to have them as numerous, intricate, and hard to be understood as possible" (140).

If early U.S. plebeian radicalism proposes "a consciousness of the identity between working men of the most diverse occupations and level of attainment" as well as a "consciousness of the interests of the working class, or 'productive classes,' as *against* those of other classes," it also gropes toward "the claim for an alternative *system*."[35] It articulates an economic egalitarianism composed of hostility toward the private accumulation of wealth *through the exploitation of labor,* and thus offers a political vision at odds with both residual Federalism and emergent liberalism. Plebeian radicalism is my name for what Sean Wilentz calls "artisan republicanism," which "was egalitarian and suffused with the ethic of the small producer—but not 'liberal' or 'petit-bourgeois,' as the twentieth century understands the terms. It was a vision of a democratic society that balanced individual rights with communal responsibilities—of independent, competent citizens and men who would soon win their competence, whose industry in the pursuit of happiness, as in politics, was undertaken not for personal gain alone but for the public good."[36] Wilentz explains that "artisan republicanism" was in tension with emerging forms of free market individualism:

> With a rhetoric rich in the republican language of corruption, equality, and independence, [artisan republicanism] remained committed to a benevolent hierarchy of skill and the cooperative workshop. Artisan independence conjured up, not a vision of ceaseless, self-interested industry, but a moral order in which all craftsman would eventually become self-governing, independent, competent masters. . . . Men's energies would be devoted, not to personal ambition or profit alone, but to the commonwealth; in the workshop, mutual obligation and respect . . . would prevail.[37]

Radical plebeians voiced a desire for a polity composed *entirely* of economically independent, civic-minded producers—for a polity free of exploiters of others' labors. For the plebeians of *Modern Chivalry,* this polity is to be achieved in part, as we will see, through the reform of U.S. legal institutions.

"A PERPETUAL WAR"

Now, it makes a certain sense to read *Modern Chivalry* as a critique of elitist political pretensions associated with Federalism. One need be familiar only with the opening chapters of the novel, in which Farrago and Teague happen upon "a place where a number of people were convened, for the purpose of electing persons to represent them in the legislature of the state" (8). The candidates are "a weaver" and "a man of education." The man of education argues for his election:

> Said he, Fellow citizens, I pretend not to any great abilities; but am conscious to myself that I have the best good will to serve you. But it is very astonishing to me, that this weaver should consider himself

qualified for the trust. For though my acquirements are not great, yet his are still less. The mechanical business which he pursues, must necessarily take up so much of his time, that he cannot apply himself to political studies. I should therefore think it would be more answerable to your dignity, and conducive to your interest, to be represented by a man at least of some letters, than by an illiterate handicraftsman like this. It will be more honourable for himself, to remain at his loom and knot threads, than to come forward in a legislative capacity; because, in the one case, he is in the sphere where God and nature has placed him; in the other, he is like a fish out of water, and must struggle for breath in a new element.

Is it possible he can understand the affairs of government, whose mind has been concentrated to the small object of weaving webs; to the price by the yard, the grist of the thread, and such like matters as concern the manufacturer of cloths? The feet of him who weaves, are more occupied than the head, or at least as much; and therefore the whole man must be, at least, but in half accustomed to exercise his mental powers. For these reasons, all other things set aside, the chance is in my favour, with respect to information. However, you will decide, and give your suffrages to him or to me, as you shall judge expedient. (8)

Farrago takes it upon himself to second these arguments:

Said he, I have no prejudice against a weaver more than another man. Nor do I know any harm in the trade; save that from the sedentary life in a damp place, there is usually a paleness of the countenance: but this is a physical, not a moral evil. . . . But to rise from the cellar to the senate house, would be an unnatural hoist. To come from counting threads, and adjusting them to the splits of a reed, to regulate the finances of a government, would be preposterous; there being no congruity in the case. There is no analogy between knotting threads and framing laws. It would be a reversion of the order of things. Not that a manufacturer of linen or woolen, or other stuff, is an inferior character, but a different one, from that which ought to be employed in affairs of state. (8–9)

Farrago then takes the weaver aside, explaining his position:

Mr. Traddle, said he, for that was the name of the manufacturer, I have not the smallest idea of wounding your sensibility; but it would seem to me, it would be more your interest to pursue your occupation, than to launch out into that of which you have no knowledge. When you go to the senate house, the application to you will not be to warp a web; but to make laws for the commonwealth. Now, suppose that the making of these laws, requires a knowledge of commerce, or of the interests of agriculture, or those principles upon which the different manufactures depend, what service could you render? It is possible you might think justly enough; but could you speak? You are not in the habit of public speaking. You are furnished with those common place ideas with which even very ignorant men can pass for knowing something. (9)

The man of education and Farrago argue that the plebeian is incapable of political thinking because his work has fit him for nothing but his work. This episode has been read as a criticism of the man of education and Farrago. Brackenridge's "satire" here, Cathy Davidson argues, "runs both ways": "It mocks an illiterate running for public office and it equally mocks another's assumption that aristocratic and dilettante education in and of itself qualifies one to rule."[38] While Farrago explains his ideas to the weaver, Teague "took it into his head, that he could be a legislator himself" (9). The electorate embraces Teague: "The thing was not displeasing to the people, who seemed to favour his pretensions" (9). Farrago responds to the electorate: "[E]ven if you think proper, now and then, to show your privilege, and exert in a signal manner, the democratic prerogative, yet is it not descending too low to filch away from me a hireling, which I cannot well spare, to serve your purposes?" (10). Farrago wants to keep Teague out of office so that he can keep his "hireling"—the laborer on whom his leisure depends. The episode thus reveals that Farrago is here anything but disinterested. The electorate articulates its favor for Teague in terms of suspicion about how elites use the law to further their own economic interests: "It is a very strange thing, said one of them, who was a speaker for the rest, that after having conquered Burgoyne and Cornwallis, and got a government of our own, we cannot put in it whom we please. This young man may be your servant, or another man's servant; but if we chuse to make him a delegate, what is that to you. He may not be yet skilled in the matter, but there is a good day a-coming. We will impower him; and it is better to trust a plain man like him, than one of your high flyers, that will make laws to suit their own purposes" (10).

Why does Brackenridge pit the man of education against a weaver? An ex-weaver, William Findley, was a thorn in the side of Brackenridge's own political career. Findley and Brackenridge served in the Pennsylvania legislature together in the 1780s. When Brackenridge let slip at a dinner party that "the people are fools," Findley attacked him in the pages of the *Pittsburgh Gazette,* painting him as elitist and self-interested.[39] In 1788 Findley defeated Brackenridge for election to the Pennsylvania ratifying convention: "Findley sent Brackenridge scurrying out of politics into literature by attacking his pretensions as a virtuous gentlemanly leader."[40]

Findley was not just a personal rival of Brackenridge. He was an important critic of Hamiltonian economics as well as a theorist of the relationship between political democracy and economic equality.[41] "According to Findley," writes Terry Bouton, "the Revolution's biggest accomplishment was giving 'citizens their right of equal protection, power, privilege, and influence.' . . . To Findley, protecting all of these different kinds of equality meant that the government must preserve a basic equality of wealth."[42] Findley was not opposed to private property or the pursuit of wealth. Findley's argument, as mapped by Andrew Shankman, was that "wealth in many hands operates as many checks": for Findley, it was "necessary to protect private property and the pursuit of wealth," but it was equally important to promote "near equality" so as to make possible "a future of widespread property ownership and independence."[43]

Yet, though the weaver defeats the man of education after Farrago successfully convinces Teague to withdraw from the election, this episode is not finally an endorsement of Findley's political vision. Dismayed by what has happened, Farrago seeks wisdom from Kolt, a "conjurer." Kolt explains the election in class terms, calling attention to Farrago's political blindness:

> There is no need of a conjurer to tell why it is that the common people are more disposed to trust one of their own class, than those who may affect to be superior. Besides, there is a certain pride in man, which leads him to elevate the low, and pull down the high. There is a kind of creating power exerted in making a senator of an unqualified per-

son: which when the author has done, he exults over the work, and, like the Creator himself when he made the world, sees that "it is very good." Moreover, there is in every government a patrician class, against whom the spirit of the multitude naturally militates: And hence a perpetual war; the aristocrats endeavouring to detrude the people, and the people contending to obtrude themselves. And it is right it should be so; for by this fermentation, the spirit of democracy is kept alive. (12)

As Ed White points out, "Kolt is no defender of the people here: [Kolt] is not condemning elites or class conflict as impediments to democracy, but rather argues that the class of rich and poor is endemic and necessary for a good democracy."[44] In fact, this election episode ultimately concludes with an argument on behalf not of plebeian rule but of what we can call liberal democracy.

In "Containing Reflections," the chapter that follows the election chapter, Brackenridge's narrator argues for a version of democracy at odds with the thrust of Findley's positions and plebeian radicalism more broadly. The narrator mediates between Kolt's position and Farrago's. On the one hand, the narrator criticizes the utltra-wealthy—indicting their "pride and arrogance"—and suggests that they should "be checked by the populace" (13). On the other hand, he holds on to an ideal of "the man of ability and integrity" as the proper legislator: "genius and virtue are independent of fortune." The narrator concludes his "reflections" by defending the right of "the people" to elect members of their own so as to produce a "medium," the balance of forces that "the man of ability and integrity" represents: "[T]he aristocratic part of the government, arrogates a right to represent; . . . the democratic contends the point; and from this conjunction and opposition of forces, there is produced a compound resolution" (13). It would be ideal, he insists, if Americans chose "virtuous" representatives. Barring this, elites and plebeians both have the right to contend for political power, their competition producing a satisfactory outcome. Dismissed, then, is a more radical argument about what the polity should be—namely, the notion that democracy is synonymous with economic equality and not merely political equality.

Modern Chivalry's dedication to a version of liberal democracy is quite explicit in later volumes. "I call myself a democrat," Brackenridge declares in part 2, volume 2, of *Modern Chivalry* (373). He then cites what he indicates to be Pericles's definition of democracy, as recorded by Thucydides and as translated by Hobbes: democracy "hath respect, not to a few, but to the multitude," which means that "though there be an equality amongst all men, in point of law, for their private controversies," citizens "are not offended at any man for following his own humour" (374). For the narrator, democracy ultimately boils down to "an *equal right of suffrage, and an equal right of office*" (376). Plebeian radicals— especially in Brackenridge's Pennsylvania—insisted that democracy had yet to be realized in Pennsylvania (and the United States more broadly), but *Modern Chivalry*'s final volumes suggest essentially the reverse. For the narrator, democracy has already been realized in the United States. I return to this below.

The drama and comedy of *Modern Chivalry*'s first three volumes derive in large measure from Teague's attempts to escape his servitude and become a member of the bourgeoisie, with Farrago in turn thwarting Teague's ambitions. When Teague is invited to become a member of a Philosophical society—to become a "Philosopher"—Farrago explains that it "is not an easy matter to get hirelings now-a-days": "It would be a very great loss to me, to have him taken off at this time, when I have equipped myself for a journey." Teague, in turn, is "a good deal incensed at this refusal of his master" and insists that he has "a right to make the best of his fortune." Farrago dupes Teague to defer his ambitions, "finding that it answered no end to dispute the matter with him, by words of sense and reason, took a contrary way to manage him" (16). Farrago convinces Teague that the Philosophical society will abuse and exploit him, skinning him so as to make him "pass" for a gigantic otter or sending him into the wilderness to collect dangerous animals. Every character is an object of satire here: the Philosophers for thinking that Teague can be one of them, Farrago for his exploitation and manipulation of Teague, and Teague for being gulled by Farrago. This episode is paradigmatic. It repeats the basic structure of the episode in which Teague makes a bid for office and Farrago insists that when "a man becomes a member of a public body, he is like a raccoon, or other beast that climbs up the fork of a tree" (11). When Teague wants to become a minister, Farrago convinces him that he will thus provoke the vengeance of "Belzebub" (24). When Teague wants to marry a wealthy heiress, Farrago leads him to believe she is "a witch, and inchantress" (61). In each of these episodes the structure of the satire is the same: Teague's "ambition," Farrago's duplicity, and those who would have Teague are all derided. Ultimately, though, Teague is, finally, allowed to "rise." Farrago, "wearied with the preposterous ambition of the bog-trotter . . . by the advice of a gentleman . . . consented to let [Teague] try his luck of getting some employment under government" (139).

Yet, Teague's "rise" does not do away with the "perpetual war." The novel continues to pit Farrago against plebeians. By promoting Teague to the position of excise officer, *Modern Chivalry* motivates Brackenridge's novelization of the Whiskey Rebellion, which "was triggered by an excise tax on grain alcohol passed by the federal Congress in 1791."[45] Congress designed the excise as a way to pay down debts accrued by the U.S. government during the Revolutionary War. Brackenridge found himself at the center of the conflict over the excise. Though "he opposed the excise tax and had defended a group of rioters against a suit by an aggrieved tax collector, he regarded the rebels as irresponsible radicals."[46] (In 1794 he published *Incidents of the Insurrection* in order to justify his position in the rebellion.) When Farrago encounters a "mob" intending to tar and feather Teague (in his new role as excise officer) and shouting "*Liberty and no excise, liberty and no excise; down with all excise officers,*" he tries to "reason" with it:

> Gentleman, said he, the law may be exceptionable on general principles, or unequal in its operation to you in this district. Nevertheless, it is the law, and has received the sanction of the public voice, made known through the constitutional organ, the representative of the people. It is the great principle of a republican government, that the will of the majority shall govern. . . . The law in question may be odious, and great allowance ought to be made for the prejudices of the people. By soft measure, and mild words, prejudices may be overcome. (206)

"Is it not a principle of that republican government which you have established," he asks the mob, "that the will of the majority shall govern; and has not the will of the majority of the United States enacted this law?" (213). The spokesman of the mob responds: "'The will of the majority,' said he; 'yes, faith; the will of the majority shall govern. It is right that it should be the case. We know the excise officer very well. Come lay hands upon him'" (214). The mob promptly seizes Teague, strips "him of his vestments," pours "tar upon his naked body" and "a bed of feathers on his head" (214). The Whiskey Rebellion episode concludes with Farrago discussing the rebellion with the Marquis de Marnessie (in exile in western Pennsylvania, we are informed, as a result of the French Revolution). Farrago, it turns out, has "read the pamphlets of Thomas Paine, entitled, 'Rights of Man,' and was a good deal disposed to subscribe to the elementary principles of that work" (218). Farrago supports the "doctrine" that "at no time can the pact or customs of ancestors forestall or take away the rights of descendants to frame whatever kinds of government they think proper" (218). The Marquis takes the opposite position, arguing that "our ancestors, having established an hereditary monarchy, it is not in the power of the descendants to change it" (220). The Marquis figures the whiskey rebels as "sans culottes" who "wish to bring all things to a perfect level" (221). Farrago argues that it is impossible "to preclude [man] from all right to think, or act in affairs of government, with a view to improve, and to improve is to change" (220). In fact, "it is conducive to an amelioration of the state of life, and likely to produce a greater sum of happiness, to innovate upon established forms" (220). This conversation, imagined to occur in midst of the Whiskey Rebellion, cannot help but have resonance for that conflict, just as the language of the French Revolution was used from all points on the U.S. political spectrum as a vehicle for talking about conflicts like the Whiskey Rebellion.[47] While Farrago's defense of "the rights of man" to design their own governments might be read as a covert endorsement of the Whiskey Rebellion and even political transformation, the narrative presentation of the whiskey rebels follows suit with conservative tropes of the whiskey rebels as "the ignorant poor, who had yet to learn the meaning of virtue, had confused licentiousness for liberty."[48] The rebels have failed to recognize the value of Farrago's advice about how they should execute their desires. Plebeians, in other words, still need counsel from gentlemen.

A few final words on *Modern Chivalry*'s representation of Whiskey Rebellion are in order. According to Thomas Paine, "there are two classes of men in the nation, those who pay taxes, and those who receive and live upon taxes."[49] Along these lines, Teague has become the class enemy of the Whiskey Rebellion, one who "lives upon taxes." Farrago as classical republican is threatened by Teague's social mobility. But Farrago becomes a moderate Democratic-Republican when he begins to embrace Teague's ambition. When he does so, he helps remake Teague as an elite. When the Whiskey Rebels get their hands on Teague, they tar and feather him. Volume 3 asks, Can a lowborn, uneducated servant become a member of the elite? The Federalist would answer "no," the liberal egalitarian "yes." The rebels in volume 4 disregard this question entirely: plebeians have become the enemies of upward mobility.

From the Whiskey Rebellion episode on, Farrago is no longer the target of satire—and *Modern Chivalry* abandons its criticism of educated elites. As Emory Elliott points out, "The three volumes of Part II of *Modern Chivalry* cannot be read in the same way or evaluated with the same criteria as the books of Part I." Part 2 amplifies the narrator: "The story," writes Elliott, "is secondary to the preaching. . . . In these books the narrator becomes the hero."[50] As Grantland Rice observes, "The pronouncements of Brackenridge's narrator become more and more didactic."[51] Or, as Cynthia S. Jordan puts it, "For the remainder of the novel, the authorial voice intrudes with increasing preachiness into the narrative proper to promote the mode of authority [Farrago] represents."[52] Time and again the narrator intrudes to offer lengthy defenses of Farrago's criticisms of plebeian political desires and to inveigh against plebeian attempts to exclude Farrago and educated elites from political decision making or—what amounts to the same—plebeian arguments on behalf of a kind of workers' state.

While the post-1800 volumes of *Modern Chivalry* do not suggest that elites exclusively should rule, because they make a point of insisting upon elite voices within political decision making as a check upon what both Farrago and the narrator describe as the dangerous excesses of plebeian political desires, they participate in the defeat of oppositional notions of democracy that emerged in the 1790s and first decades of the nineteenth century. The "real meaning of Jeffersonian democracy," writes Richard Ellis, "is to be found in the political triumph of the moderate Republicans and their eventual amalgamation with the moderate wing of the Federalist party."[53] According to Seth Cotlar, "While the election of 1800 made 'democracy' a word that respectable leaders could use without apology, this transformation came at a cost. Together, leading Jeffersonians and Federalists sheared the word 'democracy' of its previously revolutionary and leveling implications. Such ideas were transformed into perversions of democracy; they became Jacobinical."[54] For Terry Bouton, both the Federal Constitution and the Pennsylvania Constitution were "designed to impede popular reform," and thus their ratifications "weakened democracy's meaning—primarily in the way the elite founders attempted [through them] to eradicate the idea that concentrations of wealth pose a threat to the republic."[55]

"In America the Law Is King": Law, Letters, and Democracy in *Modern Chivalry*

Andrew Shankman, in his detailed study of late eighteenth- and early nineteenth-century Pennsylvania politics, wherein Brackenridge's *Modern Chivalry* makes a short but significant cameo, finds that Jeffersonian democracy "drove from the mainstream a set of political ideas and concerns articulated as part of an effort to critique and curb what future generations would call capitalist excess" (230). "Jeffersonian politics," Shankman argues, "narrowed [political] options and made certain ideas and concerns dangerous to think and voice" (238).

Shankman documents how Pennsylvania radicals expressed the belief that "commerce" "required democratic control and access," without which it was proposed that destructive levels of economic inequality would develop in the new nation (79). In newspapers like the *Aurora*, figures such as William Duane argued that "key economic decisions" should be part of "a purely popular and immediately responsive political realm" (80). Only then could "widespread access to productive property" be ensured and massive, unjust, democracy-imperiling private fortunes be prevented from coming into being (81). Philadelphia radicals were especially critical of the structure of "an independent judiciary and the centrality of English-inspired common law in American jurisprudence" (84). Philadelphia radicals conceived of the independent judiciary of the Pennsylvania Constitution as an unwarranted bulwark against popular sovereignty, one that perpetuated—and would make possible even greater—economic inequality. While Pennsylvania radicals suggested that democracy had thus not yet in fact been realized in the United States, moderate Jeffersonians—or Quids—argued essentially the opposite (112). And according to the Quids, to tamper with or dismantle the independent judiciary would be to imperil property rights themselves (112).

As Brackenridge himself avers, part 2 of *Modern Chivalry* is in part a commentary on "the convulsion of public opinion . . . with regard to the formation of a new constitution" in Pennsylvania (441). "The talk of *abolishing* the courts, and the judges, is a language which I put into the mouth of Tom the Tinker," Brackenridge notes earlier, "yet [it] is more general than is imagined" (316).

In part 2 of *Modern Chivalry* (the volumes published in 1804, 1805, and 1815), plebeian antipathy toward the law is an abiding theme, as Farrago encounters a number of plebeian characters that express disaffection for the law. One such character, identified as a "mad democrat," insists that the Revolution has not in fact produced a "free government": "Down with all law, and give us free government," he demands (271). "Abolish the courts, and demolish the judges," proposes Tom the Tinker (292). "Down with the sessions, and down with the laws," commences a song likened by Brackenridge to "Ca Ira, or the Marsilles hymn" (that is, to one of the French Revolution's anthems) and sung by a character dubbed "O'Dell the revolutionist" (296).

Yet, while a host of plebeian figures in part 2 demand the abolition of the law, they are not in fact opposed to law in general; instead, they are opposed to existing legal processes and structures, especially judicial checks on legislation. What Tom the Tinker and O'Dell the revolutionist demand is the *revision* of the Pennsylvania Constitution. Plebeians in part 2 demand a new version of the law—which is to say, a new version of how laws are made and enforced. Indeed, if early U.S. plebeians "expressed considerable antipathy to the law and its agents," notes Tomlins, they did not "set their faces against law in its 'proper' form of democratically constituted laws—majoritarian legislative government."[56]

Modern Chivalry's plebeians demand the abolition of existing legal structures, especially legislative review by an independent judiciary, because they see these structures as antithetical to their economic interests—because they see the law as an institution of economic oppression. The "mad democrat," for example, rails against "all law," because a "man's nose is just as much upon the grind-stone as it was before the revolution" (271). The plebeian critique of the law is two pronged: plebeians indict existing legal structures as impediments to genuine democracy, but they also impugn the officers of existing legal structures as exploiters of labor. Plebeian animus toward the law in *Modern Chivalry* includes mistrust of lawyers and judges, who are accused by plebeian characters of exploiting plebeians. "De Lawyers," says "an honest German," "are de tyvil . . . and sheats people for de money" (368). This criticism of lawyers resonates with Manning's *Key of Liberty*, which numbers the "lawyer" and "the judicial and executive officers" among the Few who find ways of appropriating wealth from the Many and from hindering the sovereignty of the Many (136). Like the plebeians of *Modern Chivalry,* Manning supposes that the "greatest danger [to free government] is from judicial and executive departments of governments, especially from lawyers" (137). For Manning, such "officers, all depending upon their fees and salaries for a living, are always interested in having money scarce and the people in distress," (137); "free governments are commonly destroyed by the combinations of the judicial and executive powers in favor of the interests of the Few" (41). In *Modern Chivalry,* a "man with a long chin, and a pale visage" gives cogent expression to the two-pronged plebeian critique of the law: "Can there be anything more simple," he asks, "than *for the people to just govern themselves?* What needs all this talk of checks and balances? Why keep up laws, and judges, at an expence, as if the people were not competent to give laws and to judge for themselves?" (356). The thrust of these rhetorical questions is quite plain: according to plebeians in the novel, neither an independent judiciary nor lawyers and judges are necessary to democracy, and thus the existing structure of governance merits reform.

It perhaps bears repeating here that the political consciousness of *Modern Chivalry*'s plebeians—and of the radical Pennsylvania democrats to which they point—is not to be confused with something like a Marxian class consciousness: nowhere in the novel will a reader find a plebeian critique of wage labor. As Shankman points out, radical Pennsylvania democrats "had no conception of class as Marx taught the world to understand that term. Indeed, they did not think that the market, or economic activity itself, was the chief source of inequality." Instead, radical Pennsylvania democrats "believed that the primary source of inequality was the unequal distribution of political power," and thus that the "solution to inequality was not a redistribution of property, an assault on private property, or a breakthrough in class consciousness that allowed wage laborers to fashion a common identity" (115).

Yet, despite the limitations of plebeian focus on the law as an instrument of unequal distribution of political power and thus the source of economic inequality, we should not discount the insightfulness of the plebeian critique of the law. According to Jennifer Nedelsky, for the Framers of the U.S. Constitution, "inequality became both a presumption and an object of protection which skewed the conception of limited government that underlies our Constitution"—as well as, I would add, the state constitution against which *Modern Chivalry*'s plebeians rail. "For the Framers," Nedelsky writes, "the protection of property meant the protection of *unequal* property and thus the insulation of both property and inequality from democratic transformation."[57] Cotlar seconds Nedelsky, arguing that "America's propertied elite staved off what they perceived to be the most dangerous possibilities of the age of democratic revolutions by constructing a legal and intellectual firewall that cordoned off private property from the collective political will of the people." This legal firewall was judicial review, which "pushed questions of property rights out of the realm of political consideration and relegated them to the realm of the law"; this meant that "non-elected judges" were responsible for "guarding the boundary that protected existing private property from the potentially redistributive policies of legislatures."[58] That the Constitution was designed in part to protect unequal property is apparent in Madison's *Federalist* No. 10, according to which "the most common and durable source of factions has been the various and unequal distribution of property. Those who hold and those who are without property have ever formed distinct interests in society." For *Federalist* No. 10, "an equal division of property" is one of the "wicked project[s]" that the Constitution prevents.[59] If the Constitution—and the independent judiciary—were designed to block democratic intervention in the distribution of wealth, lawyers in the early United States, Charles Sellers points out, came to function as "the shock troops of capitalism," very much serving the interests of capital accumulation.[60] And law in the early United States, Tomlins explains, "played a major role in concretizing, while simultaneously obscuring, asymmetries of power and exchange arising in the social relations of employer and employee and the organization of employment."[61] The plebeian critique of the law may very well be part of the larger story of what Marx in *The Manifesto of the Communist Party* called "the development of class antagonisms," because plebeians were, in their own fashion, contesting "the exploitation of one part of society by the other."[62]

Yet, as Robert Ferguson has pointed out, *Modern Chivalry* stands as "an elaborate defense of the law"[63]—of lawyers, and of existing state and federal constitutions. This is especially true of part 2, where a number of other characters join Farrago in defending the law against plebeian critiques of it. For a character called "the blind lawyer," for "the Chief

Justice," and above all for the narrator, "the law" (by which is meant both existing legal structures and the state and federal constitutions) is synonymous with functioning commerce and "free government." According to "the blind lawyer," to tamper with the constitutions and abolish the independent judiciary means that "[s]ecurity of person, property, and reputation, the great end of civil institutions, will be rendered precarious. . . . A free government is a government of laws" (274). Likewise, on the estimation of the Chief Justice, to abolish the independent judiciary and install "simple arbitration" would "shake the security of property, real and personal" and thus "put a stop to all [economic] improvement" (398). The narrator offers similar arguments: "In the present commercial state of society, and where property is not held in common," he surmises, "the people" would not be "safe and prosperous without law altogether" (276). "There is a strange coincidence," he continues, "between liberty, and an established jurisprudence" (277). The blind lawyer, the Chief Justice, and the narrator thus agree with *Modern Chivalry*'s plebeians that current laws and legal structures function to protect existing economic relations and processes. But unlike the novel's plebeians, theirs is a celebration of these economic relations and processes—and thus, too, of current laws and legal structures. And for the blind lawyer, the Chief Justice, and the narrator, preserving existing economic relations and processes is tantamount to preserving "liberty."

According to Farrago, acting on the desire to abolish the independent judiciary may very well lead to the overthrow of democracy itself:

> *Nor is it democracy, that I have meant to expose; or reprehend, in any thing that I have said; but the errors of it: those excesses which lead to its overthrow.* These excesses have shewn themselves in all democratic governments; whence it is that a *simple* democracy has never been able to exist long. An experiment is now made in a new world, and upon better principles; that of *representation and a more perfect separation, and near equipoise of the legislative, judicial, and executive powers.* But the balance of powers, is not easily preserved.— *The natural tendency is to one scale.* The demagogue is the first great destroyer, of the constitution, by deceiving the people. He is no democrat that deceives the people.—He is an aristocrat; and seeks after more power than is just. He will never rest short of despotic rule. (356)

For Farrago, paradoxically enough, the movement to overthrow democracy is internal to democracy. Equally paradoxical is his insinuation that
the plebeian who wishes to rewrite existing constitutions is an "aristo-
crat." Yet, these are not really paradoxes for Farrago, once we recognize
that for him there are essentially two kinds of people in the U.S. polity:
"democrats" who wish to preserve existing constitutions, and "demagogues" who want to abolish these constitutions.

Crucially, for the narrator, as much as for Farrago, there are essentially two kinds of people in the U.S. polity: there are those who want
to preserve democracy, and those who do not—and those who want to
reform current government structures, or abolish existing legal apparatuses or the legal class, are in fact a threat to democracy. Comparing the
United States to China and "Arabia," whose governments, he says, "are
arbitrary, not free," the narrator concludes that *a free government, and
the exclusion of lawyers, cannot well be reconciled*" (315). But the narrator
is defending here not just lawyers but also the existing constitution: he
tells us that the "overthrow of a judiciary tribunal" "militates against a
branch of government," and abolishing a branch of the existing government leads to "Despotism" (315).

As I pointed out earlier, Brackenridge does not suggest that plebeians
have no right to participate in government—either as voters or elected
representatives. Yet, *Modern Chivalry* refuses to countenance radical
claims like those of the "man with a long chin, and a pale visage," its
narrator instead applauding "the great struggle to preserve" the Pennsylvania Constitution (441). The narrator's point throughout part 2, which
toes the Quid line, is that tampering with "established jurisprudence" is
to imperil what for him is democracy as it has already been realized in
the United States. While the plebeians of the novel want to abolish the
class of lawyers and judges in the United States—while they want to
abolish what they consider to be an exploitative class—*Modern Chivalry*
goes to lengths to insist upon the need for a class of lawyers and judges
in the United States to shepherd the populace through the legislative
process and thus to preserve democracy.

In fact, Brackenridge's narrator occupies copious pages arguing
against constitutional reform "from below": "[I]f constitutions are played
with like battle-dores," the narrator posits, "there is an end of stability"
(441). In part 2, volume 2 (again, 1805), the narrator professes himself a
"reformist" and not opposed to "reform in principle, or practice." Yet he

qualifies this position: "To reform with safety requires a perfect knowledge of the subject of the reform. To reform the law, either in its principles, or administration, requires a lawyer; a scientific, and philosophic lawyer" (383). If the narrator says that he is not opposed to reform, he explains that he nonetheless wishes "to see the democracy move in the groove of our noble constitution" (385). In part 2, volume 4, the narrator expresses similar ideas:

> It is the balancing with stays and braces of distributed powers that gives safety. This distribution of power is the highest effort of the mind, and yet you will find but few, who, like my bog-trotter, will not conceive that they could form a constitution that would give energy and guard liberty. . . . [The] formation of a government, is not a matter to which the bulk are competent: or if they will indulge caprice in changing, and they will go to change; whenever a change is made, it will be but a majority that is satisfied, and perhaps that not great; and it is to be expected that a portion of the majority, not finding their account in the change, will associate with the former minority, and hence a change, and so toties quoties, until only one remains that is to be satisfied. (486–87)

The narrator once again argues that what he considers hasty, capricious, not-thought-through reform unbalances society, giving opportunities to would-be demagogues and tyrants. These moments are exemplary of the narrator's deliberative style. He claims to weigh the costs and benefits of constitutional reform. Though he is not in theory opposed to reform, he insists that reform is a science that requires specialized knowledge and intellectual caution. According to *Modern Chivalry*'s narrator, only a small fraction of what Manning would call the Few—lawyers, judges— are capable of designing reform, and thus it is better to do with the status quo, which does guarantee individual freedom, rather than gamble on a constitution drafted by those without such knowledge and temperament.[64]

In part 2, volume 2, Farrago is elected governor of a settlement in western Pennsylvania (393). Before his election, Farrago admires this settlement's political ethos: "The inhabitants are a very happy people, no demagogues having yet arisen among them, to propel to licentiousness, as for instance, to propose agrarian laws, or an equality of goods or chattles" (371). Eventually, though, a craze for constitutional reform manifests in the settlement, despite "the revolutions in France about this time [having] created some alarm, at the idea of changing rapidly all at once from one constitution to another" (491). Farrago's election thus sets up—motivates—an episode that functions to satirize plebeian desires for constitutional reform, and that doubles down by different means on the narrator's argument against constitutional reform "from below." A weaver (*another* weaver) proposes a constitutional amendment to raise "the price of weaving." In turn, "the cord-wainer, and the brick-layer could easily see that . . . the course of deliberation [on the amendment of the constitution] . . . would naturally take a wider range, and introduce a clause providing for them also." Thus "it had become a cry pretty much prevailing, that the sitting of the people should be permanent: and the constitution revolutionary; so that whenever, and wherever the shoe was found to pinch it might be altered" (491). "The common mechanic, and laborer," Brackenridge writes, "were led away both in speaking and acting, with an enthusiasm for a change of constitution":

> A tailor was asked what he was now making? He said a suit of constitution.
> A tinker what he was now mending? He said the constitution.
> All that could write had drawn up forms; all that could not write, had meditated forms, and were reciting them to their neighbours. It was amusing to attend to the various suggestions of the fancy of these improvasatori; or extempore makers of constitutions. Some proposed for an article, the having a provision to fatten hogs without corn; and it was in vain to explain to them that this did not depend upon the constitution of the government; but on that of the hog. Some wanted chickens hatched without eggs: others, harvests raised without the trouble of sowing seed. All were an amelioration of things in the natural or moral world. (494)

Constitutional reform here entails plebeian desire for a state that would better promote plebeian economic interests: in demanding constitutional reform, plebeians want to subject the economy to plebeian legislation. Yet, plebeian ideas about constitutional reform and legislative control of the economy are here a comic combination of particularized material activities and fantastic imaginings. *Modern Chivalry*'s plebeians insist that they are "competent to give laws and to judge for themselves" (356), but this episode teaches *Modern Chivalry*'s readers to think otherwise. "For all time," writes Jacques Rancière, "the refusal to consider certain categories of people as political beings has proceeded by means of a refusal to hear the words exiting their mouths as discourse. The other way consists in the simple observation of their material incapacity to occupy the space-time of political things—as Plato put it, artisans have time for nothing but their work."[65] Farrago is at times patently guilty of such a refusal; to Tom the Tinker, for instance, he says: "I would rather hear your voice in your shop . . . and the sound of your hammer, on a coffee pot, or a tea kettle. You can patch a brass candle-stick, better than the state, yet, I take it, Tom" (292). This episode about constitutional reform in part 2, volume 2, reveals, though, that *Modern Chivalry* itself—as much as Farrago—refuses to consider plebeians capable of occupying "the space-time of political things," and in so doing rejects the notion that the economy should be subjected to plebeian governance.

On one level, *Modern Chivalry*'s narrator denies the plebeian notion that lawyers and judges are the enemies of plebeians. According the narrator, "the law" (that is, existing legal structures) should be seen as universalistic, egalitarian, class-blind—and thus the friend of the poor. "It seems to me," he argues, "that a poor man is safer in a country of laws, than one without laws." The trial itself requires lawyers "to make as free with the character and conduct of a rich rogue in a cause, as with one of a more circumscribed estate" (279). In the United States, "every man is brought up to the bull-ring in a court of law, be he rich or poor" (314). But it is not merely that the law treats the rich and poor equally; in addition, the law and lawyers are a thorn in the side of the wealthy, organically predisposed to side with democracy. According to the narrator, "there is a natural alliance between liberty and letters" (281). For Brackenridge's narrator, "men of letters" and lawyers are the same thing. Because men of letters—which is to say, lawyers—are "seldom men of wealth," they "naturally ally themselves with the democratic interest in a commonwealth" against "power, springing from family interest, and large estates" (281). In this fashion, Brackenridge's narrator dismisses the notions of class conflict that we find in Manning's *The Key*, for example.

Yet, while Brackenridge's narrator works to dispel plebeian notions of class conflict between plebeians and lawyers, throughout the later volumes of *Modern Chivalry* Brackenridge nonetheless makes the case that legal knowledge is by necessity a specialized field. The blind lawyer, who appears first in part 2, volume 1, of *Modern Chivalry* (1804), argues that it is necessary to have learned men in the position of lawyers and judges: "Security of person, property, and reputation, the great end of civil institutions" will otherwise be rendered "precarious." "The law parliamentary," he continues, "or rules of a legislative body, is not learnt in a day. And yet without a knowledge of it, there is a want of order, as well as dispatch in business. . . . But when we come to the rules of property, the laws of tenure and of contract, a field opens, that startles the imagination. Even the study of years, makes but a sciolist" (274). The narrator agrees: "The knowledge of our rights, and capacity to prosecute, and defend them, does not spring from the ground; but from education and study. . . . We stand in need of law, learning, and legal abilities" (281). Again, the United States needs a class of individuals with specialized learning to protect property rights; *Modern Chivalry* is thus making the case that the kind of legal knowledge that reform or legislation about the economy requires is something that plebeians themselves cannot attain.

"A man may not be a scholar himself; but he may have son," writes Brackenridge's narrator, "that may. . . . The offspring of a plain farmer may be a philosopher; a lawyer; a judge. Let not the simplest man therefore set light by literary studies" (303). (For Brackenridge "literary studies" means "[l]egal knowledge, and political learning" [303]). Such a pronouncement on class mobility in the United States taps the autobiographical: Brackenridge was "the son of a poor Scottish farmer" who graduated from the College of New Jersey; he became a prominent lawyer, was elected to the Pennsylvania Senate, and was appointed to the Pennsylvania Supreme Court.[66] Yet, by suggesting that philosophers, lawyers, and judges may have been the children of plain farmers, Brackenridge deploys class mobility here as part of an argument on behalf of the legal class and existing constitutions (Pennsylvania state and federal): "Legal knowledge, and political learning," he writes, "are the stamina of the constitution. The preservation of the constitution is the stability of the state" (303). By suggesting that philosophers, lawyers, and judges may have been the children of plain farmers, Brackenridge again invites plebeians not to see either the educated elite or "existing constitutions" as their enemies. Yet, I want to emphasize what may seem a rather obvious point: Brackenridge does not say that the plain farmer himself might be also, and at the same time, a philosopher, lawyer, or judge.

While for *Modern Chivalry* "learning" is required for "reform," the novel also insists that the plebeian desire to rid the country of lawyers and the law would ultimately entail a fulfillment of the desire to rid the country of learning itself. "Larning," says the "honest German," "ish goot for noting; but to make men rogues. It ish all a contrivance to sheat people" (368). The song of "O'Dell the revolutionist" iterates this sentiment:

Down with the sessions, and down with the laws;
They put me in mind of the school-master's taws.
There's nothing in nature that gives such disgust,
As force and compulsion to make a man just.

. . . .

As lawyer's a liar; old Sooty is father;
He talks all day long, a mere jack-a-blather.
His books, and his paper may all go to hell,
And make speeches there, sing Lary O'Dell.

. . . .

The state is a vessel, and hooped like a tub;
And the adze of the cooper it goes dub, a dub.
But hooping and coopering, is fitting for fools;
Away wid all learning, and shut up the schools. (296)

While Manning called for the democratization of learning—for free, universal public education[67]—*Modern Chivalry*'s plebeians want to abolish learning altogether. According to *Modern Chivalry*, the world that plebeians desire is a world without learning.

Traveling west again in part 2, volume 2, Farrago and Teague, as well as Tom the Tinker, Will Watlin, Harum Scarum, O'Fin, and Clonmel, enter "the Lack-learning settlement." The inhabitants of Lack-learning would have no "*Scholars and Lawyers*" among them, and believing Farrago's band to include such types, "a multitude had got together, with sticks and stones, to obstruct" their "march into the country" (367). Farrago insists there "are no scholars amongst us." But he also argues that it would not matter if there were: "After all," he asks, "what harm could learning do you, provided that you did not learn yourselves?" Likening the residents of Lack-learning to animals, he argues that "the bears and the foxes of these woods do not learn; but they do not hinder men to read books. They have no objections to schools or colleges, or courts of justice; because it does not prevent them running into holes, or climbing upon trees." However, after offering this "[e]very man in his humor" defense of "learning," Farrago then argues that learning is in fact a higher state of being—that is, that it is more human, more evolved—than lack-learning: "I acknowledge that men were at first like beasts of the wood, and the fowls of the air, without grammars or dictionaries; and it took a great deal to bring them out of that state, and give them what is called education. At the revival of letters in Europe, after the dark ages, it was thought a great matter to get to be a scholar. Peculiar privileges were attached. Hence what is called 'the benefit of the clergy'" (367). It is in this context that the "honest German" denounces learning: "Larning ist goot for noting; but to make men rogues" (368). Certainly, Farrago's remarks are revealed to be anything but innocent: the presence of educated professionals in Lack-learning would change the settlement's balance of power. But if Farrago is not innocent, Lack-learning is demagogic.

In the "Observations" that follow the chapter on Lack-learning, the narrator quickly undercuts the "honest German": he is, for the narrator, a minion of "the Demagogue amongst the multitude." The critic of learning deploys anti-learning as a way to remain in power: he "did not wish to lose his influence by the competition of a lawyer, or a scholar" (368). By revealing this information about the power structure of Lack-learning, the narrator insinuates that anti-learning is itself antidemocratic, that it is potentially in the service of autocracy, and thus that Farrago's argument on behalf of learning, while perhaps duplicitous and manipulative, might paradoxically enough be necessary for the preservation of liberty. The narrator explains that the "demagogue of all times" always deploys in his rhetorical arsenal "the oppression of the laws, and the inequality of the justice of the poor." Again, the narrator splits the imagined polity into two kinds of people: on the one side are demagogues, who attack learning and who happen to be plebeian radicals, and on the other are defenders of liberty, who happen to be educated elites. Because the demagogue takes aim at the law in general, the demagogue cannot help but attack "science"—that is, education—precisely because "where there are laws, there will be science." The narrator quotes Ecclesiastes: "Of the making many books, there is no end, and much study is weariness of the flesh." The narrator argues that scholarship and writing do not give "perfect happiness," in part recapitulating Farrago's earlier argument that "it requires some resolution, and much perseverance, to become learned." Yet, whereas for Farrago the difficulty of learning warrants "peculiar privileges," for the narrator the incomplete satisfaction of learning speaks to "the inanity of the noblest of all enjoyments; the mental gratification, of *making or reading a book.*" All told, the Lack-learning episode positions learning inside a decidedly undialectical political struggle. Either the United States will have "the learned professions"—by the novel's definition necessarily a social minority—and with them "democracy," or it will have neither.

"WHAT NEEDS ALL THIS TALK?" POLYPHONY AND/AS INEQUALITY

Dana Nelson maintains that *Modern Chivalry* "makes political diversity central to the health of a democratic representative order."[68] Grantland Rice likewise contends that Brackenridge advocates "*belles lettres* as a guarantor of representative government because its cacophony of voices and mixtures of literary forms worked to diffuse the arrogation of centralized power."[69] Yet, just as the conflict between Farrago and Lacklearning is undialectical, so too is *Modern Chivalry* in general. While *Modern Chivalry* is committed to a version of vocal pluralism, it is a version of pluralism that limits democracy to a debate between elites and plebeians—between the Few and the Many. Whereas Farrago can hold conversations with other elites, plebeians can never hold conversations among themselves without the critical interjections of Farrago or the narrator. Democracy in *Modern Chivalry* requires elites and plebeians to argue with one another. It cannot be a dialogue among social equals.

In its last chapters as much as its first, *Modern Chivalry* tells the same story. Over and again, plebeians demand full control of political decision making, and Farrago interposes. Over and again, one set of plebeians chase Farrago out of a particular settlement, but we stick with Farrago—who lives to debate another set of plebeians. Over and again, plebeians say that they do not want to hear what Farrago and his ally, the blind lawyer, have to say—but we do indeed hear what they have to say. Because *Modern Chivalry*'s plebeians find Farrago's voice and his ideas maddening, they would rather a world in which there were no Farragos;

but this means that the novel's plebeians are on some level opposed to the pluralism to which the form of *Modern Chivalry* is desperately committed.

Farrago defends himself time and again. "I am a democrat myself," he insists; "It is true, I have not undervalued learning, or exclaimed against lawyers. . . . Did I engross lots of ground? Has there been a necessity for an agrarian law in my case? Have I speculated on the wants of men, by forestalling, or regrating? Have I *made haste to be rich?* . . . Is my hat off to a rich man, sooner than to the poor?" (355). Farrago may not be an exemplary capitalist, but he is nonetheless a *rentier.* A rentier, Bruce Robbins reminds us, "'lives *off*' income from property or investments. In other words, she or he does not depend on income from work that she or he actually performs."[70] And Farrago puts his weight behind professionals—lawyers and judges—that plebeians denounce as living off of others' work. While plebeians do not want to listen to Farrago and the blind lawyer, Farrago and the blind lawyer are apportioned plenty of space in the novel to talk. And the narrator buttresses and iterates and extends and rationalizes their arguments at every turn. My sense is that this novel desires to go on—to have the United States go on—forever in the same fashion, repeating the same conflict forever: even though plebeians continually run Farrago and his allies off, they cannot really succeed. Farrago and the narrator live to fight—to talk—another day. The novel does not just make the case against the plebeian desire for constitutional reform, for greater democratic control over the economy, or for the abolition of the Few. Rather, it makes the case against plebeian desires again, and again, and again. This novel comes to feel like an endless repetition of the same debate between the rentier (and his allies) and plebeians. If *Modern Chivalry* offers its readers pleasure, then, the pleasure it offers is the pleasure of this endless repetition of the same. In inviting its readers to take pleasure in this endless repetition of the same—of the continuing existence of Farrago and his attempts to put drag on plebeian political self-expression, the form of *Modern Chivalry*—as much the content of any one speech in which plebeian desires are contested— invites its readers to take pleasure in the continuing presence of class itself in the early United States. The novel's form is committed to history staying in its current groove, to use the narrator's phrase about his desires for the perpetuation of existing constitutions.

Modern Chivalry ends where it begins: toward the close of part 2,

volume 4 (1815), Teague once again—as he had near the beginning of
volume 1 (1792)—thinks about running for elected office. Yet, while
in volume 1, Teague "took it into his head, that he could be a legislator
himself" (9), in part 2, volume 4, he now aims for the position of governor in the "new settlement" "bordering on the Indian country" (379)
where Farrago has been elected governor—and thus seeks to dispose
Farrago. In volume 1, Farrago talks Teague out of running for state legislator; in part 2, volume 4, he talks the plebiscite out of installing Teague
as governor. *Modern Chivalry* ends, then, with the rentier class checking
plebeian political desire.

On one level, Teague's bid for governor represents one last occasion
for Farrago (and the novel in general) to lampoon what Brackenridge
calls "the folly of the people" on matters of political economy (516).
Teague is cajoled into his bid for governor by what Brackenridge dubs
"the Visionary Philosopher": this character is informed that Teague has
discovered "the *philosopher's stone*"—that Teague is capable of "making gold and silver in the present scarcity of specie" (515). Teague's bid
for governor at the close of *Modern Chivalry* thus has everything to do
with political economy: Teague-as-governor represents a fantasy of not
just liquidity and state solvency but also of universal abundance. Yet,
because Teague's solution to problems of liquidity, state solvency, and
the distribution of wealth is a "philosopher's stone," from the perspective of Brackenridge's novel, Teague—and the plebiscite's support for
Teague—are plagued by fantasy. Farrago responds to "the people of his
government" who support Teague and his philosopher's stone with yet
another speech, a speech propelled by Farrago's "very powerful lungs"
and transmitted by his "stentorian voice" (516):

"Good people, said he, I care no more about my popularity with you;
or whether I am again to be chosen governor or not, than I care about
whether you are fools or knaves; it all comes to the same thing; for in
both cases, you mistake your own interest. If this fool fellow, Teague
O'Regan, that has been one day popular with you, so as to be fit for
any office, and at another day not fit to be your hangman, has found
a stone, which this politician, the visionary philosopher, gives out as
having the virtue of transmuting metals, and changing wood or shells
into gold and silver; if this ragamuffin, I say, has found such a stone,
which I no more believe than my horse's hoof has the virtue of chang-

ing the earth he treads upon, into gold; what good would it do you, when the very thing that makes such metal precious, scarcity, would take away all use, or benefit of it? If you would make gold and silver as plenty as bank notes, would it be of more value? Do you take me for one that, for the sake of keeping my place, would consult a temporary popularity?" (517)

Farrago insists upon his own disinterestedness—on his own transcendence of "popularity." Moreover, he argues not only that the philosopher's stone is imaginary but also in effect that the desire that subtends belief in the philosopher's stone—a desire for a world not of economic scarcity, but abundance—is unrealistic.

On another level, Teague's bid for governor occasions the modeling of what Brackenridge's novel dubs the "great secret" of governing men. Laying bare *Modern Chivalry* as kind of anti–*Don Quixote,* Farrago again accuses the plebiscite of being unrealistic:

"You may have my bog-trotter, and welcome, for a governor; I am pretty well tired of bothering myself with him, to make use of a phrase of his own; I have has as much trouble on my hands with him as Don Quixotte had with Sancho Panza; and I cannot but acknowledge, as some say, that I have resembled Don Quixotte myself, at least in having such a bog-trotter after me; save that Sancho rode upon an ass and this O'Regan trots on foot. But I hope I shall not be considered as resembling that Spaniard in taking a wind-mill for a giant; a common stone for a magnet that can attract, or transmute metals. It is you that are the Don Quixottes in this respect, madcaps, and some of you from the madcap settlement, Thady O'Connor and several others, tossing up your caps at every turn, for a new constitution; not considering that when a thing gets in the way of changing, it will never stop until it gets to the end of liberty, and reaches despotism, which is the bourne from whence no traveller returns. Do you take me for *Jefferson?* You are mistaken if you think I have so good opinion of you. I would ill deserve your confidence if I made your whims my guide; or regarded popularity obtained in such a way. It never came into my head that, because I got the chair of government, there was a millenium about to come, when all men would do justice, and there would no occasion for judges and lawyers . . . " (517–18)

Proclaiming himself politically anti-utopian, Farrago strikes the keynote of part 2: constitutional reform, which for many plebeians was thought necessary if the United States were to move beyond class exploitation, should instead be understood as the first step toward despotism. Farrago concludes his harangue by insisting that with Teague as governor he "should not be surpized, if some of you should have your necks in the guillotine before a fortnight. . . . This happened in the French revolution, and it will happen with you, if you give way to reveries" (518). Farrago's message is clear: if the plebiscite acts on its political desires and does away with figures like Farrago, revolutionary violence will likely redound on the plebiscite itself. Farrago's message here, I have tried to show, is one that *Modern Chivalry*'s narrator vocalizes throughout its final installments. Crucially, this episode ends with the "the legislative body" and "the multitude without" entreating Farrago "to retain his place as governor," but moreover also insisting that "the bog-trotter should be guillotined" (518). Farrago himself thwarts this form of political violence, channeling it instead into the deportation of Thady O'Connor—one of the plebeian figures in the final installments of *Modern Chivalry* that speaks up on behalf of constitutional reform.[71] Equally as crucial, then, Farrago triumphs by instilling fear in the members of his audience. Though they do not really understand the events of the French Revolution or indeed what a guillotine is, "all apprehended some bad consequences" (518). The members of the audience imagine themselves as potential victims of revolutionary violence.

This episode operationalizes what Brackenridge's narrator a few pages earlier dubs a "moral truth," or "that which depends upon the nature of man, and is the foundation of his actions" (503). According to Brackenridge's narrator, it is a "moral truth" that "[a]ll government must be . . . founded in *fear*" (504). "Fear," the narrator explains, "is the foundation of government, of man, as much as of a horse, or an ass. The great secret is to govern him, not just as you would a beast; but by the *fear of suffering a distant evil*" (504). The narrator explains why this is the case:

> Who would comprehend without feeling it, that it is of all things the most difficult to govern men? The most simple way, and doubtless the best, is the same by which you would govern a beast; the *bridle and the whip*. An *individual* at the head of an *organization* may command millions, and keep them in subjection: but in this case, no one can be

allowed a will of his own, to the smallest extent. If the *two legged thing* that calls himself a man under such a government, should attempt to *speak or act* for himself, off his head goes, scalp and all, and there is an end of the disturbance. There is one way, which is to the let the multitude alone together, and then there is anarchy, or no government. If you let them alone, it does not suit very well, for in that case, they rob; and there being no security, there is no industry; and consequently, no improvement in the arts, or amelioration in the condition of man. If you undertake to restrain their passions, how will you go about it; but by force or persuasion? Persuasion will go but a little way with a man that is hungry to hinder him from putting his paw upon whatever eatable there is before him. It is but a conceit in Montesquieu, to found a republic upon the principle of *virtue;* a monarchy upon that of honour; and despotism upon that of *fear.* Fear, is the foundation of government, of man, as much as of a horse, or an ass. The great secret is to govern him, not just as you would a beast; but by *the fear of suffering a distant evil.* The reason and reflection of a man can comprehend this; that of a beast not so much. What we have seen in this new settlement, is a picture of the credulity, and restlessness of man, and his constant struggle to break through that organization of *power* by which he is restrained from that to which his passions prompt. He will endeavor to break through, by talking of changing the modes of government. But it is not the mode, but the being governed at all that displeases him. A *constitution* is that organization by which a man is governed *by rules that apply to every individual of the community;* and from which no one is exempt, but all bound to obey. That is what is called a republican government. The changing a constitution begets the desire of change, and like a dislocated bone, must produce a *weak joint.* It ought to be some great defect that would justify a change.

This passage is exemplary of the narrator's deliberative style. He speaks as a political theorist, insinuating that he is interested in what is "good" for society in general. He addresses his audience likewise as individuals interested in the question of government in the abstract, drawing his conclusions from what he insists are laws of human nature. He does not appeal to fear, but instead appeals to what for this narrator would be his audience's reason—to the members of his audience's capacity to think not only about their own individual interests but also, again,

about the interest of society in general. There are certainly "bad" forms
of government, forms of government that rob subjects of their "will."
But, nonetheless, government is necessary, for without it there is anarchy: if individuals are not governed, then they will not be guaranteed
civil protection, and as result there can be no civil society (culture or
commerce). By the same token, constitutional reform in itself is not to
be dismissed out of hand; yet, we need to be careful about constitutional
reform, since it may lead to a situation equivalent to "anarchy"—since it
may let loose the passion to resist government altogether and undo the
material "progress" that has been made under an existing constitution.
And, so, when the polity reveals symptoms of the propensity to anarchy,
fear—which plays upon both man's passion and his reason—is socially
necessary, which is to say, good for the polity in general. In *Modern Chivalry,* it is the voice of the rentier that can generate this socially necessary
fear. And as we know, the narrator has argued at length that existing constitutions are free from the "defect" that would necessitate their reform.
Under them individuals are politically "free" and "equal"; under them,
all individuals are equally ruled and protected. Good thing, then, that
there are rentiers in the first place to raise their voices against plebeian
political desires, desires which might if actualized lead to the abrogation
of existing freedom and equality, and reduce the polity to a Hobbesian
state of nature.

That *Modern Chivalry*'s narrator invites us to laud Farrago's suppres-
sion of plebeian political desire—but also that the narrator defines constitutional reform as the antithesis of intellectual and economic progress—is again evident in a short inset narrative toward the close of the
novel about, in essence, the disciplining of labor via what Brackenridge
dubs "moralizing." "Obedience to the laws, is a Christian duty," Brackenridge's prefaces this inset narrative, "and the support of government
is favourable to that settled state of society, in which alone any system
of mental cultivation can be the object of attention" (523). He continues:

> In the late commotion of the public mind in this new government,
> respecting the calling of a convention to alter the constitution, we
> had an instance of what might be done by an honest open hearted
> clergyman, of good sense, among his profession. He had a few acres
> of ground to clear, by cutting down the timber and rolling it away;
> and for this purpose, made what is called a frolic: that is, an assem-

blage for labour, and a feast at the same time for; the feast was in the fete champetre way; though they did not give it that name. A pile of wood had been set on the fire, and the kettle suspended over it on a cross beam, supported by a fit arm at each end. The maker of the frolic, the owner of the clearing, going forward, had told the men, as the truth of the case warranted him in doing, that as the female part of his family had not come out to the settlement as yet, nor would until he could get some shelter built and improvement made, they must cook themselves. There were fleshes of venison, and beef, and pork, and some fowls, and vegetables, and articles of seasoning: each might put in according to his liking. Each did put in according to his notion of making broth; and like the weird-sisters in Macbeth, they stirred the kettle, singing as they stirred, till the pot was boiled, and taken off the hanger, to assemble round and put their ladles in. Some thought the broth had too much salt, or pepper, or cabbage; others too little. The proportion of every article of fish, flesh, or fowl was found fault with by some one. My ingredient, said the master of the entertainment, is yet to come, that is a flask of whiskey; to which they all assented to have poured in. A ladle of the broth enlivened the spirit, put them in good humour; and it was a safe thing to jest with them, and to slur good hints under the veil of parable. "Good folks, said he, being of an occupation which the wags in their humour sometimes call pulpit whacking, it is not difficult for me to strike a doctrine out of anything, as easily as Moses did the water fall out of the rock at Melba; and hence it is, that we are apt, even on common occasions, though not in the pulpit, to spiritualize. This I am not about to do at present, but rather, if you please, to moralize a little. We have a constitution, or frame of government, which has stood some time, and for anything I can see, might stand a while yet. It was framed by men of great political skill, at least, great information; and it was with great deliberation that it was formed. It was not until lately that any one thought to disturb, and new model; and in fact to make another. Reform is a popular word, and it is that which is chosen. But every one must foresee an entire overhauling. Now, as I would wish to see our young timber sawed into planks to line houses, or to make floors; or by hewing, made fit for harrows or ploughs and beams, rather than erected into guillotines, I am for putting up with the constitution until we get our fields cleared, and our meadows made; until we look about us, and get time to think a little, lest going hastily about it we make worse. For you see, in making this broth, where every thing was put in that any one said he liked, it was not savoury, until a dash of whiskey made it palatable——." (524–25)

Like Farrago, the clergyman is a wealthy, educated landowner that acts to manipulate his audience: he gets the workers he has hired drunk (presumably) and holds up the possibility of the guillotine to dissuade them from desiring constitutional reform. Moreover, he intimates that he—as much as the existing constitution that he defends—represents the glue that allows the activities of the assembled workers to come together in a satisfying whole: without him, the dish would not be "savoury." Yet, like Brackenridge's narrator, the clergyman suggests, first, that writing constitutions requires a specialized knowledge that plebeians do not possess; second, that the existing constitution works well enough for the polity to let it alone; and, third, that reforming the constitution might unleash political violence and derail economic progress. It bears emphasizing, then, that for Brackenridge's narrator, this figure is "honest," "open hearted," and "of good sense." Once again, Brackenridge's narrator encourages us to relish—to take pleasure in—the voice of the Few. *Modern Chivalry* can be read, I have been arguing, as teaching a lesson that the Few would like to hear: the Few, their voices, and their resistance to plebeian political desires are necessary parts—indispensable ingredients—of the United States whole, and not, as plebeian radicals would have it, an impediment to the realization of truly "free Government."

3   THE PROVIDENCE OF CLASS
Catharine Maria Sedgwick, Political Economy, and Sentimental Fiction in the 1830s

In the last two chapters, I have tried to show that unwieldy U.S. novels published in the final decade of the eighteenth century and the first two decades of the nineteenth century work as rejoinders to Enlightenment-era and radical plebeian varieties of economic egalitarianism. This chapter moves to the 1830s, a decade in which socialism as a political perspective begins to edge onto the stage in the United States. More particularly, this chapter argues that two of Catharine Maria Sedgwick's 1830s sentimental novels, *The Poor Rich Man, and the Rich Poor Man* (1836) and *Live and Let Live* (1837), should be read as responses to early forms of socialist thinking in the United States—but, also, that these novels continue the project of legitimating class inequality in the United States.

Sedgwick is now recognized as a central figure of U.S. literary culture in the decades preceding what F. O. Matthiessen famously called the American Renaissance of the 1850s. Yet, even though *The Poor Rich Man* and *Live and Let Live* "went through a score of more editions" after their initial publications and "proved to be [Sedgwick's] bestselling works,"[1] these novels have received nowhere near as much attention from scholars as her *Hope Leslie* (1827), a historical novel which has secured Sedgwick's reputation as an opponent of her moment's racial and gender ideologies. [2] *The Poor Rich Man* and *Live and Let Live* reveal another facet to Sedgwick's writing. These novels represent an inegalitarian version of sentimentalism, keyed as they are to counteracting arguments on behalf of a fundamental transformation in the way wealth is produced and distributed in the antebellum United States.[3]

Moreover, these once very popular though now largely overlooked novels challenge the equation of northern antebellum sentimental fiction with a liberal democratic disavowal of permanent class inequality in the United States. If 1850s sentimental novels posit locations and persons "outside class"[4] by focusing on characters that are not clearly participants (as buyers or sellers) in the market for labor, Sedgwick's earlier approach to class offers us something quite different: in Sedgwick's *The Poor Rich Man* and *Live and Let Live* characters are very much "inside class"—but it is a good thing that they are. The few critics who have written on *The Poor Rich Man* and *Live and Let Live* at times suggest that these novels are quite radical, going so far as to suggest that Sedgwick is "anticipating and hastening the time when equality will exist in fact and not just in theory,"[5] and that she "unquestionably resists the quickly developing market society."[6] I would contend, instead, that Sedgwick's novels, like Charles Brockden Brown's and Hugh Henry Brackenridge's, ask us to reconsider the story that the early United States told about itself. Here, the U.S. novel does not hide economic inequality by insisting upon an expansive middle class with "rich" and "poor" as inconsequential minorities; rather, for Sedgwick, the United States both is and ought always be marked by the division of "rich" and "poor"—by fundamental economic inequality among whites.

"THE GREAT SUBJECT OF INEQUALITY OF CONDITION": SENTIMENTALISM VS. "THE AGRARIAN PRINCIPLE"

The narrator of *The Poor Rich Man* observes that the "great subject of inequality of condition . . . puzzles the philosopher, and sometimes disturbs the Christian" (39). Sedgwick solves this puzzle by insisting "Providence" has made "this inequality the necessary result of the human condition" and that "the true agrarian principle" is "to be found in the voluntary exercise of those virtues that produce an interchange of benevolent offices." "If there were a perfect community of goods," she asks, "where would be the opportunity for the exercise of the virtues, of justice, and mercy, humility, fidelity, and gratitude?" (39). Casting economic inequality as a providential logic, Sedgwick's novels represent economic inequality as the precondition of ethical feeling and action. Her novels tap the "rich" and "poor" to "exercise" what are construed as different but equally essential "virtues": "justice, and mercy" are the province of the rich; "humility, fidelity, and gratitude" are the province of the poor. The "voluntary exercise" of Christian virtues arising from within economic inequality, Sedgwick maintains, entails a kind of reciprocal exchange ("interchange of benevolent offices") that quashes the need for economic equality.

This moment exemplifies the didactic, polemical flavor of Sedgwick's short 1830s novels. It also indicates her participation in a discourse of class that extends back at least as far as John Winthrop's 1630 *A Model of Christian Charity:* "God Almighty in His most holy and wise providence," Winthrop begins, "hath so disposed of the condition of mankind, as in all times some must be rich, some poor, some high and eminent in power and dignity; others mean and in subjection."[7]

Yet, Sedgwick's novels were very much of their moment, self-conscious responses to the first wave of socialist politics in the United States. "Agrarian principle" might call to mind the Jeffersonian ideal of a yeoman republic, but "agrarianism" in this era denoted "utopian socialist solution[s]."[8] Sedgwick's use of the term invokes projects like New Harmony, the Owenite community in southern Indiana, and texts like Thomas Skidmore's 1829 *The Rights of Man to Property,* which called for the radical redistribution of land. In the 1820s and '30s, a number of radicals and working-class activists buttressed their claims by declaring that Christianity necessitates the abolition of economic inequality, but Sedgwick instead holds Christianity to be a matter of individual actions *within* economic inequality. Sedgwick will not countenance the "agrarian principle," because, for her, economic inequality benefits the United States ethically and spiritually.

That Sedgwick explicitly seeks to defend economic inequality explains why, I would suggest, *The Poor Rich Man* and *Live and Let Live* do not offer the same kind of narrative focus and architecture we find in later sentimental novels. This is not to say that later forms of literary sentimentalism do not function to legitimate capitalism. Indeed, Gillian Brown and Lori Merish have argued that antebellum literary sentimentalism consecrates forms of "possessive individualism."[9] Brown and Merish reveal sentimental fiction to work as an essentially middle-class cultural form that upholds middle-class hegemony; and it does so in large measure, they show, by disavowing class inequality under capitalism by promulgating a fantasy of "classlessness."[10] Amy Schrager Lang has explicitly proposed "classlessness" as the ideology of antebellum sentimentalism. Extending Karen Halttunen's observation that the U.S. middle class conceived of the United States as "a classless society,"[11] Lang argues that sentimental fiction is "the story not of moving up but of moving out of class."[12] For Lang, Susan Warner's *The Wide, Wide World* (1850) and Maria Cummins's *The Lamplighter* (1854) stage "classlessness" via stories about women who come to have "no particular class location." Even though Ellen in *The Wide, Wide World* and Gerty in *The Lamplighter* move out of poverty and into the middle class, they are finally "presented as unclassed" on Lang's reading.[13] While the center of focus of major 1850s sentimental novels is on characters that come to evade easy class categorization, in Sedgwick's novels the focus is instead on characters that are always categorized as rich or poor.

Lang contends, furthermore, that "to publicly admit the reality of class in America was to open the nation to the threat of class conflict."[14] Certainly, to invoke class could be to summon class conflict: "What distinguishes the present from every other struggle in which the human race has been engaged," wrote Frances Wright in 1830, "is, that the present is, evidently, openly and acknowledgedly, a war of class, and this war is universal."[15] Yet, Martin Burke has established that antebellum Americans "did not simply espouse a liberal ideology of classlessness that denied the presence of actual socioeconomic divisions."[16] Instead, a number of antebellum writers "created a durable convention in public discourse that represented the United States as a society formed by classes, but freed from class conflict."[17]

Many antebellum writers advanced class as inescapable. For Rev. G. W. Burnap, it is the unavoidable price of economic productivity: the "comforts and luxuries which are now brought to the door of the humblest cottage," he argues, would not exist if "the agrarian principle prevailed." (Here, too, "agrarian principle" refers to utopian socialism.) "It is only by large revenues falling into few hands, that those treasures can be amassed, which react upon society with such benignant power." "Nothing, then, can be more unreasonable or unwise," Burnap concludes, "than the wish, that there were no rich men, even when cherished by the poor."[18] Productivity is likewise central to James Fenimore Cooper's defense of economic inequality in *The American Democrat* (1838): "Where there is a rigid equality of condition . . . that condition must necessarily be one of a low scale of mediocrity."[19] Because "rights of property" are "an indispensable condition of society," on Cooper's account, it follows that "[o]ne [man] is reduced to serve, while another commands, and, of course, there can be no equality in their social conditions" (45). Yet, for Cooper, "societies, or religious sects, in which a community of property prevails, are content with merely supplying the wants of life, knowing little or nothing of its elegancies, refinements, or mental pleasures" (135). For Thomas Cooper writing in 1830, economic inequality would be impossible to maintain, because "natural" differences between individuals would eventually lead to economic inequality "within the short period of twenty-five years" after equality was imposed.[20]

Sedgwick's *The Poor Rich Man* and *Live and Let Live* work in tandem with justifications of economic inequality to be found in contemporaneous political economy, including her own brother Theodore's 1836 *Public and Private Economy* (to which I return later in this chapter). While Catharine Sedgwick's novels deny class conflict by insisting upon the possibility of sympathetic relationships between rich and poor, these novels neither castigate those individuals who do not transcend relative poverty nor trade in the promise that everyone could become "middle class."[21] In point of fact, Sedgwick deploys a binary class lexicon in which the United States forever consists of rich and poor, making patently clear that in her ideal nation there will always be poor families and individuals who must sell their labor to the rich in order to survive.

Sedgwick's binary class lexicon of rich and poor, which both her narrators and her working-class characters deploy, might be said to mystify antebellum socioeconomic realities. Certainly, the complexity of social stratification and the intersections of class, race, gender, and region in the antebellum United States exceed this simplifying dichotomy. Yet, Sedgwick's lexicon of rich and poor represents and naturalizes the very real fact of class inequality.[22] And it does so without displacing class with race and gender in order to produce the idea of "classlessness" among whites. While antiessentialist approaches to class reject the presupposition that "shared forms of life—whether cultural or political—stem from an anterior economic determination,"[23] the instability of class identities does not make class go away. Again, as Eric Schocket explains, "class can be both an objective reality and a discursive construct."[24] Perhaps it is counterintuitive that she does so, but Sedgwick uses a language of economic polarity as the means by which to imagine an organic society at a time when workers and some intellectuals were already using binary class vocabularies to protest economic inequality.

With the rich in Sedgwick's novels expressing their virtues by caring for the poor, Sedgwick brandishes a version of economic paternalism: here, the relationship between rich and poor can be like that between a loving parent and obedient child.[25] The liberal culture of the Revolutionary era, as Jay Fliegelman and others have argued,[26] helped to delegitimize political paternalism, to legitimate individual economic ambition, and to bring into being "a vision of classlessness" (to use Joyce Appleby's phrase).[27] What we discover in Sedgwick's fiction, though, is that "the market revolution" (Charles Sellers's term) breathed new life into paternalism in the North. As Ellen Meiksins Wood explains of England and the United States, paternalistic conceptions about the economy and liberal-democratic political ideals were not necessarily antithetical: "patriarchalism" (Wood's term for paternalism) "remained in place long after 1832, surviving [the] ancien régime and the development of industrial capitalism, even coexisting, particularly in the United States (well beyond the abolition of slavery), with an official ideology of universal equality."[28] "The early development of capitalism," she continues, "gave the patriarchal conception of the master-servant relation a new lease of life, as the most readily available and adaptable ideological support for the inequality of the wage-labour contract."[29] Sedgwick's novels deploy a vision of social hierarchy grounded in Christianity that is akin to classical republicanism, where the "people" are not "an undifferentiated mass" but hierarchically organized, "performing complementary roles and practicing complementary virtues."[30] Sedgwick's idea of Christian capitalism—committed both to capitalism and to hierarchical, paternalistic relationships between rich and poor—mediates between republicanism and liberalism, if we take "republicanism" to mean an anticommercial, hierarchical social vision and "liberalism" to mean a procommercial one.[31]

"The principal theme of the sentimental text," writes Joanne Dobson, "is the desire for bonding."[32] Even so, sentimentalism may be structurally obligated to forms of inequality, demanding social difference rather than dissolving it. "To the extent that sentimentalism asks those who witness suffering to act on behalf of those in pain," Susan Pearson explains, it "replicates the vertical, hierarchical logic of benevolence rather than the horizontal logic of democracy or equal rights."[33] Sedgwick's novels ask their readers to desire economic inequality, because this inequality can lead to the flourishing of positive affect which bonds individuals who are not members of the same family or class.[34] If 1820s and '30s Christian socialists challenged market society by insisting that economic inequality leads to hardened hearts and to rich and poor despising one another, in Sedgwick's novels, the rich can—and do—manifest Christian "sympathy" for the poor, and so the poor in turn have cause to love the rich.

Indeed, Sedgwick's novels graft consent, in a republican fashion, onto the working class, imagining that it accepts an economically hierarchical social order. Previous studies of Sedgwick's 1830s novels have not given imagined working-class speech in them its due, but this speech is central to these novels' ratification of an unequal economic order, and so a key formal device by which these novels do their cultural work has been overlooked. At the end of both *The Poor Rich Man* and *Live and Let Live,* poor characters make the case that the United States needs to have rich and poor alike. Economic inequality, it turns out, is something that the poor themselves desire. Sedgwick's novels participate in debates about the meaning of economic inequality by staging a working class that is, and will remain, bonded to economic inequality, exactly when working-class militants are increasingly promoting a contrary position.

The Poor Rich Man and *Live and Let Live* can be read, then, as mediating formally between the rhetorical strategies for legitimating class on display, on the one hand, in Brockden Brown's bildungsromans and, on the other, in Brackenridge's *Modern Chivalry.* Like Brown's *Ormond* and *Arthur Mervyn,* Sedgwick's novels do their cultural work with respect to class in part by purporting to represent the subjective experience of economic subalternity. Here again we get narratives according to which poverty is itself a beneficial state of being for the individual subjected to it. Yet, like Brackenridge's *Modern Chivalry,* Sedgwick's novels also trade in an abstract language of class—according to which class is construed as not merely unavoidable but necessary for collective well-being. Indeed, Sedgwick's novels ratify economic inequality by suggesting that this abstract understanding of class as socially necessary is itself a way of thinking about class in the United States that emerges from the experience of economic subalternity.

THE CHALLENGE OF CHRISTIAN EGALITARIANISM

In 1835 Alexis de Tocqueville acclaimed the "equality of condition" in the United States vis-à-vis Europe.[35] Yet the American 1820s and 1830s witnessed increasing economic stratification as well as labor unrest.[36]

Working-class advocates in the United States perceived something quite different from what Tocqueville did. Theophilus Fisk's 1835 address "Capital against Labor" begins: "The history of the producers of wealth, of the industrious classes, is that of a continual warfare of HONESTY against FRAUD, WEAKNESS against power, JUSTICE against OPPRESSION."[37] Decades before *The Communist Manifesto*, a language of protest arose in the United States that, first, defined U.S. capitalism as a domain of conflict between exploitative owners and productive workers and, secondly, painted the United States as a polarized society of economic extremes. This discursive attack on economic inequality nourished and was nourished by working-class political organization (an increase in unions and union membership) and action (over 100 strikes in the Northeast through the 1830s).[38]

The 1820s and the 1830s were the decades when something on the order of anticapitalist class consciousness emerged in the United States.[39] A parallel and related development is what I call Christian egalitarianism. Figures like Cornelius Blatchly construed Christianity as a gospel of economic equality. In his 1822 *An Essay on Common Wealth*, Blatchly argues that wealth is produced by society, not by isolated individuals, and so wealth should be common to all:

> The *gifts* which society bestows, belonged to her before she *gave* them; and she is religiously obligated to use and bestow her blessings and donations in the most wise, just, equal and social manner;—In other words, the productions and wealth produced by society, should not be *individual, selfish*, and *exclusive property*, but *social* and *common* benefit and wealth. . . . A *pure common wealth* would put an end to the vast riches of a *few*, and the miserable indigence of *many*. *All* would have what Agur prayed for, when he said, *"Give me neither poverty nor riches." Great wealth*, as well as *great penury, is a great evil.*[40]

Here, economic inequality is a sin in need of structural remediation. Unequal wealth, Blatchly says, is "evil" (87). Thus, "love to God" requires economic equality (85).

"The society that produced the first American labor movement was," Jama Lazerow reminds us, "a deeply pious one—and likely the most Christian anywhere in the world at the time."[41] In 1832 Charles Douglas began an address to the New England Artisan Society by asking if God has "resolved that one portion of his creatures, made of the same materials, and subject to the same laws of our common nature, should riot in wealth and luxuriate on his bounties, while the great number should be poor and miserable, the hewers of wood, and the drawers of water to their more fortunate but less honest oppressors."[42] (Not for nothing, the phrase "hewers of wood and drawers of water" was also central to seventeenth-, eighteenth-, and nineteenth-century English artisan protest against proletarianization, according to Peter Linnebaugh and Marcus Rediker.)[43] To fight against economic inequality was, in Fisk's words, to fight against "the apostles of Mammon."[44]

Prominent antebellum intellectuals joined working-class activists in treating Christianity as a gospel of economic equality. Notably, Orestes Brownson, in an 1835 review of *An Essay on the Moral Constitution and History of Man*, writes that "he who is himself, rich, enjoying ample pleasure" cannot help viewing "the manual laborer" "not as a fellow immortal, with rights, duties, interests, and feelings, sacred as his own, but as a mere instrument of his wealth or pleasure." If the wealthy disregard the humanity of workers, workers themselves are plagued by discontent: "The poor man who trudges daily to his toil," Brownson continues, "will believe society as it is" to be "very imperfect," and "hard and bitter thoughts will pass through [the poor man's] mind as he gazes on the palace of the rich." While Brownson refuses to "censure or approve" both class viewpoints alike, he nonetheless insists that economic inequality makes it impossible for individuals to be good Christians: "All over the world, even in its most favored portions, there is an inequality of wealth, in moral, even intellectual, and social advantages, which we believe wholly inconsistent with the full exercise of Christian love."[45] In his better-known "The Laboring Classes" (1840), Brownson iterates this argument: "[T]he great work for this age and the coming, is to raise up the laborer, and to realize in our own social arrangements and in the actual condition of all men, that equality between man and man, which God has established between the rights of one and those of another."[46] For Brownson, "no man can serve both God and Mammon"; "to resuscitate the Christianity of Christ" requires an egalitarian distribution of wealth (440).

The interpretation of Christianity as economically egalitarian led to proposals for radical programs of economic reorganization. The "mischievous effects of [economic] inequality," Brownson contends, "do not result from the personal character of either rich or poor, but from itself, and they will continue, just as long as there are rich men and poor men in the same community" (440). Which is to say, individual actions cannot solve the problem. For Blatchly, "God's will would be done on earth as it is in heaven" only when wealth is "*common*" (88).[47] Introducing Americans to the ideas of Robert Owen, whose writing circulated in Transcendentalist circles, Blatchly helped to inspire 1840s utopian socialist projects like Brook Farm.[48] According to David Harris, Blatchly "made the first significant contribution to modern socialist theory in the United States."[49] The link between Christian economic egalitarianism and utopian socialism is on full display in George Ripley's preamble to the "Constitution" (1844) for Brook Farm, wherein Ripley explains that Brook Farm's goal is "to establish the external relations of life on a basis of wisdom and purity; to apply the principles of justice and love to our social organization in accordance with the laws of Divine Providence."[50]

Received wisdom about the main political currents in the antebellum period has marginalized the tradition of socialism Blatchly represents.[51] Of course, Karl Marx argued against utopian socialism in *The Communist Manifesto* (and elsewhere), suggesting that socialism can only arrive when the productive forces that capitalism unleashes finally outgrow capitalism's relations of production. But the Christian socialists of Sedgwick's day were primarily questioning whether the private accumulation of wealth and attendant economic inequality were compatible with "the principles of justice & love"—not productivity. Sedgwick's novels and Christian egalitarianism both understand economy in ethical terms. In fact, Sedgwick may owe the terms of her defense of economic inequality to Christian critique of economic inequality, insofar as she tries to imagine inequality as the very foundation of Christian virtue.

"We Are All of Us . . . Labourers in Our Father's Field"

The Poor Rich Man is structured as a series of complementary portraits of two New York City families: on the one side are the "poor" Aikins; on the other side are the "rich" Finleys. The poor Aikins are charitable and humane, participating in the civic life of their community by such generous actions as nursing back to health a "poor English curate" (90) who has come to America in search of his seduced daughter but finds unemployment and crippling illness. The rich Finleys are selfish and ma-terialistic, even refusing to support Morris Finley's mother-in-law and sister-in-law when the death of Finley's father-in-law leaves these kins-women "penniless" (76).

As the title indicates, *The Poor Rich Man, and the Rich Poor Man* de-constructs "rich" and "poor" by suggesting that it is better to be poor than rich. On one level, *The Poor Rich Man* seems to offer an especially bald version of the antebellum notion that poverty is "a form of spiri-tual richness that contains the seeds of its own negation, a blessed state that purifies honesty and opens the heart to generosity and nobility—a condition inevitably soiled by false gold."[52] The novel even suggests that the poor are healthy *because* they are poor, while debilitating decadence plagues the rich. Early in the novel, a doctor explains: "The poor have many facilities for health over the rich" (43–44). Yet, Sedgwick's por-traits of the Finleys and the Aikins imply a potentially damning cri-tique of America's socioeconomic order: since the poor are in many ways more ethical than the rich, and since the merchant capitalist comes off as a blight on American society, perhaps a truly ethical society is one in which there is no such thing as merchant capitalists? Sedgwick's novel occasionally leads its readers to revile the rich and to desire a different economic order.

High-pitched lament overtakes the typically balanced and re-strained tone of the novel's narrator when Morris Finley—the merchant capitalist—does not help Paulina Clark (a friend of the Aikins and a former love interest of Morris) in her time of need. The narrator here strikes a chord consonant with radical Christian egalitarian attacks on capitalism:

And what time has a New-York merchant, who is making his thou-sands and tens of thousands engrossed as he is with projects and cal-culations, and beset by the hopes and fears that accompany the accu-mulation of riches, and their possible loss—what time has he for the claims of human brotherhood?—what time to obey the injunction, "Bear ye one another's burdens?"—what time to imitate his Divine Master in going about doing good? . . . He may find time for a passing alms, but for protection, for advice, for patient sympathy, for those ef-fective charities that his knowledge, station, and influence put within his power, *he has no time.* (92)

This tirade lays bare the problem for which the novel must find a solution: if rich merchant capitalists can be so unethical, and if the accumulation of wealth obviates Christian sentiment and action, how can U.S. capitalism and economic inequality be legitimated? A similar question lurks behind the grumblings of Gabe Miner, a working-class friend of Aikin. "A poor man, and a poor man's children have but few privileges in this life; work, work, and no play; while the rich have nothing to do but enjoy themselves" (111). Why, in other words, should some have to sell their labor while others do not?

Henry Aikin, the novel's "rich poor man," responds with a three-part rebuttal to Miner. First, he explains that he has more free time than the capitalist and fewer worries: "I often drive home at nightfall with a light heart, for my work is done, my wages earned and paid; and I leave the merchants who employ me standing over their desks, their brows drawn up to a knot with care and anxiety; and there they stay till seven, eight, or nine o'clock" (111). Second, Aikin rebuffs Miner's complaint by offering a notion of class mobility: "We must remember that . . . the poor family of this generation is the rich family of the next; and, more than that, the poor of to-day are the rich of to-morrow" (111). At this point, Aikin is making a case according to which the United States is in certain ways classless: capitalists are overworked workers, and the United States is marked by social mobility. Third—and, most important—Aikin adds that some of the rich are "among the very best persons in society": "[T]here is Mr. Beckwith, he has ten talents, and a faithful steward is he; he and his whole family are an honour and a blessing to their country— doing in every way all the good they can" (111–12).

In this final rejoinder, Sedgwick may be revealing her sense that the justification for economic inequality requires more than the notions of the rich as overworked and the possibility of social mobility. There will be some workers, Aikin implies, who are forever relatively poor. "We are all of us," Aikin thus concludes, "from the highest to the lowest, labourers in our Father's field" (112). In describing wealthy merchants like Beckwith and workers like Miner and himself as members of one family united in the collective labor of cultivating God's property, Aikin in part emphasizes the idea that the rich and poor are members of a single class, since they are both "labourers." Even so, he is making the case that there should be some who are relatively high and others who are relatively low, that wealth should not be distributed in an egalitarian fashion among this imagined single class of workers who all do equally important work.

Beckwith is a supplement to the binary of "poor rich man" and "rich poor man." We could call him a rich rich man. He does what Morris Finley does not: he figures out how to accrue personal profits while simultaneously helping the working class. He does so by building better-quality low-income housing. Working-class families in New York were more likely than not to live in cramped, run-down rental properties, the outcome of a housing market defined by "artificial scarcity created by concentrated ownership of vast stretches of vacant land," competition for limited property that played to "the purchasing power" of "elite New Yorkers" to buy up property, and "the diminishing power of mechanic families to acquire property" as competition drove up prices and effectively "reduce[d] the value of labor."[53] In other words, the New York housing market fed off of and deepened economic inequality in the city. "Four hundred and sixty-nine dollars is paid for the rent of this house," Beckwith says to the Aikins of their first home, while "the property is not worth four thousand five hundred. But so it is all over the city; the poor pay rents out of all proportion to the rich" (157). That is, the poor pay a larger percentage of their incomes for their housing and higher rent relative to the values of the properties they inhabit than the rich.

Yet, when the Aikins move into Beckwith's rental property, their rent is the same. Beckwith does not help the Aikins to save money, nor does he completely rectify the disproportionate amount they pay relative to the rich. Moreover, the housing project is no charitable venture: as Beckwith says to Susan Aikin, "capitalists will be attracted to" it (158). In point of fact, Beckwith stands to make an 8 percent profit on his investment in the housing project from the rent his tenants pay (177). Economic inequality is left intact, perhaps exacerbated. As Theophilus Fisk argued, building was itself one of the primary locations of potential class exploitation: houses are built, he writes, "by the hard hand of labor, in sweat, and toil, and fatigue."[54] And Beckwith's sympathy has its limits. It is "inevitable," he suggests to Aikin, "that the very poor and vicious" pay rents "out of all proportion to the rich": "they are transient tenants, and their pay uncertain" (157–58). Beckwith claims to want to help working-class families, but he is primarily interested in helping those, the "industrious and honest" poor, who appear already to embody his values (158).

To him, the Aikin family deserves a reward since they seem middle-class in spirit and behavior despite being poor.[55]

At the same time, Beckwith also wants to change the behavior of the "poorer classes" who do not appear to embody his values. For him, "the want of comfort and convenience" experienced by the poor leads to "intemperance" (176). We may think of Beckwith's housing invest-ment as Sedgwick's attempt to reform investing practices by orienting them toward "the welfare of others" (as opposed to the highest rate of return).[56] But this would be to overlook how Beckwith's plan to invest in better housing for "the poorer classes" is also a plan to create con-ditions that produce more compliant workers. Beckwith's approach to the "poorer classes" rests on the notion that workers should be orga-nized into well-regulated homes wherein reside families incapable of class antagonism because they consist of hardworking men and happy, homebound women. And while we might read his project as an attempt to remake workers in the image of the middle class, Beckwith does not seek to eradicate class divisions.

Significantly, Aikin reads Beckwith's plan as disinterested. Through Aikin's appreciation of Beckwith's plan, Sedgwick teaches her readers that workers are supposed to be cheerful as permanent renters—to be content as not exactly middle class. They are then supposed to see the rich who profit from the rent they pay as their paternalistic benefactors, and thus more fundamentally to see the private accumulation of wealth as the precondition of Christian action. Although Beckwith's housing plan implies that economic inequality can lead to better living condi-tions for the working class (insofar as Beckwith uses his privately ac-cumulated wealth to invest in better housing), the point of this episode extends beyond demonstrating something like trickle-down economics *avant la lettre*. Paradoxically enough, Beckwith's housing plan carries with it a noneconomic justification of economic inequality as much as an economic one. In the final pages (to which I will return shortly), Aikin uses Beckwith's housing plan to teach his children the lesson he teaches Miner—namely, that rich and poor exist to enact different but comple-mentary Christian virtues.

Beckwith's housing plan and Aikin's reading of it manifest a principle laid out in *Public and Private Economy*, a well-received work of political economy by Sedgwick's older brother, Theodore. The first volume of

Public and Private Economy was published in the same year, 1836, and with the same press, Harper & Brothers, as *The Poor Rich Man*. According to Theodore Sedgwick, "[E]very rich man's money may be well employed, not only for his own advantage, but for that of the poor also."[57] Investing both to his own as well as the poor's advantage, Beckwith represents what Theodore Sedgwick calls "the perfection of the Christian character" (17).

On the one hand, Theodore Sedgwick proposes that the United States can become something of a classless society, first because social mobility already defines the national spirit ("the power of *self-elevation* . . . is one of the grand distinctions of the people of the United States"), and secondly because no laws create a leisured class in the United States (despite a very small number, "the whole people are compelled to labour") (225). On the other hand, Theodore Sedgwick also suggests that there will always be classes in the United States: "[T]here ever have been, and ever will be, high and low, rich and poor, masters and servants" (227–28). Jacksonianism, Richard Hofstadter wrote, was "not the philosophy of a radical leveling movement that proposes to uproot property or to reconstruct society along drastically different lines. It proceeds upon no Utopian premises—full equality is impossible, 'distinctions will always exist.'"[58] *Public and Private Economy* reflects this same anti-utopianism. *Public and Private Economy* endorses a proprietary model of selfhood: "Civilization may said to be property, or to proceed from it" (15). It thus makes sense, if we follow Macpherson, that Theodore Sedgwick would also be committed to the asymmetrical accumulation of wealth.[59] Yet, *Public and Private Economy* also very early on mobilizes Christianity to defend economic inequality and the continuing existence of at least relative poverty. "Nothing is more striking in the Christian religion than the constant condemnation of all injustice to, and robbery of the poor, who are labourers for small wages," Theodore Sedgwick concedes; nevertheless, the "Christian religion equally forbids, on the part of the poor, all hatred of the rich. . . . There have always been rich and poor—there must be rich and poor. The people have been most miserable in those countries where there are no rich" (23). Thus does Theodore Sedgwick try to legitimate U.S. economic inequality according to logics similar to his sister's.

Yet, *The Poor Rich Man* has what *Public and Private Economy* does not: working-class speech and, more particularly, a member of the working class to make the case for economic inequality. Working-class consent to economic inequality happens from below in Catharine Sedgwick's writing.

In the concluding conversation between Aikin and his daughters, the novelist shows working-class consent to economic inequality to be an ongoing, intergenerational process of education within the working class. Aikin's daughter Ruth tells her father that if "the scholars at our school" knew Beckwith, then "they would not call rich people so hateful" (178). Subject at school to arguments against economic inequality, the Aikin children are ultimately swayed by what they learn from their working-class father at home. Aikin supports Ruth's point, telling his children not to "trust what others tell you" and see "that Providence has bound the rich and the poor by one chain. Their interests are the same; the prosperity of one is the prosperity of all. . . . The enterprise and success of the merchant give us employment and rich rewards for our labour. We are dependant on them, but they are as quite dependant on us. If there were none of these hateful rich people, Ruth, who, think you, would build hospitals, and provide asylums for orphans, and for the deaf and dumb, and blind?" (178). Aikin is teaching his children how to read economic relations, just as Sedgwick's novel instructs its readers to look at the world they live in through her fictional characters. His representation of U.S. class relations does not at first completely satisfy his children: "But 'tis a comfort, father, to the poor," his daughter Susan responds, "to remember that the greatest, wisest, and best Being that ever appeared on earth had no part nor lot in the riches of this world; and that, for our sakes, he became poor" (179). Susan wants to decouple poverty from moral failure, which is a move that Sedgwick's novel also enacts (and confirms). Yet, Aikin's figure of the providential "one chain" also effectively makes space for the existence of the rich in the moral order. Blatchly might oppose Aikin's logic and the feelings he means to inculcate: if wealth were held in common, the community would take care of children, the ill, and the disabled. Aikin, however, comes off as a loving father who has his children's best interests in mind. He can convince his children that God wants there to be people who have more money than other people and may make money off of poor people. Again, Aikin is the voice of economic paternalism, but his version of it is sanctified by kinship and routed through a particular version of Christian ethics according to which economic inequality makes possible Christian virtue.

That Aikin succeeds in teaching Miner and his children what to think about the relationship between rich and poor—as well as its continuing existence—points to how Sedgwick's novel works formally. If, as D. A. Miller and others have argued, the relationship between narrator and character is a site of potential antagonism internal to novels with implications for how novels represent extrinsic social conflict and power relations, in Sedgwick's novel narrator and central character, tellingly, speak with the same voice.[60] Aikin's philosophy of economic inequality as social harmony is the same one the narrator of *The Poor Rich Man* explicitly articulates, but, crucially, it is a member of the poor who explains to the poor how to think about economic inequality. The message of economic division as social harmony that both the narrator and Aikin express is thus manifest on the level of form: first, because a central poor character and the narrator say essentially the same thing about economic inequality, and, secondly, because poor characters seem to teach themselves the very ideas about economic inequality the narrator offers. Thus Aikin makes the narrator's formulations about "inequality of condition" being a matter of providence look like anything but a bourgeois manipulation.

"Unfortunate Friends"

Although Sedgwick spends little time representing the experience of working-class labor in *The Poor Rich Man,* in *Live and Let Live* she focuses on women as workers and hirers of labor through a narrative of the tribulations of a young domestic servant in a series of different homes. In this later novel, women are decidedly inside the market, as sellers and buyers of labor, even if they are still primarily inside homes. Both *The Poor Rich Man* and *Live and Let Live* index that the growth of capitalism did not sequester women (especially working-class women) in the homes of their fathers or husbands but instead sent women (again, especially working-class women) onto the market for labor.[61] And the "most common wage employment" of women in New York City, the location of Sedgwick's 1830s novels, was domestic service.[62] If in *The Poor Rich Man* Sedgwick represents the possibility of a sentimental, Christian relationship between capitalist employer/landlord and worker/tenant, she does something very similar for mistress/employer and domestic employee in *Live and Let Live.*

The brunt of *Live* details the hardships of its protagonist, Lucy, as the employee of a series of cruel employers who do not view her as an equal and who treat her accordingly. Her first employer, the *nouveau riche* Mrs. Broadson, aims to get "the greatest possible service for the least possible compensation."[63] Lucy's second employer, Mrs. Ardley, "the wife of a rich merchant," "had always lived in affluence," so she believes that "this was the station Providence had allotted her" and that "there was a certain class born to understand and perform domestic service, while she and all in her category were to enjoy its results" (74). Mrs. Broadson, Mrs. Ardley, and Mrs. Simson (Lucy's last "bad" employer) all treat their domestic workers the same: providing only cramped living space, paying as little as they can, forcing their workers to work all hours of the day, and refusing them free time and vacations.

To the extent that these employers are examples of what employers should not be, they might perform a reformist function by eliciting the self-reflection of middle-class readers and providing Sedgwick an occasion to solicit sympathy for female servants like Lucy. In the preface, Sedgwick announces that "her business has been to illustrate the failures of one party in the contract between employers and employed" (v). The purpose of *Live,* Laurie Ousley argues, is "to 'illustrate' the proper role of the mistress-employer to those housekeepers who too readily seek to exploit their domestics."[64] For Ousley, Sedgwick's solution to the paradox posed to democracy by women's wage labor is better contracts: "Sedgwick does not reject capitalism and its concomitant class relations so much as she embraces the contract as a means of addressing the social repercussions of class struggle."[65] Ousley rightly argues that Sedgwick imagines individual, voluntary action as the salve for class exploitation.

Yet, Sedgwick imagines an employer-employee relationship ultimately abrogating the need for the legal protection of domestic servants and making actual legal agreements between mistress-employers and domestic servants unnecessary. As Sedgwick's narrator observes, "if young women were educated for their household duties," and if they approached their domestic employees as "their 'unfortunate friends,' whom it was their religious duty to instruct, to enlighten, to improve, to make better and happier," then "domestic economy" would be "perfected" and "there would be no need of political economy" (120). Ideal employers in *Live* do not need contracts because they already follow a higher law of compassion. And all mistress-employers, *Live* suggests, could follow this higher law, because there is nothing inherent in economic inequality preventing them from imitating Christ in overseeing their employees. Recall that for Brownson "inequality of wealth" is "wholly inconsistent with the full exercise of Christian love."[66] Likewise, Brownson argues that individuals cannot become full Christians without "a radical change" in "our social arrangements" ("Laboring Classes," 439). For Sedgwick, when employers act like the novel's Mrs. Hyde, Christian love is already manifest. Sedgwick embraces Christian sentiment as already working against class exploitation, counteracting its effects instead of being tarnished by them.

Although the vast majority of *Live* is dedicated to Lucy's time with exploitative, unsympathetic employers, she does find two good ones. The first, Mrs. Lovett, who eventually becomes Lucy's mother-in-law, is the wife of a "prosperous baker" and "emits an atmosphere of affection and kindness" (121). She is just as wealthy as Mrs. Simson, but, while Mrs. Simson's "cupidity and selfishness" "have made a moral waste around her," Mrs. Lovett's temperament—her "good sense, affectionateness, and sweet temper"—is akin "to those blessed fountains well called 'diamonds of the desert,' that minister to the life and beauty of everything within their reach" (132). By including Lucy in outings to hear lectures, for instance, the Lovetts make her feel like a member of their family. During the year she works for Mrs. Lovett, Lucy is "reminded by nothing but the regular receipt of her wages that she was at service" (141). Lucy's second good employer, Mrs. Hyde, the wife of one of "the wealthy and busy merchants of the city of New-York" (181), is "a Christian woman" for whom "the want of her fellow-creatures were claims, and who judged and felt in their affairs as if they were her own" (178). Governed by sympathy for her employees, Mrs. Hyde is the consummate sentimental employer, embodying what Sedgwick calls, in a moment of fascinating gender reversal, "Wordsworth's beautiful description of the man of Christian sympathy" (178).[67]

A "fellow-worker" in "the love of God," who cares about her employees' welfare during their service to her as well as their future economic prospects, Mrs. Hyde distinguishes herself from Lucy's other employers by appointing herself as an instructor of domestic skills: "My girls all get married after a while," she explains to Lucy, "and I wish that, while they are serving me, they should have a sort of education that will enable them to make their own homes prosperous and happy" (188). The

narrator iterates Mrs. Hyde's mission: "[O]ne of her objects was to qual-
ify those she employed for the happier condition that probably awaited
them—to be the masters and mistresses of independent homes" (201).
Like Beckwith in *The Poor Rich Man,* Mrs. Hyde assigns herself the
mission of promoting middle-class domesticity and its gender norms.
Training Lucy to become what she considers to be a proper woman in a
proper home, she too believes that society should be organized into individual economic units of families comprising husbands that sell their
labor on the market and wives who aid those husbands by tending to
household affairs. In this way, Mrs. Hyde forms Lucy for the role of her
future husband's unpaid worker, helping to replicate antebellum class
relations.[68]

"Sentimental didacts," writes Barbara Ryan, "taught that service relationships could and ought be family-like."[69] Nowhere is this more the
case than in *Live and Let Live,* Ryan suggests.[70] Mrs. Hyde seems like
anything but a capitalist spending wealth accumulated from others' labors: though she buys labor with the wealth her family has accumulated,
she veils accumulation by using this wealth to disperse what the novel
construes as Christian love.[71] Mrs. Hyde's training of Lucy is represented
by both the narrator and Lucy as Christian mothering. Lucy even thinks
Mrs. Hyde is "just as kind as mother" (189). The narrator explains that
Mrs. Hyde's "vigilant" watch on Lucy is like "the keen perception of the
parent, and the admonition that followed it was gentle; for, in imita-
tion of Him who she served, 'love was her motive and reformation her
object'" (204). Again, narrator and character speak in the same terms
and tones.

By the close of *Live and Let Live,* Lucy has turned her experience as
Mrs. Hyde's employee into a blunt justification of class inequality in
Christian terms:

> "Oh, mother, what a happy world this would be if there were plenty
> such as you and Mrs. Hyde—if the rich and the poor, in their respec-
> tive stations, *felt* and *acted* right. How foolish and wicked are those
> who try to set one against the other; when, by being friends, and act-
> ing in agreement, so much good could be done, so much happiness
> gained. It seems to me as if it were necessary there should be rich
> and poor, to make all those seeds of virtue which God has planted in
> our hearts spring up and grow. If Mrs. Hyde was not rich, how could

she manifest such humility and self-denial, such wise generosity and such wise economy? and, dear mother, had you not been poor, *very* poor, could you have given us an example of such gentleness, long-suffering, patience, and self-reliance?" (214)[72]

Lucy's defense of inequality directly rejoins the critiques we find in Christian economic egalitarianism. Granted, Lucy suggests that her poverty was materially beneficial to her, since it put her in Mrs. Hyde's service and consequently has "qualified" her to "take charge" of her own family and "contribute" to her new husband's "prosperity as well as his happiness" (214). According to Lucy, poverty is a necessary phase of her individual education and preparation for her life as a middle-class wife. Her story does conclude with mobility into the middle class. Yet, Lucy ultimately claims that economic inequality—the very dichotomy between rich and poor—benefits the spiritual life of the community. Harriet Beecher Stowe's *Uncle Tom's Cabin,* Gillian Brown argues, imagines the day when there will be no more servants.[73] Sedgwick, for her part, does not: Lucy is not saying there should come a day when all women are members of the middle class, but instead that there should always be some white Americans who are poor. Although people from different classes appear to share the same values and beliefs in Sedgwick's novels—while "sentiment subsumes class differences"[74]—it would be a mistake to suppose that Sedgwick's United States is classless or should be heading toward classlessness. Again, "Mobility changes the experience of class," Schocket writes, "but it does not make it go away."[75] Despite her mobility, Lucy herself refuses to make class go away.

It bears emphasizing, then, that in *Live and Let Live* the concluding defense of inequality is voiced by a character that has experienced poverty and, as a result, hardship, anxiety, and exploitation, just as the poor Aikin justifies economic inequality in *The Poor Rich Man.* That Lucy has emerged from poverty is very much a matter of accident, so it is conceivable that she would come to different conclusions about the distribution of wealth. Yet, it is a person with experiences of poverty who rails, first, against those who think of the relationship between classes as conflict and, second, against the desire for a world without divisions of rich and poor. For Theophilus Fisk in 1835, "There is a period in the affairs of men, when forbearance ceases to be a virtue, when patient endurance becomes criminal."[76] That period is now, Fisk contends, but for Lucy that period will never come. According to Lucy, to "feel right" is to believe in the justness of economic inequality; to believe in class conflict, on the other hand, is to feel wrongly. She implicitly criticizes the rich who do not live up to Mrs. Hyde's example of Christian virtue, but, unlike Christian economic egalitarians, she refuses to define the essence, or even the tendency, of economic inequality as un-Christian actions. Were there no rich and no poor, Lucy explains, then humanity would be, paradoxically enough, incomplete: it could not realize the manifold variety of Christian virtues.

"THE MOTE IN MY BROTHER'S EYE"

In Rebecca Harding Davis's 1861 *Life in the Iron Mills,* mill worker Deb picks the pocket of a wealthy industrialist named Mitchell and then gives the money to Hugh Wolfe, a fellow mill worker but also a sculptor of korl. Wolfe initially decides to return the stolen money, even though Deb tells him it is his "right to keep it."[77] But while on his way to return the money, Wolfe observes well-to-do churchgoers, and he decides otherwise. For Wolfe, to keep the stolen money means the possibility of escape from the brutalizing conditions of being a mill worker that Davis's story has sought to depict: "He need not go, need never go again, thank God!" (48). Yet, to keep the stolen money is not to escape the iron mills for a life of mere leisure; in escaping the mills, Wolfe might be able to realize a better version of himself: "Was it not his right to live as they,—a pure life, a good, true-hearted life, full of beauty and kind words? He only wanted to know how to use the strength within him. His heart warmed, as he thought of it. He suffered himself to think longer. If he took the money?" (46). Observing the well-to-do churchgoers, Wolfe sees "himself as he might be, strong, helpful, kindly" (46). Ultimately, his thought evolves into something on the order of a religiously inflected, radical class consciousness: "A thief! Well, what was it to be a thief? He met the question at last. . . . God made this money—the fresh air, too—for his children's use. He never made the difference between rich and poor" (47). For Wolfe, to keep the stolen money is thus to expropriate what has been wrongly expropriated, but also to obey God.

Davis reports Wolfe's belief that all should have access to wealth through free indirect discourse. While we become privy to the deepest thoughts of a working-class character at this climactic moment, Davis invites her readers to look through Wolfe's eyes but through her language:

> There were times when the soft floods of color in the crimson and purple flames, or the clear depth of amber in the water below the bridge, had somehow given him a glimpse of another world than this,—of an infinite depth of beauty and of quiet somewhere,—somewhere,—a depth of quiet and rest and love. Looking up now, it became strangely real. The sun had sunk quite below the hills, but his last rays struck upward, touching the zenith. The fog had risen, and the town and river were steeped in its thick, gray damp; but overhead, the sun-touched smoke-clouds opened like a cleft ocean,—shifting, rolling seas of crimson mist, waves of billowy silver veined with blood-scarlet, inner depths unfathomable of glancing light. Wolfe's artist-eye grew drunk with color. The gates of that other world! Fading, flashing before him now! What, in that world of Beauty, Content, and Right, were the petty laws, the mine and thine, of mill-owners and mill-hands? (47)

Wolfe catches a glimpse of heaven, and this glimpse allows him to question the private, asymmetric accumulation of wealth in his world.

Yet, while Davis invites her readers to assume temporarily Wolfe's angle of vision and the flash of economically egalitarian desire that goes with it at this key moment in his life, her narrator is not entirely sympathetic to Wolfe's point of view:

> Then he saw himself as he might be, strong, helpful, kindly. The night crept on, as this one image slowly evolved itself from the crowd of other thoughts and stood triumphant. He looked at it. As he might be! What wonder, if it blinded him to delirium,—the madness that underlies all revolution, all progress, and all fall?
>
> You laugh at the shallow temptation? You see the error underlying its argument so clearly,—that to him a true life was one of full development rather than self-restraint? That he was deaf to the higher tone in a cry of voluntary suffering for truth's sake than in the fullest flow of spontaneous harmony? I do not plead his cause. I only want to show you the mote in my brother's eye: then you can see clearly to take it out. (46)

The same rhetorical double movement takes place in both paragraphs of this passage. In each paragraph, Davis's narrator first invites us to sympathize with Wolfe's viewpoint, but then concludes by insisting on his blindness. We are to have sympathy for Wolfe's outrage and his desire, we are to be critical of easy dismissals of him, and we are invited to understand why he choses theft; yet, we are also encouraged not to exonerate entirely his theft or the politics entailed by a full exoneration. To exonerate fully Wolfe's theft is to follow a delirious, mad path—the path of revolution and fall as much as progress: the narrator does not "plead [Wolfe's] cause." Wolfe, the narrator insists, has a "mote" in his eye; his discontent, while understandable, is a matter of distorted vision. What does it mean that we are to remove the "mote" for him? It means that Davis's imagined middle-class audience is called upon, on the one hand, to alleviate the effects of economic asymmetries that have inspired Wolfe's discontent, and, on the other hand, to make Wolfe (and those who might come to think like he does) recognize that his vision is flawed. We may sympathize with Wolfe, but we should also realize that what he wants of this world is not precisely what God wants of the world. Is not this the logic that Sedgwick had already established in her 1830s novels?

4   No Apologies for the Anti-Renters
Class, James Fenimore Cooper, and Frontier Romance

Whether you think of the issue of Palestine or of gentrification and zoning in American small towns, it is that peculiar and imaginary thing called private property in land which is at stake. The land is not only an object of struggle between the classes, between rich and poor; it defines their very existence and the separation between them.
—Fredric Jameson, "The Aesthetics of Singularity"

After the publication of [*Homeward Bound* and *Home as Found*], he became much interested in the well-known Anti-Rent agitation by which the State of New York was so long shaken; and three of his novels, "Satanstoe," "The Chainbearer," and "The Redskins," forming one continuous narrative, were written with reference to this subject. Many professed novel-readers are, we suspect, repelled from these books, partly because of this continuity of the story, and partly because they contain a moral; but we assure them, that, if on these grounds they pass them by, they lose both pleasure and profit. They are written with all the vigor and spirit of his prime; they have many powerful scenes and admirably drawn characters; . . . and in all the legal and ethical points for which the author contends he is perfectly right.
—"James Fenimore Cooper," *Atlantic Monthly* (1862)

"To marry a man against the movements of his will is to do a violence to human nature!"
—Dr. Obed Battius in James Fenimore Cooper's *The Prairie*

Sedgwick's *The Poor Rich Man* and *Live and Let Live,* I argued in the previous chapter, legitimate economic inequality in part by imagining the working class as politically docile: in Sedgwick's 1830s novels, the working class assents to an economically hierarchical social order, discovering in economic inequality the manifestation of "providence." Yet, what if U.S. workers do not assent to economic inequality? What if U.S. workers understand economic inequality as a violation of "natural law"? These are questions that animate James Fenimore Cooper's now (also) largely forgotten 1840s Littlepage novels—*Satanstoe* (1845), *The Chainbearer* (1846), and *The Redskins* (1846). In this chapter, my goal is to detail how these novels push back against the threat of working-class insurgency and thereby exonerate what Cooper would call "inequality of condition." Like Brackenridge's *Modern Chivalry*, Cooper's Littlepage novels figure economic egalitarianism as a threat to "liberty." But Cooper adds a twist: in the Littlepage novels, economic egalitarianism is a threat to affective autonomy—to what the antebellum bourgeoisie considered "democratic" courtship and marriage practices.

"THE MOST CLASS-CONSCIOUS OF ALL AMERICAN WRITERS"

The name James Fenimore Cooper tends to conjure up what Philip Fisher has called "the primal quarrel of American history . . . between white settlers and Indians over the white claims to land that they found already peopled by the Indians."[1] While Cooper was his era's most prolific novelist of this "primal quarrel," he was also, Leslie Fielder long insisted, "the most class-conscious of all American writers."[2] Whether or not Fiedler's estimation that Cooper was the *most* class-conscious of all American writers is true, Cooper's 1840s Littlepage novels are decidedly class-conscious. These novels were Cooper's response to the Anti-Rent War, which rocked the Hudson Valley from 1839 and 1847. The Anti-Rent War was the first in a series of violent class conflicts in the United States that Howard Zinn in *A People's History of the United States* collects under the suggestive title of "The Other Civil War."[3] Especially with *The Chainbearer* and *The Redskins,* Cooper takes up overt, intraracial class war as the theme of his fiction.

The Littlepage novels—and *Satanstoe* in particular—were once central both to accounts of Cooper's career and to the rise of the American novel in general. They figure prominently, for instance, in Richard Chase's *The American Novel and Its Tradition* (1957) and Marius Bewley's *The Eccentric Design* (1959). For Chase, "*Satanstoe* suggests but does not present fully the fundamental contradiction of Cooper's thought." "The forest sequences of the novel," he continues, "imply that the ideal young man of the New World, though his values will be formed by a traditional society, will also be at home on the margins of society where all social values disappear and are replaced by a strict code of the woods."[4] Bewley deems *Satanstoe* "perhaps Cooper's best novel after the Leatherstocking tales," and like Chase he argues that *Satanstoe* and the other novels of the Littlepage trilogy reveal the contradictions at the heart of Cooper's worldview: here we see that Cooper was simultaneously antiaristocratic and opposed to "a leveling interpretation of democracy."[5]

Literary historians today rarely read or write about the Littlepage novels, perhaps because these novels seem to express a quasi-aristocratic—and thus atavistic—political sensibility vis-à-vis the democratic ethos of the Jacksonian/post-Jacksonian era.[6] It's true that the Littlepage novels are no celebration of the so-called common man. In fact, they avowedly side with the landlords in the Anti-Rent War. "Cooper," writes Chase, "wanted to demonstrate the social and cultural advantages to democracy of private estates and aristocratic families."[7] "Cooper's aim," writes Bewley, "was to praise landed wealth, transmitted through families, at the expense of wealth gained by speculation or industrial enterprise."[8] The Littlepage novels would thus seem to be significant only as antiquarian detritus in the dustbin of history, unlike *The Last of the Mohicans* and the other Leatherstocking novels, which have been kept alive as much by American culture at large as by professional literary historians.

A few contemporary critics have tried to rescue the Littlepage novels from oblivion by suggesting that they are politically unstable, at odds with their author's own political allegiances but also critical of the Indian dispossession that Cooper in other novels rationalizes. Ken Egan contends that the Littlepage trilogy deconstructs the opposition between landlords and anti-renters, painting both as uncourageous usurpers of Native American lands.[9] Lance Schachterle and Jerome McGann proffer consonant arguments. For Schachterle, the Littlepage novels testify against Indian dispossession.[10] For McGann, likewise, the Littlepage trilogy is a send-up of the landlords' racism. "Given his own history," McGann observes, "Cooper strongly sympathizes with the land-owner position. But when he translates himself into Cooper the editor, his formal move completely reshapes how his sympathies function in the trilogy."[11] For McGann, Cooper's choice to narrate the Anti-Rent War from the first-person perspective of imagined landlords works to expose the landlords as "narrow and privileged men whose bigotry toward 'niggers' and recent Irish immigrants is on full view."[12] For Egan, Schachterle, and McGann, the Littlepage novels are thus out of step with Jacksonian ideology. They merit recovery not because they express obsolete class interests, but because they tender critiques of landlords and racialist apologetics for Indian dispossession.[13]

Yet, to read the Littlepage novels as ultimately condemnations of settler colonialism and its racialist logics is, I want to argue, not precisely right; moreover, doing so is to underappreciate both the significance of the Anti-Rent War to the terrain of class struggle attending the development of American capitalism in the 1840s and the work these novels do on behalf of the antebellum bourgeoisie. Because Cooper's novels deal directly with anti-rentism, in attending to them we cannot help being reminded of the presence of oppositional political economy in the antebellum United States. In other words, these novels especially undercut the literary historical common sense according to which liberalism is so thoroughly pervasive—so entirely hegemonic—in the antebellum United States as to make outright class struggle unthinkable as a concern of antebellum literature.

The landlords did not "win" the Anti-Rent War. Neither, though, did the anti-renters. The outcome of the Anti-Rent War was not the economic egalitarianism for which so many of the anti-renters and working-class radicals sympathetic to their cause had hoped.[14] Indeed, many prominent working-class radicals and critics of capitalist inequality in the 1840s claimed anti-renters as fellow travelers, insisting that the Anti-Rent War played both a symbolic and a material role in the struggle against economic inequality and exploitation in the newly industrializing United States. While the Littlepage novels might be read as offering a rearguard defense of a soon-to-be-obsolete Hudson Valley leasehold system (and class of landlords), they are significant because they wage ideological war not only against anti-renters but also against a radical tendency in the antebellum United States that claimed anti-renters as a version of itself. Put differently, though these novels might at times express nostalgia for a premodern past, in doing battle against the economic egalitarianism of anti-renters they legitimate future class inequality for the ascendant U.S. bourgeois order as much as they proselytize on behalf of the quasi-feudal landlord/tenant system of the Hudson

Valley. Thus it makes sense that the *Atlantic Monthly*—a bourgeois literary institution par excellence—lauded "all the legal and ethical points for which [the trilogy] contends" as "perfectly right": for the *Atlantic Monthly*, these novels should be celebrated because of their entertaining stories and well-wrought characters, but mostly for their "moral."[15]

I am not alone, I want to point out, in conceptualizing the conflict animating the Littlepage novels as one between economic egalitarianism and capitalism (as opposed to merely tenants and a soon-to-be obsolete, quasi-aristocratic leasehold system). Dana Nelson has recently suggested that the Littlepage trilogy, by forcing us to reckon with the meaning of the Anti-Rent War and the notions of democracy subtending anti-rentism, "helps us track historically the substantive, if diminishing threat that the power of commons democracy posed to the growing economic power of liberalism in the early United States" (*Commons Democracy* 136). For Nelson, the Littlepage trilogy dramatizes the 1840s conflict between "plebian political economy" and "liberal democracy" (157). On Nelson's reading, the trilogy records the defeat of a "localist, informal, equalitarian" political economy by a brand of "legal formalism" "that protects the economy from the political power of the people"—by a "legal formalism" "where the economy was shielded from the political power of the democratic majority by the simultaneous divorce of land from its political status *and* the downsizing of citizenship" (155, 152, 170–71). Here, Cooper's Littlepage trilogy "helps us remember" the "complex historical struggle to place the economic sphere out of the political reach of the democratic mass" (152–53).[16]

On my reading, in contrast to Nelson's, Cooper's trilogy not only reminds us of a historical process that has been largely been forgotten (i.e., class struggle in the United States, and the political project that grows out of this struggle of throwing up barriers against interventions into the economy on behalf of greater equality) but also actively *participates* in this process. Which is to say, my goal here is to highlight precisely *how* Cooper's novels militate against a new articulation of U.S. economic egalitarianism, and thus how Cooper's *novelistic* representation of the meaning of economic egalitarianism helped the U.S. bourgeoisie to consolidate itself ideologically against economic egalitarianism in the 1840s.

In his preface to *The Redskins,* Cooper makes clear that he is writing against economic egalitarianism broadly. He writes:

The notion that every husbandman is to be a freeholder, is as Utopian in practice, as it would be to expect that all men were to be on the same level in fortune, condition, education and habits. As such a state of things as the last never yet did exist, it was probably never designed by divine wisdom that it should exist. The whole structure of society must be changed, even in this country, ere it could exist among ourselves, and the change would not have been made a month before the utter impracticability of such a social fusion would make itself felt by all.[17]

Passages like this one reveal that not only did Cooper go to great lengths to defend a particular leasehold system; he tells us that his defense of the leasehold system in the Littlepage novels is also a defense of U.S. inequality in general.

The narrators of the Littlepage novels unsurprisingly instruct their readers to believe that economic egalitarianism represents a threat not only to the accumulated fortunes of elites but also to the sanctity of private property itself. "Throughout his career," Robert Lawson-Peebles writes, "Cooper defended the rights of property-owners."[18] As much as any other early U.S. novelist, Cooper was a spokesman for the inviolability of private property. In his 1838 *The American Democrat*, he writes: "The first great principle connected with the rights of property, is its inviolability in all cases in which the laws leave it in possession of the proprietor. Every child should be taught to respect the sanctity of his neighbour's house, garden, fields and all that is his."[19] According to Cooper, "[A]ll who love equal justice, and, indeed, the safety of free institutions, should understand that property has its rights, and the necessity of rigidly respecting them. It is the right of the possessor of property to be placed on an equal footing with all his fellow citizens, in every respect. If he is not to be exalted on account of his wealth, neither is he to be denounced."[20] And, what Cooper discerned in the anti-rent movement was an attack on the inviolability of private property, insofar as from his perspective anti-renters meant to expropriate—for him, steal—what was the landlords' legally sanctioned private property: anti-renters were "striving," he writes in *The Redskins*, "to deprive a particular class of its rights of property, directly in the face of written contracts" (228). By insisting that the landlords' estates should be broken up and redistributed, anti-renters were, on Cooper's account, denying minority rights and thus enacting what Tocqueville dubbed "the tyranny of the majority": "[T]he great principle which lies at the bottom of anti-rentism," Cooper suggests, "if principle it can be called, is the assumption of a claim that the interests and wishes of numbers are to be respected, though done at the sacrifice of the clearest rights of the few. That is not liberty, but tyranny in its worse form, every right-thinking and right-feeling man must be fully aware" (*Redskins,* vi). As John McWilliams puts it, "Cooper conceive[d] of Anti-Rentism as a threat to liberty."[21] What Cooper rails against, then, is a form of democracy in which citizens mobilize—in which citizens can mobilize—on behalf of laws and practices that would redistribute wealth, especially productive property.

Perhaps more surprisingly, the Littlepage novels also stage anti-rentism as a threat to democratic marriage practices and the affective autonomy of middle-class women. As a result, these novels do their ideological work in large measure by activating one of the tenets of the culture of the American Revolution. As Jay Fliegelman has argued, the American Revolution as a public, political act was shaped by—was made thinkable by—ideals about how individual families should be put together. According to the writers that helped create the culture behind the American Revolution, families should be formed out of affectionate and voluntary "unions." The "cause" of the American Revolution, Fliegelman contends, was "the cause of 'union,' of liberty not as a final autonomy but as the freedom to choose one's bond."[22] In *A Treatise on Domestic Economy* (1841), Catherine Beecher describes "a truly democratic state" as one in which "each individual is allowed to choose for himself, who shall take the position of his superior." "No woman," Beecher continues, "is forced to obey any husband but the one she chooses for herself. . . . So every domestic, and every artisan or laborer, after passing from parental control, can choose the employer to whom he is to accord obedience, or, if he prefers to relinquish certain advantages, he can remain without taking a subordinate place to any employer."[23] We can imagine anti-renters and other working-class radicals bristling at the notion that the prerogative of a worker to "choose the employer to whom he is to accord obedience" constitutes "a truly democratic state." In Cooper's novels, though, economic egalitarians are unconcerned with respecting a woman's right to choose her husband. Seeing certain "poor" but "virtuous" heroines as the means by which they might secure their economic desires, economic egalitarians in these novels do violence to these "poor" but "virtuous" heroines. Economic egalitarians in Cooper's novels believe that such heroines should be *their* "property," even if these heroines desire to wed economic elites. Economic egalitarians in Cooper's novels are thus individuals who refuse to abide by the logic of companionate marriage. They refuse to acknowledge the heroine's affective autonomy, or her right to choose which "master" to serve.

Indeed, *The Chainbearer* and *The Redskins* imbricate narratives of agrarian insurgency and love plots. While critics who have reopened these novels have little to say about their love plots and the women around whom they turn, they are central both to the form and to the ideological work of the Littlepage novels. As Ian Watt long ago taught us, marriage predicated on "the free choice of the individuals concerned"[24] is part of the novel form's DNA, and frontier romance is no exception. Here, economic egalitarianism must be "put down" (to use Cooper's phrase) if the basic narrative contract of the frontier romance—a concluding romantic marriage—is to be observed. Moreover, Cooper's Littlepage novels also draw on the frontier romance's racial logic. Because economic egalitarians here threaten the romantic autonomy of "virtuous" women, these characters occupy the position that "bad" Indians occupy in Cooper's earlier frontier romances. Economic egalitarians thus become not quite "white." And though Cooper's novels position agrarian insurgents as "bad" Indians, they also construct plots in which blacks and Native Americans are the foes of white anti-renters and vice versa, even though land reformers insisted that the anti-rent movement and the claims of Native Americans and abolitionists were all part of the same egalitarian project.

The Rights of Man to Property

"One thing must be obvious to the plainest understanding; that as long as property is unequal; or rather, as long as it is so enormously unequal, as we see it at present, that those who possess it, *will* live on the labor of others, and themselves perform none, or if any, a very disproportionate share, of that toil which attends them as a condition of their existence."[25] So wrote Thomas Skidmore in his 1829 *The Rights of Man to Property!* "Skidmore's argument for the recognition of men's equal right to property," David Harris explains, "rests above all upon his perception that there can in practice be no equal right to life, liberty and the pursuit of happiness if there is no equal right to property."[26] The title of Skidmore's book—a book that Sean Wilentz calls "the most thoroughgoing 'agrarian' tract ever produced by an American"[27]—gives a name to a defining feature of radical working-class discourse in the 1840s. Often paying direct homage to Skidmore, working-class activists and social reformers in the 1840s argued that if the United States was to surmount class exploitation it would be by reconsidering how land, that most basic form of productive property, is and should be distributed.

"By the mid-1840s," Wilentz explains, "land reform had captured the imagination of every labor radical still active in New York."[28] Beginning in the 1840s, Adam Tuchinsky similarly points out, "land reform became a part of the basic vocabulary of Northern political life, uniting intellectuals, workers, and small farmers across the region."[29] For 1840s land reformers, the reason that some men are forced into life-consuming labor while other men are able to lead lives of leisure is due to an unnatural, arbitrary distribution of land. George Henry Evans, perhaps the most prominent land reformer and the leader of the National Reform Association, came to argue in the 1840s (as Jonathan Glickstein aptly explains) "that free access to land would rectify the injustice and exploitation inhering in existing wage labor because the laborer would no longer be '*dependant* on the employer': the hireling 'would receive the full value of his labor, because he would have the ready alternative of laboring for himself.'"[30] If land were available to all who wanted it, land reformers suggested, then a producers' republic—a society of independent farmers and fully compensated, self-determining workers—would be the outcome.

Land reform writers based their arguments on two basic conceptual schemes. First, they adhered to a version of natural rights discourse, according to which all men have a right to land. The intellectual heritage of land reform in the 1840s thus extends back to eighteenth-century thinkers like Thomas Paine and Thomas Jefferson. In *Agrarian Justice* (1797), Paine argued "that every man had a natural right or birthright in the soil, and linked the distribution of land to the balance of political power or the existence of corruption in society."[31] For Paine, "dispossession represented a denial of the individual's natural right to land, necessitating an elaborate scheme of redistributive taxation in order to compensate the landless for their lost inheritance."[32] In a 1785 letter to James Madison, Jefferson outlined his own variety of agrarianism: "Whenever there are in any country, uncultivated lands and unemployed poor, it is clear that the laws of property have been so far extended as to violate natural right. The earth is given as a common stock for man to labor and live on." "It is not too soon," Jefferson continues, "to provide by every possible means that as few as possible shall be without a little portion of land."[33] The notion that "the earth is given as common stock" is at the foundation of Skidmore's *Rights of Man to Property!* For Skidmore, property is "the whole material world . . . just as it came from the Creator." Each individual, Skidmore thus argues, has the right "to partake of and enjoy equally with his fellows, [the earth's] fruits and its productions."[34]

Second, land reformers deployed a version of the labor theory of wealth, according to which all wealth is the product of labor—and according to which a just society is one in which workers receive the "full fruits" of their labors. Here, too, land reformers drew on a philosophical tradition extending back at least as far as John Locke.[35] By recognizing and articulating an affinity between a natural rights theory of land ownership and a labor theory of wealth, land reformers produced an oppositional politico-economic discourse. To eradicate exploitation, all workers must own productive property—or have the opportunity to own productive property. Wrote George Henry Evans: "[I]f any man have a right on earth, he has a right to land enough to raise a habitation on. If he has a *right to live,* he has a right to land enough for his subsistence. Deprive anyone of these rights, and you place him at the mercy of those who possess them."[36]

While land reformers saw the asymmetric distribution of productive property as the source of exploitation, they did not contend that private ownership of productive property itself was the root cause of exploitation. Land reform might thus be dismissed as a theoretically deficient form of oppositional political economy. From one perspective, it hewed too closely to bourgeois individualism to stand as a genuine alternative to the logic of capitalism.[37] Certainly, land reform expresses a desire for what Marx calls "private property of the worker in his means of production"—a desire for private property "which is personally earned, i.e., which is based, as it were, on the fusing together of the isolated, independent working individual with the conditions of his labour."[38] As

such, land reform "excludes the concentration of these means of production," but it "also excludes co-operation."[39] But if, as C. B. Macpherson
argues, Lockean ideas about property, land, and labor served to justify
individual accumulation and economic inequality, land reformers' pleas
for "private property of the worker in his means of production" involved
turning Lockean notions against the culture that Locke helped to legitimate.[40] As Tuchinsky observes, "In the largely pre-Marxist context of the
1840s, '50s, and '60s, the question of property was not yet the polarizing
litmus test it would become, and most labor radicals viewed the democratic extension of property, rather than its destruction, as central to
labor's emancipation."[41] Yet, if land reform was decidedly pre-socialist,
it can also be thought of as a precursor of social democracy: "Committed to economic rights, land reform was among the first initiatives
that explicitly promoted the state as an agent of economic welfare and
wealth redistribution."[42] Indeed, even though land reformers, like late
eighteenth-century plebeian radicals, expressed a desire for "a smaller
and more decentralized political order" and were suspicious of "large-
scale governments," they wanted nonetheless a government that would
intervene in the economy to promote greater economic equality.[43] Moreover, land reform was, as I pointed out in the introduction, an inspiration for European radicals: by a somewhat circuitous path, Skidmore
himself influenced Marx's critique of capitalism.[44]

In 1844 Lewis Masquerier, a member of the National Reform Association, penned the "Declaration of Independence of the Producing from
the Non-Producing Class," a document that makes clear how land reform's combination of the languages of natural rights and a labor theory
of wealth entailed a decidedly radical social vision. Masquerier writes,
signifying on Jefferson's legacy, just as Skidmore had Paine's:

> We hold these truths to be self evident: That as the natural wants
> and powers of production of all men are nearly equal, all should be
> producers as well as consumers. That, as nothing but labor bestowed
> upon the natural elements and products of the earth can produce
> property, nothing else can give title to it: and hence every man is en-
> titled, with the same exertion, to an equal share of the soil, water, air,
> and light.[45]

Masquerier continues:

The history of the aristocratic [non-producing] class, is nothing but a continued series of usurpations of the produce of laborers through all ages, all having the direct tendency of reducing them to the utmost degradation, want, and misery. . . . Thus have [the non-producers], in the character of land-*lords* and usurers, reduced the great body of the people in subsequent ages to a state of abject tenantry and vassalage. (67)

By drawing on a natural rights theory of land ownership and a labor theory of wealth, Masquerier's "Declaration" produces a social ontology and historical narrative that equates the most unfree forms of labor with the accumulation and distribution mechanisms of finance. Here, there is no difference between "military and manor services, feuds, rents, tythes, deodans, interest, dividends, profit, and personal slavery" (67).

Of particular note is Masquerier's invocation of "land-*lord*" and "tenantry." This vocabulary of class is a strategic reference to the Anti-Rent War, which was taking place just as Masquerier wrote. The Anti-Rent War was, writes Reeve Huston, "the largest farmers' movement in the United States before the 1870s": "Some 260,000 men, women, and children—over 8 percent of New York's population—lived on scores of estates along the Hudson, Delaware, and Mohawk rivers. These estates ranged in size from 6,000 to 750,000 acres. Tenants leased their farms in perpetuity, for a number of years, or as long as those named in the lease remained alive. Beginning in 1839, many of these farmers built a movement that aimed at destroying these estates and distributing the land among themselves." Before the 1820s, Huston explains, landlords "refrained from prosecuting tenants for unpaid rents"; though "landlords routinely dunned and cajoled leaseholders," they "seldom sued them." But in the 1820s and 1830s, "these habits of benevolence and deference declined": landlords, "who were falling increasingly into debt, began prosecuting tenants for their unpaid rents." The Anti-Rent War was set off in 1839 when landlord Stephen Rensselaer died, "leaving debts worth $750,000 and a will that directed his executors to pay his obligations by collecting his tenants' overdue rents." Rensselaer's tenants, in turn, "organized a movement that aimed at ending Van Rensselaer's and other landlords' claims to their estates." By 1845 this movement had gathered "tens of thousands of supporters in eleven counties" in New York.[46]

As Masquerier's "Declaration" reveals, labor activists in New York

City imagined themselves as fellow travelers with the anti-renters in the Hudson Valley (and vice versa). For Masquerier, landlord and tenant are synonyms for capitalist and laborer, and his "Declaration" seeks to produce at least imagined solidarity between rural tenant farmers and wageworkers in urban centers. Masquerier writes, he tells us, on behalf of "the producers and would-be producers, of the City of New York" (69). Prominent land reformer Thomas Devyr visited the Hudson Valley and gave speeches at anti-renter rallies. The movement garnered support from Horace Greeley, who made the case for the anti-renters in the *New-York Tribune*, the newspaper that under Greeley's editorship helped turn land reform into the central focus of urban working-class politics in the 1840s. According to Masquerier's "Declaration," anti-rent very much counts as part of what Jameson calls "the single great collective story" of the "struggle to wrest a realm of Freedom from a realm of Necessity." Indeed, for the proslavery writer George Fitzhugh, anti-rent was affiliated with opposition to another form of social inequality—slavery: "No one who reads a newspaper can but have observed that every abolitionist is either an agrarian, a socialist, an infidel, an anti-renter, or in some way is trying to upset other institutions of society, as well as slavery at the South."[47]

That urban working-class activists trumpeted the anti-renters makes sense, because many of the most radical beliefs of the anti-renters dovetailed with the tenets of land reform. If the landholding elite of the Hudson "saw property in land as originating in the grant of land by a sovereign," writes Huston, the anti-renters in turn "insisted that property was created by the labor that improved the land. They believed that independent proprietorship was the natural status of free men, and that as long as unimproved land existed, everyone willing to improve it had a claim to a portion of it."[48] For the anti-renters, like land reformers more generally, ownership of land was the natural right of every man: land ownership was the source of freedom, because to own land was to be in a position to control one's labor.

In fact, it can be argued that the anti-rent rebellion catalyzed the larger movement for land reform among working-class activists and reformers elsewhere in the United States: "In triggering a more general discussion of land, monopoly, and property rights," Tuchinsky argues, the anti-rent movement "was a gateway to more radical reform movements," inspiring "others outside the movement . . . to link the lands question in New

York and eventually the entire West to the fate of urban workers." If U.S. working-class activism was flagging in the late 1830s, "the Anti-Rent movement revived it."[49]

In his preface to *Satanstoe,* a novel set in 1758 in which the Anti-Rent War only looms on the horizon, Cooper informs his readers that the three Littlepage novels will "relate directly to the great New York question of the day, ANTI-RENTISM."[50] As he puts it in this preface, "no apology is necessary for treating the subject of anti-rentism with the utmost frankness. Agreeably to our views of the matter," he continues, "the existence of true liberty among us, the perpetuity of the institutions, and the safety of public morals are all dependent on putting down, wholly, absolutely, and unqualifiedly, the false and dishonest theories and statements that have been boldly advanced in connection with this subject" (4). I will demonstrate that the Littlepage novels figure economic egalitarianism as "uncivilized" through their marriage plots, but the meaning of the Littlepage novels extends beyond the Anti-Rent War, just as for National Reformers the meaning of the Anti-Rent War had to do with the fate of class itself in the United States. Because working-class radicalism in the 1840s was so often articulated through claims for land redistribution, Cooper's literary campaign against anti-renters could not help but also be a symbolic attack on the larger historical frame of working-class radicalism in this decade.

THE AMERICAN DEMOCRAT: PROPERTY AND INEQUALITY

Of course, property rights and the right to the ownership of land in particular are central concerns in Cooper's writing before the Littlepage novels. And twenty years before the Littlepage novels, Cooper had already begun to wrestle with a version of economic egalitarianism through the figure of Natty Bumppo. In *The Pioneers* (1823), Natty, in opposition to Judge Temple, argues for a natural rights theory of land use and ownership: for Natty, Richard Godden observes, "land and its creatures are common; the killer of the deer owns the deer because he has put his labour into it—but all men must have right of access to the deer."[51] Dana Nelson also suggests that Natty stands for an economic commons rather than antisocial individualism (*Commons Democracy* 84–104). Yet, already in *The Pioneers,* Cooper figured economic egalitarianism and "civilization" as mutually exclusive. Though Natty vocalizes ideas about property as a "common" right, he also casts them as tenable only *before* white "civilization" in North America.[52] Natty himself believes that his ideas about land ownership and its distribution are incompatible with civilization, where he has no place.

In *The American Democrat*, which appeared just a few years before the Littlepage novels, Cooper argues that "property is the base of all civilization, its existence and security are indispensable to social improvement."[53] Here, Cooper explicitly decries communitarian projects, insisting that the production of surplus wealth is only possible under conditions of guaranteed private ownership of property of all kinds: "Were it possible to have a community of property, it would soon be found that no one would toil, but that men would be disposed to be satisfied with barely enough for the supply of their physical wants, since none would exert themselves to obtain advantages solely for the use of others. . . . Thus we see that the societies, or religious sects, in which a community of property prevails, are content with merely supplying the wants of life, knowing little or nothing of its elegancies, refinements, or mental pleasures" (135). Cooper relies on a static view of the human subject, unable to imagine a situation in which individuals operate beyond self-interest: "The principle of individuality, or to use a less winning term, of selfishness, lies at the root of all voluntary human exertion." He contrasts "civilization" and its commitment to "the rights of property" with the "savage state," where "land is without owners," and to "pastoral, or semi-barbarous states," where land is owned not by "individuals" but by "tribes" (135–36). These observations, from the chapter "On Property," iterate arguments from the chapter "On Equality": there we find Cooper telling us that "equality of condition is incompatible with civilization," and that "equality of condition" is "found only to exist in those communities that are but slightly removed from the savage state" (42). A justification for Indian dispossession is implicit in all of this: because there is no private property in land in the "semi-barbarous" state, Natives may need to be displaced to create room for "the rights of property" and their attendant comforts.

The dominant voices of *The Chainbearer* and *The Redskins* speak the language of *The American Democrat*. In *The Chainbearer*, Cooper repeats almost verbatim his arguments from *The American Democrat* about property and civilization. He places them in the mouth of Mordaunt Littlepage, this novel's protagonist-narrator, who explains to Sureflint, his Indian comrade, why the "white man" is so much "stronger" than the "red man":

> Now, all the knowledge, and all the arts of life that the white man enjoys and turns to his profit, come from the rights of property. No man would build a wigwam to make rifles in, if he thought he could not keep it as long as he wished, sell it when he pleased, and leave it to his son when he went to the land of spirits. It is by encouraging man's love of himself, in this manner, that he is got to do so much. Thus it is, too, that the father gives to the son what he has learned, as well as what he has built or bought; and so, in time, nations get to be powerful, as they get to be what we call civilized. Without these rights of property, no people could be civilized; for no people would do their utmost, unless each man were permitted to be master of what he can acquire, subject to the great and common laws that are necessary to regulate such matters.[54]

Like Cooper in *The American Democrat,* Mordaunt celebrates "the rights of property" as the cause and foundation of civilization, justifying Indian dispossession in the name of "knowledge" and "the arts of life." Of particular note in Mordaunt's lecture on property rights is his deployment of a version of the labor theory of wealth: "A man must work for himself to do his most; and he cannot work for himself unless he enjoys the fruits of his labor. Thus it is, that he must have a right of property in land, either bought or hired, in order to make him cause that land to produce all that nature intended it should produce. On this necessity is founded the rights of property; the gain being civilization; the loss ignorance, and poverty, and weakness" (124). It is precisely this kind of argument about the relationship between wealth and labor—which Mordaunt uses to justify Indian dispossession—that the squatters of *The Chainbearer* and the anti-renters of *The Redskins* deploy in order to insist upon their own rights to a portion of already owned land. According to these characters, exclusion from land ownership means that one is not "working for himself," and thus that one cannot be said to "enjoy the fruits of his labor." The conversation between Sureflint and Mordaunt helps to reveal, then, how the ideological justification for Indian dispossession could be adapted into an argument for land reform. Paradoxically, the philosophical basis of landlords' claims to their right in property vis-à-vis displaced Natives contains within it an argument on behalf of wider land distribution. In the *American Democrat,* Cooper already deployed a "fruits of labor" argument on behalf of private property: "We toil for food, for clothes, for houses, lands, and for property, in general. This is done because we know that the fruits of our labor will belong to ourselves, or to those who are most dear to us" (136). But if land ownership is the backbone of civilization, guaranteeing its worker the fruits of his labor, why should not more people — why shouldn't everyone — be landowners?

Indeed, a paradox riddles Cooper's ideas about the rights of property: property must be inviolable, because otherwise no one would produce wealth; however, the inviolability of property means that some individuals will forever be without property and thus forced to transfer the wealth they produce through their labor to those who do own property. "One man must labor," he writes in *The American Democrat,* "while another may live luxuriously on his means; one has leisure and opportunity to cultivate his tastes, to increase his information, and to refine his habits, while another is compelled to toil, that he may live. One is reduced to serve, while another commands, and, of course, there can be no equality in their social conditions" (45).[55] For Cooper, private property by definition cannot be taken away and redistributed by the state; if it could be, then no one would seek to increase his wealth. But Cooper, unconvinced by dreams of upward mobility and boundless opportunity, also does not believe that everyone will necessarily accumulate property. The paradox of Cooper's notion of the rights of property is, then, that while the rights of property guarantee individuals the fruits of their labor, they also produce a situation in which some need not labor at all while others eke out subsistence. Precisely because the rights of property are a human construction — the right to ownership of land being especially "artificial and extended" — it is impossible to argue, Cooper duly acknowledges, that economic inequality of the kind he describes is founded in nature: "As regards all human institutions men are born equal, no sophistry being able to prove that nature intended one should inherit power and wealth, another slavery and want" (136, 47).

According to Ezra Tawil, Cooper's *The Pioneers* preemptively resolves the contradiction in his theory of property by recourse to race. The revelation of Oliver Edwards's white blood at the end of *The Pioneers* makes possible his ascent to property ownership, "linking ownership to blood of a particular kind": "There is no such thing, the resolution of *The Pioneers* tells us, as a man's natural right to property, for strictly speaking, there is no political being such as 'man' as the Enlightenment conceived him. Instead, Lockean 'man' has been displaced by distinct varieties of men with different claims to property. . . . Oliver Edwards's right of property, the novel suggests, rests not on his political status as a 'man,' but on his racial status as a 'white man.'"[56] The Littlepage novels, I want to argue, work to resolve the contradiction in Cooper's theory of property at a time when it was becoming clear that not every white man would in fact be a property owner under market capitalism, and thus they offer an important supplement to the ideological work of *The Pioneers*.

Domestic Frontier Romance; or, the Class Politics of the Marriage Plot

Musing on the belief system of his nemesis Jason Newcome, Corny Littlepage, the protagonist-narrator of *Satanstoe*, suggests that a "disposition to regard the human family, as so many tenants in common of the estate left by Adam, will lead in the end to something extraordinary" (288). *The Chainbearer* and *The Redskins* prove Corny right, insofar as this idea—that the right to property is *common* to all—leads to the "extraordinary" fact of violent social conflict. "Family" is, however, the very terrain on which these novels do battle with such egalitarianism, insofar as they construe economic egalitarianism as at odds with the notion that families should be made out of the romantic love between husband and wife.

Cooper puts the language of every man's right to land ownership into the mouths of lower-class white characters. Aaron Thousandacres, a squatter "renegade" whose name alone signals an excessive acquisitiveness, is the voice of "the rights of man to property" in *The Chainbearer*. The dialect in which Thousandacres speaks encodes the content of his speech as unruly, deviant, and uneducated, despite his protestations that his theory of property is founded in religious principles:

I begin at the beginnin', when man was first put in possession of the 'arth, to till, and to dig, and to cut saw-logs, and to make lumber, jist as suited his wants and inclinations. Now, Adam was the father of all, and to him and his posterity was the possession of the 'arth given, and by Him whose title's worth that of all the kings, and governors, and assemblies in the known world. Adam lived his time, and left all things to posterity, and so has it been from father to son, down to our day and giniration, according to the law of God, though not accordin' to the laws of man. (335)

This belief in the natural, God-given right to land stands behind Thousandacres's decision to set up a lumber enterprise on land owned by the Littlepages: "Here is the 'arth, as I told you, given to man, to be used for his wants. When you and I are born, some parts of the world is in use, and some parts isn't. We want land, when we are old enough to turn our hands to labor, and I make my pitch out here in the woods, say where no man has pitched afore me" (336). While Thousandacres explains himself, Chainbearer—Mordaunt Littlepage's ally of "gentle" stock who has been reduced to a wageworker—constantly interrupts, attempting to deconstruct Thousandacres's logic. Chainbearer asks, to how much land then does any man have a right? Thousandacres responds: "[E]ach man would take as much as was necessary to his wants" (336). Thousandacres here blurs the distinction between want and need, and it would seem that his philosophy has no way of adjudicating between conflicts predicated on limited resources. Nor is he simply a subsistence farmer: he is in the process of deforesting part of the Littlepage lands to sell lumber on the market. Even so, Thousandacres articulates a belief in limitations on land possession:

> If [Mordaunt Littlepage is] a fri'nd of liberty, he should be a fri'nd of liberty's people; should give liberty and take liberty. Now, I call it liberty to let every man have as much land as he has a need on, and no more, keepin' the rest for them that's in the same sitiation. If he and his fathers be true fri'nds of liberty, let 'em prove it like men, by giving up all claims to any more land than they want. That's what I call liberty! Let every man have as much land as he's need on; that's my religion, and it's liberty too. (386)

Thousandacres endangers American political economy because he redefines "liberty" not as suffrage or free competition, but as an economic principle that guarantees ownership of the means of production to every man.

While *The Chainbearer* is set in the 1780s, *The Redskins* is set in the present, during the Anti-Rent War. Now Cooper's imagined anti-renters use "the rights of man to property" discourse. Disguised to protect themselves from the anti-renters, landlords Roger and Hugh Littlepage attend an anti-rent meeting. There they listen to one of the lecturers, a caricature of a Thomas Devyr, who, recall, visited the region during the conflict. The lecturer's oration strings together hatred of the land-lords, a labor theory of wealth, and something on the order of Skid-more's scheme for generational redistribution of land. The lecturer is, according to Hugh, "fluent, inflated, and anything but logical. Not only did he contradict himself, but he contradicted the laws of nature" (250). The lecturer asks, "Now, who will say that a freeman hasn't a right to air, hasn't a right to water, and, on the same process, hasn't a right to land?" (253). "He has, fellow-citizens—he has,'" the lecturer insists. "These are what are called in philosophy elementary rights" (253). The lecturer thus calls for "a just division of [the Littlepage] property" (275).

Josh Brigham is one character especially excited about the lecturer's visit. He is, as Hugh disparages him, an "anti-rent disposed hireling," "the very *beau ideal* of the suspicious school, being envious and malignant, as well as shrewd, observant, and covetous" (197). Brigham reveals to the disguised Hugh that he has "'been dealin' in speckylation,'" and that he "'means to make anti-rentism get me a farm cheap'" (199). Brigham is no yeoman farmer or republican artisan, but a wageworker who nonethe-less aspires to possessive individualism. With Seneca Newcome, Brigham later attempts to set the Littlepage house on fire, and to strangle Hugh Littlepage to death in the bargain. As Hugh says, Brigham is "almost an inmate of my family," and yet he "had not only conspired to rob me of my property, on a large scale, but he had actually carried his plot so far as to resort to the brand and the rifle" (403). Brigham's violence, we are told, is not merely "the result of the vulgar disposition to steal; it was purely a consequence of a widely-extended system, that is fast becoming incorporated with the politics of the land" (403). Cooper calculates his portrait of Brigham to inspire fear in a bourgeois urban audience at a moment when land reform was becoming the mantra of urban working-class politics as well. The novel implicitly warns that urban wageworkers might also commit politically motivated acts of violence against their employers. Yet, because there are plenty of "good" and dutiful lower class characters like Chainbearer in the Littlepage novels, ones who do not become agrarian insurgents, they suggest that radical working-class agrarian ideals are not the natural expression of a class position so much as an ill-formed belief system that inspires violent behavior in "bad" individuals. Indeed, Thousandacres (in *The Chainbearer*) and the anti-renters (in *The Redskins*) are villains not by virtue of their class status. They are villains because their beliefs about property compel them to what for their respective novels are immoral acts. Importantly, characters that believe in every man's right to property are especially villainous because they would interrupt the fulfillment of their novels' respective love plots.

Assuming that Cooper's great contribution to American literature is the unmarriageable Nathaniel Bumppo, literary historical common sense suggests that Cooper's project is at odds with domestic fiction and its emphasis on marriage. According to Leslie Fiedler, Cooper's frontier romances, like Natty himself, "turn from society to nature or nightmare out of a desperate need to avoid the facts of wooing, marriage, and child-bearing."[57] For Fiedler, marriage represents "a kind of *emasculation*" for Natty, since his "virility . . . is not genital but heroic and cannot survive in the marriage bed any more than beside the hearth."[58] As Tawil observes, "Most accounts of American literary history proceed on the assumption that the cultural impulse behind the frontier romance opposes that responsible for domestic fiction."[59] Even if this is so, the fact remains that all of Cooper's novels end with a marriage—a marriage between a gentleman hero or sidekick and a "virtuous" woman.[60] As Henry Nash Smith reminds us, "A novel, according to the canons which [Cooper] considered binding, was a love story. The hero of the novel was the man who played the male lead in the courtship."[61]

If there is any wonder about Cooper's relationship to domesticity as a value system, in the Littlepage novels praise for the domestic sphere finds space within frontier romance. In *Satanstoe*, domestic space enchants Corny Littlepage, as does the woman who tends it:

> I was as much delighted with the appearance of things in the interior of Lilacsbush, as I had been with the exterior. Everywhere, it seemed to me, I met with the signs of Anneke's taste and skill. I do not wish the reader to suppose that the residence itself was of the very first character and class, for this it could not lay claim to be. . . . I know not how it was, but the china appeared to me richer and neater than common under Anneke's pretty little hand, while the massive and

highly-finished plate of the breakfast service, was such as could be wrought only in England. In a word, while everything appeared rich and respectable, there was a certain indescribable air of comfort, gentility, and neatness about the whole, that impressed me in an unusual manner. (126)

Corny leaves Lilacsbush "deeply in love" with Anneke: to his mind she is blessed with "beauty and modesty, and grace, and gentleness, and spirit, and sense, and delicacy, and virtue and piety" (129, 134). However much Corny recounts his martial adventures on the frontier, the telos of his plot is domestic life with Anneke. According to Lora Romero's reading of *Last of the Mohicans*, Cooper's anxiety about the "threat woman's invisible power poses to the male subject produces the need for some space (the frontier) in order to elude her miasmic influence and hence makes imperative the macropolitical controls effecting Indian removal from contiguous territories."[62] Yet, in the Littlepage novels, frontier adventures are required in order to open up territories in which there are spaces in which women, fortunately, preside.

Furthermore, *Satanstoe*, *The Chainbearer*, and *The Redskins* each unfold around a central courtship and marriage plot, and all are stories of sexual rivalry. In *Satanstoe*, Corny competes with Bulstrode for the hand of Anneke. In *The Chainbearer*, Mordaunt Littlepage falls in love with Ursula ("Dus") Malbone, the niece of the novel's eponymous Chainbearer. Though Dus is gentle born, educated, sings wonderfully, and is possessed of every feminine "virtue," she has been reduced to poverty, at times assisting her uncle with his physical labor. Mordaunt's rival Zephaniah, the son of Thousandacres, also desires Dus. In *The Redskins*, Opportunity Newcome has designs on Hugh Littlepage, who in turn falls in love with Mary Warren. Mary Warren is the daughter of the Reverend Warren; she is as beautiful and "virtuous" as Anneke and Dus, and like Dus is educated but lacks money. Seneca Newcome stands as Hugh's rival, proposing to Mary (in addition to all of Uncle Roger Littlepage's wards). If *The Chainbearer* and *The Redskins* offer novelistic pleasure, it is in their final matrimonial couplings, both of which are quasi cross-class alliances predicated on mutual desire. Dus does indeed marry Mordaunt, and Mary marries Hugh.

Scholars who have recognized the importance of marriage plots to Cooper's Leatherstocking novels have pointed out that these novels do not permit either interracial or interclass marriages. Nina Baym, for example, tells us that "the content of the marriage statement" in the Leatherstocking novels is "deeply conservative: marriage takes place within the boundaries of the group. Neither extending or modifying the social structure, it confirms the group's previous membership, and tightens the group's solidarity and exclusiveness."[63] Charting which women are "marriageable" in the Leatherstocking novels, Baym concludes that "the conception of a flexible social structure evaded" Cooper, for in "every book his rigid hierarchical view of society eclipses the romantic sympathies which he embodies in loners and outcasts."[64] This assessment would seem to hold true for the Littlepage novels, in which characters scoff at interclass marriages. In *The Chainbearer,* Chainbearer himself protests a marriage between Zephaniah and his niece Dus on the grounds that Zephaniah is socially inferior to Dus: "[S]he shalt nefer marry a squatter—she shalt nefer marry any man t'at ist not of a class, and feelin's, ant hapits, ant opinions, fit to pe t'e huspant of a laty!" (396). In *The Redskins,* Roger Littlepage suggests that Seneca Newcome deserves to be hanged not because of his attempt to burn down the Littlepage home but because of his disregard for "proprieties" about who can marry whom: "How is it possible," Roger exclaims, "or where could the chap have been bred, to fancy for an instant that a young woman of fortune and station, would marry *him*" (464).

What I want to point out, though, is that in the Littlepage novels the marriages desired by male economic egalitarians—the marriages desired by figures who give voice to the oppositional political economy against which Cooper's narrators protest quite loudly—are figured as coercive. When Thousandacres is caught logging on Littlepage land, his plan to get himself out of trouble turns on a coerced marriage. Though Dus is in love with Mordaunt, Thousandacres—having imprisoned Mordaunt, Chainbearer, and Dus—tries to force a marriage between Dus and his son, Zephaniah: "[W]e'll have the young folks married on the spot," he says to Chainbearer (who is Dus's uncle), "and that will make etarnal peace forever, as you must suppose, atween you and me. Wa-a-l, peace made atween *us,* 'twil leave but little to accommodate with the writin' owners of the sile, seein' that you're on tarms with 'em all" (394). Since Chainbearer is a friend of the Littlepages, Thousandacres reasons, the Littlepages will not prosecute him if marriage connects his family to Chainbearer's.

It is worth noting that, in construing working-class men as a threat to female autonomy, Cooper prefigures Nathaniel Hawthorne. The sexual rivalry between Mordaunt and Zephiniah in *The Chainbearer* anticipates Nathaniel Hawthorne's anxious narrative of sexual rivalry in *The Blithedale Romance*. Miles Coverdale, the bourgeois narrator of *Blithedale*, expresses dismay over the power of working-class men over Priscilla, who—like *The Chainbearer*'s Dus—is of bourgeois extraction but has fallen into poverty. Thousandacres's attempt to coerce a marriage looks forward to the mesmeric coercion of Priscilla in *Blithedale* by man-on-the-make Westervelt. Likewise, it looks forward to Matthew Maule's mesmeric coercion of Alice Pyncheon in *The House of the Seven Gable*'s inset story, "Alice Pyncheon." Matthew Maule—"bitter with the sense of hereditary wrong, because he considered the great Pyncheon House to be standing on soil which should have been his own"[65]—revenges himself on the Maules by mesmerizing Alice into a state of servitude. "While Alice Pyncheon lived," Hawthorne writes, "she was Maule's slave, in bondage more humiliating, a thousand-fold, than that which binds its chain around the body."[66] Hawthorne echoes Cooper's penchant for stories in which working-class men would coerce and even enslave women in order to accomplish their ends.

Thousandacres's attempt to force a marriage between Dus and Zephiniah in *The Chainbearer* is mirrored by the opportunistic marriage proposals of anti-renter Seneca Newcome in *The Redskins*. We learn toward the end of the novel that Seneca has proposed to every young woman in the Littlepage circle. These youth all laugh off Roger's anger at Seneca's presumptions. All laugh, that is, except Mary, who cries out that Roger's proposals are a reflection of "the great Anti-Rent principle, after all. In the one case, it is only a wish to get good farms cheap—and in the other, good wives" (465). Roger emends Mary's comments, but does not this time encounter resistance from the Littlepage circle youth: "In the one case, other men's farms—and in the other, other men's wives," he explains (465). Roger insinuates that the anti-renters would do what Thousandacres tries to do, namely, take a woman away from the man to whom she has already committed herself. "Here's a fellow who first endeavours to raise a flame in the hearts of no less than four young ladies," Roger continues shortly after, "failing of which, he takes refuge in lighting a fire in Hugh's kitchen" (466). While the Littlepage youth do not agree with Roger's assessment that it is impossible for a "woman of fortune and station" to desire a man without property, they nonetheless agree that Seneca's marriage proposals are "anti-rentism" by other means. According to Roger and Mary, Seneca would use women to secure property just as he would use arson. In *The Chainbearer,* egalitarian ideas about land ownership lead to the attempt to coerce a marriage; in *The Redskins,* they lead to a disregard for proper rituals of romantic courtship. Certainly, Seneca does not "get to know" the women to whom he proposes; he makes no attempt to know about their "insides." He does not do the requisite work, as it were, of courtship: he tries to "get" a wife "cheap," in Mary's formulation. In contrast, Mary and Hugh engage in a series of conversations that allow them to learn that they have similar ways of thinking and feeling. "Good wives" are a kind of property in these novels, but they are a kind of property to which not every man has a rightful claim. Indeed, they are kind of property that reserves the right to determine its owner.

And although no one tries to coerce a marriage in *The Redskins,* here, too, Cooper frames economic egalitarianism as a threat to a woman's right to choose her "owner." Because the anti-renters want to rid the region of landlords, they are willing to destroy landlords' homes, and even to kill them. However, Mary cannot leave the region, for her father commits to serve his parish, and she in turn commits to assist him. Furthermore, when agrarian insurgents come very close to inadvertently depriving Mary of her beloved Hugh, Hugh explains that the anti-renters in the novel would—had they the power—intentionally prevent their marriage. He explains that the anti-renters object to the marriage between him and Mary:

> My engagement with the daughter of a poor clergyman has produced great scandal among the anti-renters, they who loudly decry aristocracy! The objection is that the match is not equal! That equality which is the consequence of social position, connections, education and similarity of habits, thoughts, and if you will, prejudices, is all thrown away on these persons. They have no notion of its existence; but they can very well understand that the owner of an unencumbered and handsome estate is richer than then the heiress of a poor divine. (532–33)

According to Hugh, then, the anti-renters' view of marriage is the truly aristocratic one, because for the anti-renters it is only parity in the respective wealth of prospective spouses that qualifies them for marriage to one another.

If the wisdom on Cooper's marriages in the Leatherstocking novels is that they are (again, Baym) "deeply conservative," Cooper in the Little-page novels is suggesting that it is economic egalitarians who harbor notions about who should marry whom that are inflexible, exclusive, and narrow. Indeed, though in *The Chainbearer*, Chainbearer expresses apprehension, not just about a match between Dus and Zephiniah, but also about a match between Dus and Mordaunt on the grounds that Dus is not Mordaunt's equal ("[S]he ist still a chainpearer's niece," he explains to Mordaunt, "and you are still General Littlepage's son ant heir" [373]), Chainbearer ultimately comes to realize that the mutual, consensual desire between Dus and Mordaunt is more significant than Dus's lack of money. So, while Chainbearer and Corny's family embrace his marriage to Dus, and Hugh's family embraces his marriage to Mary in *The Redskins,* characters in the Littlepage novels that espouse economically egalitarian ideas promise to *restrict* whom a woman should marry as a means by which to accomplish their goals. If a typical protest in the United States against economic egalitarianism holds that economic egalitarianism prohibits the *economic* autonomy of the individual, Cooper's novels furthermore construe economic egalitarianism as antithetical to the *romantic* autonomy of the individual. Indeed, while the intrusive narrators of Cooper's Littlepage novels rail against economic egalitarianism, the stories these novels tell invite readers to think of economic egalitarianism as a threat (as I said above) to "democratic" marriage practices. Or, in other words, these novels invite their readers to believe that being opposed to economic egalitarianism is also being for the right of a woman to choose her husband.

Not merely any kind of woman, though: the heroines of *The Chainbearer* and *The Redskins* are models of "true womanhood." It was in the 1840s and '50s that "woman" came to be defined as a "separate species of humanity."[67] The "attributes" of "True Womanhood," Barbara Welter taught us, were "piety, purity, submissiveness, and domesticity."[68] Or, as Mary Ryan observes, citing Frances Parkes's *Domestic Duties* (1831), the "true woman" was defined by "purity of mind, simplicity, and frankness of heart, promptness of active character, lively and warm affections, inducing a habit of forbearance and the practice of self-denial."[69] The terms by which Dus and Mary are admired come right out of the "true womanhood" lexicon. Mordaunt takes note of "the play of virtuous and ingenuous emotion" in her "lovely female countenance" (161). Dus exhibits "directness, truth, and ingenuousness," and these qualities are "blended" with "the feelings and delicacy of her sex" (166); she displays "delicacy, and sentiment, and virtue, and all that pertains to a well-educated young woman" (166); she has "a woman's instinct for the graceful and beautiful" (169). Cooper further ascribes all the virtues of "true womanhood" to Mary at various points in *The Redskins,* praising the special femininity of "the pretty, gentle, timid, yet spirited and intelligent daughter of the rector" (152). On his first meeting with Mary, Hugh notes that "the expression of her face, eyes, smile, and all put together, was . . . singularly sweet and feminine" (97).

"True womanhood" was, as has been well documented, and as I touched upon briefly in the introduction, a defining feature of nineteenth-century bourgeois ideology.[70] According to antebellum definitions of "true womanhood," women are by nature designed to be wives and mothers, and their natural sphere is thus the "private," intimate sphere of the middle-class home. True womanhood reflected and legitimated the notion that society should be composed of private economic units (the nuclear family), composed in turn by a strict division of labor: women should tend to the cares of the family, while men should provide the wealth upon which the nuclear family depends by participating in the economic sphere of the market beyond the home.[71]

Yet, while Dus and Mary are exemplary of true womanhood, the class position of Dus and Mary is not cut-and-dried. Dus may have wealthy ancestors and Mary may be "the daughter of an educated and well-connected clergyman" (182), but both heroines begin their respective novels poor. In fact, even though Dus is "a *lady,*" she has been reduced to doing manual labor for pay: she assists her uncle in carrying chain. Mordaunt recoils when he learns this about Dus: "But you, Miss Malbone—dearest Dus—who have been so educated . . . are not in your proper sphere, while thus occupied" (163). Here, economic inequality poses a threat to true womanhood, insofar as it subjects a true woman to an economic "sphere" disharmonious with true womanhood.[72] Mordaunt must reconcile himself to Dus's situation: "It is not so easy to say what is the proper sphere of a woman. I admit it ought to be, in general, in the domestic circle, and under the domestic roof; but circumstances must control that. We hear of wives who follow their husbands to the camp, and we hear of nuns who come out of their convents to attend the sick and wounded in hospitals. It does not strike, then, as so bad in a girl who offers to aid her parent" (163). While economic inequality may imperil true womanhood, in Cooper's novels true womanhood nonetheless survives the fall into material deprivation. According to Amy Schrager Lang, the model of "perfect womanhood" put forward by Hawthorne in the form of *The House of the Seven Gables*'s Phoebe "perfectly mediates between the lower and upper classes."[73] "And [Phoebe] does so," Lang explains, "not only symbolically but literally insofar as she moves effortlessly and unselfconsciously between the cent shop, the garden, the street, and the Pyncheon mansion, retaining her own identity intact." In *The Chainbearer* and *The Redskins,* "perfect womanhood" is also imagined to be somewhat independent of material circumstances: Dus and Mary move effortlessly between and among classes, preserving their femininity despite having to do things that only men are supposed to do.

Yet, while the class position of Dus and Mary is not cut-and-dried, Dus and Mary are not imagined to be—like the heroines of later domestic fiction—"outside the play of interests—economic, social, and political."[74] Agrarian insurgents in their respective novels assume that the poverty of Dus and Mary should make them sympathetic to the economically egalitarian cause, but, significantly, Dus and Mary both reject economic egalitarianism. Equally significant, Dus and Mary express their opposition to economic egalitarianism before the prospect of marriage to a landlord materializes for either one of them (though, of course, this opposition helps to make Dus and Mary attractive to their respective Littlepage suitors). On the one hand, Dus and Mary model a politicized true woman who never forgets her allegiance to the bourgeoisie, even when she is not exactly bourgeois herself. Dus and Mary teach Cooper's female readers that if you want to be recognized as a womanly woman, you will neither desire nor sympathize with economic egalitarians. What Joel Pfister says of "the ideological pearl of wisdom" in *The Scarlet Letter* also rings true of the Littlepage novels: in *The Scarlet Letter* "you cannot rebel and be feminine at the same time."[75] Dus and Mary are womanly women—they remain "feminine" even in poverty—in large measure *because,* these novels suggest, they are opposed to economic egalitarianism—*because* they are never drawn to men who espouse an economically egalitarian position.

On the other hand, that Dus and Mary are poor, virtuous women—

that poor, virtuous women are opposed to economic egalitarianism—endows opposition to economic egalitarianism with another alibi: to fight against the egalitarian distribution of wealth is to fight on behalf of—for—"womanhood." Even though the landlords of *The Chainbearer* and *The Redskins* may be less than heroic (as Egan, McGann, and Nelson suggest), their fight is construed as a vindication of true womanhood. Because "woman" and economic egalitarianism are set up as antagonists in these novels, the class politics of the Littlepage novels slipstream along behind gender ideology.

Indeed, *The Chainbearer* and *The Redskins* might be described as novels wherein poor but virtuous women are ultimately rewarded—with marriages to wealthy men—for their "natural" antagonism toward economic egalitarianism. At the end of their respective plots, Dus and Mary move into the material location—the Littlepage estate—in which their "femininity" can flourish. In fact, Dus reappears in *The Redskins* as Hugh's loving mother, presiding over the Littlepage home. *The Chainbearer* and *The Redskins* do not suggest that class conflict cannot—or will not—happen in the United States (class conflict has already happened in the United States, these novels remind us); neither do these final marriages dissolve socioeconomic inequality. Yet, through these marriages, which translate "poor" into woman and "rich" into man, Cooper's novels, like so many others that end with cross-class marriages, invite their readers to believe that "the poor" and "the rich" can love one another.[76]

RACE AND CLASS IN THE LITTLEPAGE NOVELS

"At the bottom of the moral ladder" of Cooper's Leatherstocking novels, Richard Slotkin writes, "are those plebeian types—hunters or squatters—who act like Indians in their interaction with white women."[77] For Slotkin, the Bush family in Cooper's *The Prairie* (1827) exemplifies this plebian type, kidnapping Inez and carrying her away from her husband, Middleton.[78] Ishmael Bush is a precursor of Thousandacres and the anti-renters of *The Redskins,* offering early in *The Prairie* a natural rights theory of land use and ownership: "I am as rightful an owner of the land I stand on, as any governor in the States!"[79] Ishmael only redeems his family, however, when he allows Inez to go free and when he allows

Ellen to choose her own spouse. Thousandacres and the anti-renters of *The Redskins* who would take "other men's wives" remain closer to *The Prairie*'s Mahrotee, who would force Inez to marry him, and the "bad Indians" of *The Deerslayer* who kidnap Hist.[80] By putting the "bad whites" of the Littlepage novels in the structural position occupied by "bad Indians" in his earlier frontier romances—that is, in the role of an enemy that needs to be overcome so that a companionate marriage can take place—Cooper uses novelistic means to argue that white civilization must not compromise with or accommodate economic egalitarianism.

Cooper's novels insinuate, in other words, that a belief in the right of economic equality renders egalitarians not quite "white." In so insinuating, Cooper had help from the anti-renters themselves. The title of *The Redskins; or, Indian and Injin* refers specifically to the tactics of one set of anti-renters. Though Cooper calls them "Injins," in 1841 there appeared a group of disguised anti-rent insurgents who dubbed themselves "Indians"; by 1845 "some 10,000 men had joined the Indians."[81] The disguise these "Indians" wore consisted of "a long hunting shirt or calico gown and pantaloons; masks of leather or glazed muslin with holes for the eyes, ears, and mouth with peaks, like animal ears or devil's horns, at the corners" (119). Drawing "heavily from two inextricably linked groups"—"young men and the landless and land-poor"—the "Indians" intimidated landlords and lawmen, preventing "landlords from collecting rent and lawmen from evicting tenants or conducting distress sales" (117, 119). By donning disguises and dubbing themselves "Indians," they also "served a critical ideological function": on the one hand, they "helped perpetuate the fiction of white tenants' respectability by projecting responsibility for their lawlessness and savagery onto another race;" on the other hand, "by claiming title through an appropriated 'Indian' identity," they "underscored the fraudulence of landlords' titles and made a better claim to the land than any white person could make" (121).

This is not to suggest that many of the "Indians" were not themselves, in a word, racist. Neither is it to suggest, then, that many of the "Indians" were not complicit in the ideology of settler colonialism. Many anti-renters—the "Indians" included—promoted (at times unwittingly, but at others quite intentionally and explicitly) Native American dispossession: "Like most antebellum white men, the anti-renters did not listen to actual native peoples or to African Americans," Reeve Huston explains; "rather they created an image of racial others that served their own purposes. In doing so, they gave voice to a class identity that was unmistakably white. In promoting their egalitarian class agenda, the anti-renters simultaneously helped advance the multi-class cause of white supremacy and Indian removal" (129).[82] And land reform more broadly can be understood as a version of what Mark Rifkin calls "settler common sense," insofar as it takes for granted "non-native access to Indigenous territories" as the means by which working-class whites might achieve full "personhood."[83]

Yet, it is not the racism of anti-renters (or of economic egalitarians) that is the problem for Cooper. *The Redskins* sensationalizes the tactics of anti-rent "Indians." It is as "Injins" that Brigham and Newcome attempt to burn down the Littlepage home.[84] The problem for Cooper with anti-renters is that they are, as I have suggested, like "bad Indians." Putting economic egalitarianism in the structural position of the "bad Indian" who must be overcome so that a white, not-exactly-poor and not-exactly-wealthy woman can enjoy the freedom to marry her object of desire, Cooper made whiteness and civilization synonymous with economic inequality. And he did so as much as any other early U.S. novelist, because he did so explicitly and advertently.

To this point, I've been reading the Littlepage novels as directed primarily at a white, bourgeois readership. Indeed, my argument has been that these novels "teach" a white, bourgeois readership that opposing economic egalitarianism is to defend "democratic" marriage practices. But I'd like to conclude this chapter by suggesting that we can also read the Littlepage novels as aimed at working-class readers, too—and as an attempt to prevent white workers from thinking of Native Americans and blacks as their allies.

Of particular significance in Cooper's argument against economic egalitarianism is his representation of a tribe of "real" Indians who set themselves against *The Redskins*'s "Injins." Though these "real" Indians are critical of all white claims to North American land, they come to the rescue of the Littlepages when the Littlepages are under siege by the "Injins," for whom they reserve their harshest criticisms. In the climactic scene of *The Redskins,* one of these "real" Indians, Eaglesflight, delivers a speech that homologizes property and marriage through a notion of exclusive possession that indicts the anti-renters in racial terms. Eaglesflight offers a parable to illustrate the wrongheadedness of the anti-renters' principles, narrating how Susquesus obeyed the "red-man's law" by not infringing on the rights of a sexual rival, Waterfowl, to the possession of their shared object of desire, Ouithwith. Though Chief Susquesus is the warrior Waterfowl's superior, Susquesus obeys the law according to which Waterfowl has rightful possession of Ouithwith (herself a war captive). On the one hand, this parable suggests that land possession should be like marriage: they both should be a matter of exclusive, lasting title according to which a woman cannot be taken away from a man if the law dictates he "owns" her. On the other hand, Eaglesflight's narrative suggests that the anti-renters' unwillingness to submit to "pale-face law" about property is the equivalent of a "red-man" failing to submit to "red-man law" about women. Eaglesflight's parable—like Roger Littlepage's objection to Seneca's proposals—thus links anti-renters' disregard for property rights to a disregard for norms governing marriage. Eaglesflight's parable lays bare how the laws governing property and the conventions governing courtship are both socially constructed, but it also suggests that transgressing them can be, and should be, reckoned unnatural. Transgressing these conventions is tantamount, he explains, to forfeiting one's racial identity. Here, then, the "noble savage" conveniently draws the lines of racial identity. He explains that to be a "pale-face" you must submit to inegalitarian laws governing property.

Though anti-renters were not (as I pointed out) free from white supremacist thinking, National Reformers imagined land reform as a progressive racial movement and connected questions of land distribution to Indian rights and abolition. At their most radical, land reformers insisted not just that all white men had a right to land in the United States, but that Indians and blacks—as well as women—did as well. George Henry Evans, for example, "placed the words of Black Hawk alongside those of Jefferson in his publication."[85] The audience of a New York City National Reform meeting "gave 'loud applause' to Alvan Bovay's declaration that 'the Indians have a right somewhere, and it was certainly time now that their oppression should cease'" (78). For National Reformers, abolition was only half the battle for blacks, because "genuine personal liberty and independence for blacks, as for whites, required economic and social rights" in addition to political rights (80). In 1848 National Reformer Henry Hamlin Van Amringe linked land reform to racial—as well as gender—equality: "I am an abolitionist, as well as a

National Reformer," Van Amringe declared. Land, he insisted, "should be free to each one of either sex, and of all complexions of skins," "free without money or price, to any landless actual settler, man or woman, a native of the United States or Territories, and to all foreigners who under the laws of our country may become naturalized." (80). In crucial ways, "land reform became a multiracial movement," explains Mark Lause, under the leadership of radical National Reformers (82). The novelist William Wells Brown was but one of many prominent black Americans who "wished success to the Land Reform movement" (83).

But in Cooper's Littlepage novels, there is no political solidarity to be gained for the white worker who would sacrifice his allegiance to "whiteness" on behalf of interracial social, political, and economic equality, precisely because racial Others are themselves committed to inequality among whites. Indeed, Eaglesflight's parable poisons the prospect of solidarity between Natives and those landless workers who were challenging existing regimes of property in the United States.

What's more, the "real" Indians are not the only racial Other to oppose the "Injins." Hugh's slave, Jaff, also voices his staunch disapproval of the anti-renters, beginning a lengthy harangue with the question "What you want wid Masser Hugh's land?—why dat you t'ink to get gentle'em's property, eh?" (505). Thus, in Cooper's imagined world, neither Indians nor black slaves will ally with the struggles of economically marginal whites. Slaves naturally will themselves to economic elites. All told, Cooper forecloses the prospect of interracial labor solidarity.[86]

George Henry Evans linked slave owners to northern landlords, black slaves to white tenant and wage farmers: "The slaveholder has inherited other people's *bodies,* and the Landholder has inherited other people's *land;* and thereby *holds* their bodies" (Lause, 73). In the next chapter, where my focus is on how Harriet Beecher Stowe activated the comparison between poor whites and black slaves in her antislavery novel *Dred,* I touch upon the limitations of such comparisons. Here, I want to suggest that what Cooper does in *The Redskins* is teach potential working-class readers that slaves are their enemies. Hemmed in by white elites and antagonistic racial subalterns, all the white worker of Cooper's novel has left is a notion of "whiteness" defined by internal economic inequality. Thus, at novel's end, the "Injins," as Philip Deloria puts it, "throw away their calico bags and slink home . . . leaving the field clear for the formalizing of the inevitable romantic connections among the elite Ravensnest crowd."[87] We should not underestimate the potency of Cooper's divisive novelistic strategies for playing women, reds, and blacks against the claims to economic equality of poor white men. These strategies forcefully impede a political imaginary of universal economic equality.

5   WORKING-CLASS ABOLITIONISM AND ANTISLAVERY FICTION
"White Slaves" and Harriet Beecher Stowe's *Dred*

In the final chapter of *Love and Theft: Blackface Minstrelsy and the American Working Class,* Eric Lott details how 1850s stage adaptations of Harriet Beecher Stowe's *Uncle Tom's Cabin* were indebted to blackface minstrelsy, which was one of the primary forms of working-class entertainment in the antebellum North. These adaptations, Lott writes, "could not . . . have avoided making use of blackface devices: minstrelsy was the current material condition of theatrical production in the representation of racial matters." But while these adaptations thus reproduced the problematic racial politics of blackface minstrelsy, they also refashioned minstrelsy, Lott contends, "for explicit antislavery purposes."[1] And because members of the northern, white working class attended performances of these adaptations, they may have helped to forge working-class abolitionism. "Rather than talking down to them from the abolitionist's lofty perch," Lott writes, "*Uncle Tom* dramas spoke in the idiom of popular melodrama, wedding new political concerns to familiar forms" (228). According to Lott, George Aiken's version of *Uncle Tom's Cabin* in particular accentuated the latent appeals of Stowe's novel to the white working class:

There is, of course, a great deal of room in the story of *Uncle Tom's Cabin* for mechanic accents, to borrow Michael Denning's phrase. Right off the bat George Harris loses his job in the factory to which his master has hired him out; the master has decided that George's lease on independence is getting too dear, and wants him to come back to the plantation and, despite his marriage to Eliza, an arranged marriage. This demotion is transparently a shift from artisan (George

is an inventor) to slave, and in conjoining the two, the action everywhere invokes George's status as a put-upon "wage slave." In the dramas George's speeches about his lack of freedom thus take on a specifically artisanal cast, making the freedom in question a matter of both
black and working-class relevance. (229)

Perhaps Aiken's *Uncle Tom's Cabin* rendered more overt Stowe's invita-
tion to white workers to see themselves in George Harris and thus recognize the fight against chattel slavery as their own.

Taking its cue from Lott, this chapter explores how—and to what
end—the literature of antislavery attempted to secure white working-
class solidarity with the cause of abolition. I focus here, though, not
on *Uncle Tom's Cabin* (or its adaptations), but rather on Stowe's 1856
novel *Dred: A Tale of the Great Dismal Swamp. Dred's* representations of
southern poor whites and of the relationships between planter elites and
southern poor whites function, I suggest, to imagine abolition as "of the
greatest importance to the workingmen of the United States," to borrow
a phrase from an abolitionist broadside.

Literary historians have observed that *Dred* undercuts what Tawil
calls the "particular brand of racialism"[2] that complicates the abolitionism of *Uncle Tom's Cabin.* "Instead of privileging racially defined 'blood'
lines," Susan Ryan argues, *Dred* "champions non-kin, interracial families and communities."[3] Moreover, literary historians tend to agree that
Dred represents a departure from *Uncle Tom's Cabin*'s sentimentalism.
John Carlos Rowe tells us that *Dred* "self-consciously criticize[s] . . . stereotypes of African American characters, religious sentimentalism dis-
connected from political practice, the colonial utopia of Liberia . . . , and
the white paternalism of abolition in *Uncle Tom's Cabin.*"[4] If *Uncle Tom's
Cabin* solicits white sympathy for the plight of black slaves but also proposes voluntary manumission as the solution to slavery, *Dred* in contrast
at times flirts with an endorsement of slave rebellion.

As Robert Levine puts it, "Domesticity and sympathy go only so far
in *Dred,* a novel that ultimately asks its readers to consider slavery from
the point of view of black revolutionaries lurking in the recesses of the
Dismal Swamp."[5] Likewise, David Reynolds suggests that *Dred* "shows
that Stowe, the creator of the gentle Uncle Tom, was now thinking of
violence as the solution to the slavery problem."[6]

But with *Dred,* Stowe departs from *Uncle Tom's Cabin* in another sig-

nificant way: here, southern poor whites become central to the abolitionist arguments of Stowe's fiction. "Class is a central theme in *Dred*," Sarah
Meer aptly observes.[7] By focusing attention on southern poor whites in
Dred, Stowe expands upon a theme she broached in her 1853 *A Key to
Uncle Tom's Cabin*. In the chapter entitled "Poor White Trash," Stowe
writes: "[T]he institution of slavery has produced not only heathenish,
degraded, miserable slaves, but it produces a class of white people who
are, by universal admission, more heathenish, degraded, and miserable.
The institution of slavery has accomplished the double feat, in America,
not only of degrading and brutalising her black working classes, but of
producing, notwithstanding a fertile soil, and abundant room, a poor
white population as degraded and brutal as ever existed in any of the
most crowded districts of Europe."[8] According to *A Key*, slavery produces white poverty—and thus class inequality among whites—in the
South. Stowe rehearses this line of reasoning throughout *Dred*. "All the
land that's good for anything," says the mulatto slave Harry in *Dred*, "is
taken up for large estates."[9] What's more, propertyless whites cannot find
jobs because they compete with slave labor: "Planters," Harry says, "don't
want them on their places—they'd rather have their own servants. If one
of them wants to be a blacksmith, or a carpenter, there's no encourage-
ment" (107). As Edward Clayton, a slave owner turned abolitionist in
the novel, puts it, slavery "prevents the general education of the whites,
and keeps the poorer classes down to the lowest point, while it enriches
a few" (152). Clayton at times echoes the very phrasing of *A Key*: "I don't
believe there's any country in old, despotic Europe where the poor are
more miserable, vicious, and degraded, than they are in our slave states"
(465).[10] According to *Dred's* narrator, "the wretched condition" of southern poor whites "is not among the least of the evils of slavery" (400).

Allison Hurst is correct when she observes that in *Dred* Stowe "de-
picts poor whites as lazy, shiftless, uninterested in culture and education, immoral and over-sexed."[11] I want to put pressure, though, on her
contention that "though Stowe argues passionately against the institution
of slavery, she has no problem at all with a rigid class hierarchy between
elites and the working class."[12] In fact, *Dred* is proposing something quite
the contrary, namely that abolitionism represents both a desire for the
end of class inequality among whites as well as the means by which class
inequality among whites is to be overcome in the United States. For the
character Clayton, abolition is as much about liberating poor southern

whites as it is about liberating black slaves: "Now . . . if for nothing else, if we had no feeling of humanity for the slave, we must do something for the sake of the whites, for this is carrying us back into barbarism, as fast as we can go" (464). On one level, Stowe's novel invites its northern middle-class readers to feel for poor southern whites—and to imagine that their allegiance with the cause of abolition is also a matter of caring for the plight of poor southern whites. On another level, Stowe's novel deploys southern poor whites to appeal to potential northern white working-class readers. Writes Rowe: "Like Frederick Douglass in *My Bondage and My Freedom* (1855), published the year before *Dred*, Stowe calls attention to the common cause shared by African American slaves and the white southern working class."[13] But also the white *northern* working class, I would argue: southern poor whites in *Dred* motivate a series of discussions between abolitionist and proslavery characters in the novel—and these discussions in turn reveal proslavery characters to be the enemies of northern white workers. In fact, the plantation elites of Stowe's South tell us that they desire to enslave both poor southern whites and northern white workers. According to *Dred*, white workers in the North have everything to lose from the continued existence of slavery and its ruling class. *Dred* can thus be read, I will demonstrate, as a reworking of northern working-class abolitionist arguments about the "slave-power conspiracy."

I will also argue, though, that *Dred* works to defang any emergent working-class anticapitalism insofar as it construes the primary source of intraracial economic inequality—that is, class inequality among whites—in the United States to be racial slavery. In *Capital*, Marx famously writes: "Labour in a white skin cannot emancipate itself where it is branded in a black skin."[14] *Dred* might seem to offer a parallel assessment; yet *the novel* stops short of critiquing capitalism. According to *Dred*, economic inequality among whites is fundamentally a symptom of southern chattel slavery and thus something that whites living in the capitalist North have escaped.

"White Slaves"

In the 1840s and 1850s, the analogy was frequently drawn between white wage laborers and black chattel slaves. New York representative Mike Walsh, for example, deployed the analogy in a speech in the U.S. Congress: "The only difference between the negro slave of the South, and the white wage slave of the North, is, that the one has a master without asking for him, and the other has to beg for the privilege of becoming a slave. . . . The one is a slave of an individual; the other is the slave of an inexorable class."[15] Yet, the figure of the white worker as slave summoned *both* identification and disidentification between white workers and black slaves. While some activists deployed "wage slavery," others who used the term "white slavery" to protest the economic plights of whites carried racialist baggage behind them. Indeed, condemnations of white wage labor through a comparison to black slavery often "rested on a racist underpinning": by holding that "slavery was meant for blacks, freedom for whites," this comparison implied that "what was degrading in wage labor was reducing white men to the same level as African-Americans."[16] As Roediger has demonstrated, invocations of "white slavery" did not necessarily indicate "an act of solidarity with the [African American] slave but rather a call to arms to end the inappropriate oppression of whites." Indeed, the use of the term "white slavery" to describe the economic plight of whites could suggest that it was "the 'slavery' of *whites* that deserved censure."[17] Schocket aptly deconstructs the figure of "white slavery": "the suggested alliance built around the word *slavery*," he points out, "is undercut by the modifier *white*. Hence, the 'enslavement' of whites rather than the enslavement of people emerges as the root problem."[18] Some self-professed abolitionists could describe white wage slavery as worse than black chattel slavery. Ardent abolitionist and land reformer George Henry Evans wrote that the "slave to the Land-Lord and capitalist class is in a worse, aye a *worse* condition than the slave who has a master of his own."[19] Some working-class activists went even further, denouncing abolition—as Theophilus Fisk and Ely Moore did—as inimical to the interests of labor reform.[20]

"That solidarity between working-class and anti-slavery advocates did not materialize during the antebellum period," Timothy Helwig reminds us, "is well accepted." Indeed, Helwig continues, "labor advocates were often more concerned with the material conditions of northern workers than the plight of black chattel slaves in the south."[21] Following W. E. B. DuBois's groundbreaking 1935 *Black Reconstruction in America*, Roediger, Lott, and Alexander Saxton (among others) have established that racial ideologies impeded abolitionism from taking root as a principal tenet of white working-class political identity in both the South and the

North. "To ask workers to *sustain* comparisons of themselves and Black slaves," writes Roediger, "violated at once their republican pride and their sense of whiteness."[22]

Yet, a number of antebellum writers did insist that white workers would be promoting their own interests by recognizing their solidarity with black slaves and in turn becoming the foes of black chattel slavery. In his 1855 *My Bondage and My Freedom,* Frederick Douglass claims that there should exist a natural link between white workers and black slaves, especially in the South: "The difference between the white slave, and the black slave, is this: the latter belongs to *one* slaveholder, and the former belongs to *all* the slaveholders, collectively. The white slave has taken from him, by indirection, what the black slave has taken from him, directly, and without ceremony."[23] This similarity allows Douglass to hope for the development of solidarity between white southern workers and black slaves. The novelist George Lippard, both a self-professed abolitionist and a fellow traveler of working-class militants, frequently drew the worker/slave analogy in his fiction. In his very popular 1844 novel *The Quaker City,* the character Devil Bug dreams of an apocalyptic future in Philadelphia where "the slaves of the city, white and black"— "the slaves of the cotton Lord and the factory Prince"—assemble for the end of the world;[24] in later writings, as Helwig demonstrates, Lippard would use the figure of the white slave to imagine the need for solidarity between white workers and black slaves.[25] Walt Whitman, in his 1847 *Brooklyn Eagle* editorial "American Workingmen, Versus Slavery," calls on white workers to struggle against the spread of slavery to new territories acquired in the U.S.-Mexico War. "An honest poor mechanic, in a slave State," Whitman writes, "is put on a par with the negro mechanic." "The influence of the slavery institution," Whitman continues, "is to bring the dignity of labor down to the level of slavery."[26] Corollary to the idea that wage labor represents a form of slavery, then, was the argument that racial slavery degrades white workers in both the South and the North. In "American Workingmen, Versus Slavery," Whitman appeals to the belief that slavery siphons wealth away from white workers while simultaneously reducing the prestige of manual labor. Charles Nordhoff's 1865 pamphlet *America for Free Workingmen!* iterates this version of antislavery argument, laying bare the compromised racial politics of a certain strain of working-class abolition. "The slave-labor system gives to the capitalist many unjust advantages over the poor free workman,"

Nordhoff writes; in addition to giving "a dozen slave-owners, with a thousand slaves, as many votes in the Legislature . . . as is possessed by five hundred free workingmen," it also "gives to slave mechanics, slave shoemakers, slave blacksmiths, slave carpenters, slave wheelwrights, the labor, and to their wealthy masters the profits, which of right belong to the free workingman."[27] According to Nordhoff, Lincoln's aim was "not so much to free the slaves, as *to free the workingman*."[28] For Nordhoff, the problem with black slavery is that it robs white workers of wealth that is rightfully theirs; and, thus, Nordhoff's espousal of an abolitionist politics is qualified by his subordination of the plight of black slaves to that of white workers.

"Among the more ironic conjunctures of ante-bellum American history," writes Eric Foner, "is the fact that the expansion of capitalist labor relations evoked severe criticism from two very different quarters: the proslavery ideologues of the South and the labor movement of the North."[29] Crucially, apologists for slavery frequently deployed the figure of the "white slave": it was part and parcel of their argument that slavery is a more humane economic system than capitalism and that black slaves have it better than the "white slaves" of the North. This is a central line of reasoning in George Fitzhugh's *Sociology for the South, or the Failure of Free Society* (1854) and *Cannibals All! or, Slaves Without Masters* (1857). Under the *"laissez-faire* system," Fitzhugh writes in *Sociology for the South,* "a few individuals possessed of capital and cunning acquire a power to employ the laboring class on such terms as they please, and they seldom fail to use that power. Hence, the numbers and destitution of the poor in free society are daily increasing, the numbers of the middle or independent class diminishing, and the few rich men growing hourly richer."[30] Here is a strident version of anticapitalism rarely encountered in antebellum America. Capitalism is for Fitzhugh a system "that places all mankind in antagonistic positions, and puts all society at war" (23). And capitalism is "especially injurious to the poorer class," he writes, "for besides the labor necessary to support the family, the poor man is burdened with the care of finding a home, and procuring employment, and attending to all domestic wants and concerns" (27). Slavery, on the other hand, is a boon to the slave: slavery, Fitzhugh says, "relieve[s] the laborer of many of the cares of household affairs, and protect[s] and support[s] him in sickness and old age, besides preventing the too great reduction of wages by redundancy of labor and free competition" (28).

For Fitzhugh, wageworkers are the real slaves: "The profits which capital extracts from labor makes free laborers slaves," he writes in *Cannibals All*, "without the rights, privileges, or advantages of domestic slaves."[31]

Fitzhugh was not alone in making arguments like these. The notion that white wageworkers in the North have it worse than black slaves in the South appears without fail in a number of so-called anti-Tom novels, which sought to undercut the abolitionist message of Stowe's *Uncle Tom's Cabin*. One primary strategy of these novels was to portray northern capitalism as highly exploitative of white workers and southern slavery in turn as benignly paternalistic. Charles Jacobs Peterson's 1852 *The Cabin and the Parlor; or, Slaves and Masters* anticipates Fitzhugh's arguments about capitalism and capitalists, especially in the following dialogue:

> "You make out the slave," said Mr. Sharpe, surlily, "to be no worse off than the white man."
>
> "Comparisons of that sort are not the true way of putting it. All general, arbitrary assertions are apt to mislead. The slave, be his condition as it may, *is* worse off than you, or me, Mr. Sharpe, or than any free white man, who has either a business, or a fortune, to place him above reasonable fear or want, and save him, therefore, from the anxieties of poverty. But I fear that the average condition of the mere operative, who lives on his daily wages, is not a bit better relatively than that of the slave. The worst huts I ever saw human beings inhabiting, in this country, I saw, some years ago, at the Summit Hill coal-mines. We have nothing so bad at the South."
>
> "Oh! I have never been there. But the workmen are low Irish, I am told."
>
> "They are men and brothers though, to use your own phrase: and certainly a more intellectual race than the African; as good as we are indeed. Yet a net-work of circumstances, which begins weaving at their birth, and goes on till their death, makes them, and every other penniless operative, virtually, though not in name, the slave of the capitalist. What, did a Northern manufacturer tell me, just before I sailed for Europe? I was asking him how the new revenue law, then just passed, would affect him: and his answer was, that the reduction of duty would drive his goods out of the market, unless he could manufacture them cheaper: but this, he continued, he should do. And

how? we asked. By cutting down wages, was his reply. And he did cut them down."

"Perfectly right," growled Mr. Sharpe. "The law of supply and demand. Nothing wrong about that."

"Except that it reduces the mere operative to be virtually the slave of the capitalist," said Walworth, scornfully. "And there is no concealing, gentlemen, that this is his real condition, the world over, call him by what name you will."[32]

The male protagonist of Caroline's Hentz's 1854 *The Planter's Northern Bride* harbors Fitzhugh-esque thoughts about the plight of white wageworkers respective to the plight of black slaves:

In the mean time Moreland waded through a deep current of thought, that swelled as it rolled, and oft times it was turbid and foaming, and sometimes it seemed of icy chillness. He was a man of strong intellect and strong passions; but the latter, being under the control of principle, gave force and energy and warmth to a character which, if unrestrained, they would have defaced and laid waste. He was a searcher after truth, and felt ready and brave enough to plunge into the cold abyss, where it is said to be hidden, or to encounter the fires of persecution, the thorns of prejudice, to hazard everything, to suffer everything, rather than relinquish the hope of attaining it. He pondered much on the condition of mankind, its inequalities and wrongs. He thought of the poor and subservient in other lands, and compared them with our own. He thought of the groaning serfs of Russia; the starving sons of Ireland; the squalid operatives of England, its dark, subterranean workshops, sunless abodes of want, misery, and sin, its toiling millions, doomed to drain their hearts' best blood to add to the splendours and luxuries of royalty and rank; of the free hirelings of the North, who, as a *class,* travail in discontent and repining, anxious to throw off the yoke of servitude, sighing for an equality which exists only in name; and then he turned his thoughts homeward, to the enslaved children of Africa, and, taking them as a *class,* as a *distinct race* of beings, he came to the irresistible conclusion, that they were the happiest *subservient* race that were found on the face of the globe. He did not seek to disguise to himself the evils which were inseparably connected with their condition, or that man too oft abused the power he owned; but in view of all this, in view of the great, commanding truth, that wherever civilized man exists, there is the dividing line of the high and the low, the rich and the poor, the thinking and the labouring, in view of the God-proclaimed fact that "all Creation toileth and groaneth together," and that labour and suffering are the solemn sacraments of life, he believed that the slaves of the South were blest beyond the pallid slaves of Europe, or the anxious, care-worn labourers of the North.[33]

And the following moment from Caroline E. Rush's 1852 *The North and the South; or, Slavery and its Contrasts* is particularly revelatory of the way "anti-Tom" novels trade in sentimentalism to oppose abolition:

> God forbid that you should waste your sympathies on the slaves of the South. . . . Abolish slavery at the North;—the slavery of sewing women, and of the apprentice and bound girl system; and again, the slavery that holds in chains of adamant, that low, debauched, despised portion of our community, who, on account of their many crimes and their loathsome manner of living, have cast themselves out of the pale of society, but who are not the less the creatures of God; are not the less our brothers and sisters, are not the less, oh! abolitionist, according to thy code, born fee and equal with thyself.[34]

Stowe's *Dred* is very much a response to the anti-Tom novels, as virtually everyone who has written on this novel points out: it is, as it were, an anti-anti-Tom novel.[35] If anti-Tom novels insist that capitalism produces "white slaves," *Dred* rejoins that slavery severely degrades propertyless southern whites and turns them into slaves of sorts. But *Dred* also works to paint southern plantation elites as the enemies of the northern white working class as well.

DRED AND THE SLAVE-POWER CONSPIRACY

A formal device of slavery novels—both Stowe's novels and the anti-Tom novels—is the staging of debates between abolitionists and slave owners. This is one of the central means by which the authors of slavery novels organize and condense debates about slavery and thus seek to sway their readers' opinions. The poor whites of *Dred* are on more than one occasion the subject of debate between Nina Gordon (the heiress of a southern plantation who has returned to the South as an abolitionist after time in the North) and her proslavery aunt and uncle. For Nina and other advocates of abolition in *Dred,* white poverty as well as the unsavory attitudes and behaviors of poor whites are symptoms of slavery as an economic system. For Nina's aunt and uncle, in contrast, poor whites are at fault for their poverty, and economic elites should be endowed with more control over them. In fact, according to Nina's aunt and uncle, southern poor whites should be made slaves. "I always thought," says Aunt Nesbit, "there ought to be a law passed to make 'em all slaves" (105). Likewise, Uncle John says that planter elites "ought to have absolute sway over the working classes, just as the brain rules the hand. It must come to that, at last—no other arrangement is possible" (218).

Yet—and this is critical—Uncle John's opinions about white workers extend to workers in the North as well: "Now, people may talk as much as they please of the educated democracy of the north . . . *I* don't like 'em. What do working-men want of education?—Ruins 'em! I've heard of their learned blacksmiths bothering around, neglecting their work, to make speeches. I don't like such things. It raises them above their sphere. . . . To be sure, our poor whites are in a devil of a fix; but we haven't got 'em under yet. We shall get 'em in, one of these days, with our niggers, and then all will be contentment" (289). Here, the planter class is quite baldly the enemy of northern white workers. The planter class desires to turn poor whites in the South into not figurative but literal slaves, and it is also opposed to any northern working-class desires for greater economic, political, and social equality.

Dred thus deploys a version of what Bernard Mandel identified as working-class notions of "the slave-power conspiracy." According to working-class abolitionists, the "slave-power conspiracy" sought to "destroy the liberty of the American people in general and of the workers in particular." Working-class abolitionists insisted upon the "intrinsic hostility of slavery and the slaveholders to the working class."[36] As early as 1836, William Goodell argued that southern slavery aimed at "nothing more nor less than *the subjugation of the free laboring population of the non-slaveholding states* to a despotism no less appalling than that to which the laboring population of the south are now subjected."[37] A poem entitled "Men of Labor," and published in 1856—the same year as *Dred*—in the *Anti-Slavery Bugle,* speaks on behalf of white workers against the "slave-power conspiracy":

> Men of Labor, ho! the battle
> Calls to action, calls to arms;
> Shall your toil be free or fetter'd
> In your workshops, on your farms?
> Plough and loom, ringing anvil,
> Trowel, hammer, spade and hod—
> Shall they bear the curse of bondage,
> Or the Freedom born of God?
> Lo! 'tis yours to give the answer,
> Yours to say if Slavery's night
> Wider o'er this fair Republic
> Shall extend its awful blight—
> Blight to speech, and soil, and labor,
> Blight to all that lifts and saves
> Freemen—sovereigns in their freedom—
> From the grade and fate of slaves.[38]

According to Mandel, slaveholders "never actually said that the workers should be literally enslaved."[39] Yet, slaveholders in *Dred* do precisely this. Perhaps *Dred* thus radicalizes working-class notions about "the slave-power conspiracy"?

Abolitionist characters in *Dred* take a different view of things than do their proslavery interlocutors. "'I went up into New Hampshire, once,'" Nina Gordon tells her uncle, "'with Livy Ray, to spend a vacation. Livy's father is a famer; works part of every day with his own men; hoes, digs, plants; but he is Governor of the State. . . . There are no high and low *classes* there. Everybody works; and everybody seems to have a good time. . . . Seems to me this is better than making slaves of all the working classes, or having any working classes at all" (219). Here, *Dred* casts abolition as the desire for fundamental economic equality among whites—for what amounts to a classless world of independent, educated proprietors and entrepreneurs. Nina may be terribly naive in her assessment of the North as nearly without class, but she nonetheless expresses a desire for a United States without class.

All told, dialogues between pro- and antislavery characters in *Dred* thus function to solicit northern white labor's sympathies for the cause of abolition by portraying proslavery as anything but "white egalitarianism" (to use Alexander Saxton's term), and abolition as precisely this. What's more, Stowe's novel seeks to glue together—to forge a compromise between—abolition for abolition's sake and abolition for white labor's sake, using well-to-do white abolitionists as the hinge between these two versions of abolition. In the version of labor abolitionism we find in Walt Whitman's "American Workingmen, Versus Slavery," for instance, the plight of black slaves is essentially beside the point. In *Dred*, though, Nina Gordon and Edward Clayton desire in roughly equal measure abolition for black slaves and abolition on behalf of white workers.

Conversations between pro- and antislavery characters in *Dred* also provide a key for reading the anti-antiabolitionist behavior of *Dred*'s poor white characters. Toward the end of the novel, a "mob" of poor whites is mobilized by the novel's most nefarious slave owner, Tom Gordon, to attack outspoken abolitionist Edward Clayton. "To differentiate her novel as much as possible from those of her proslavery contemporaries," Susan Ryan aptly observes, "Stowe makes Tom Gordon, her chief villain, the antithesis of proslavery rhetoric's benevolent southern gentleman."[40] And Tom Gordon views black slaves and poor whites with equal contempt. Stowe's novel works to make clear that the poor whites who follow Tom Gordon are operating according to what amounts to false consciousness: they have, as Clayton's friend Russell puts its, "bandages" over their eyes (469). They have nothing to gain from their affiliation with slave owners except continued subordination. As Rowe notes, in *Dred* "southern racism and artificial class divisions prevent poor whites from recognizing their common cause with exploited slaves."[41]

Dred's plot of poor white anti-antislavery activity thus dramatizes what Stowe—and Frederick Douglass—were elsewhere theorizing to be the self-damaging dynamic of white, working-class, especially southern, racism in the 1850s. In "Poor White Trash," Stowe writes: "Singular as it may appear, though slavery is the cause of the misery and degradation of this class [of poor whites], yet they are the most vehement and ferocious advocates of slavery. The reason is this: They feel the scorn of the upper classes, and their only means of consolation is in having a class below them, whom they may scorn in turn. To set the negro at liberty would deprive them of this last comfort; and accordingly no class of men advo-

cate slavery with such frantic and unreasoning violence, or hate abolitionists with such demoniac hatred."[42] In *My Bondage and My Freedom*,
Douglass similarly explains how slave owners co-opt the political energies of white workers in the South: "The slaveholders," Douglass writes,
"with a craftiness peculiar to themselves, by encouraging the enmity of
the poor, laboring white against the blacks, succeeds [*sic*] in making the
said white man almost as much a slave as the black slave himself."[43] In
Dred, Southern poor whites have become, to use categories Douglass
first introduced in his 1845 *A Narrative of the Life*, slaves "in form" if not
"in fact."

If *Dred* deploys a version of the southern poor white to address potential working-class readers in the North, perhaps Stowe's novel asks
these readers to dis-identify with the novel's poor whites who have been
co-opted by proslavery forces and instead to identify with the novel's
insurgent black characters and white abolitionists.[44]

Dred and Capitalism

Nina Gordon and Edward Clayton desire, in roughly equal measure, abolition for black slaves and abolition on behalf of white workers, I wrote
earlier. With Stowe's *Dred*, then, something very important—something
not just on the level of theme but of morphology—has changed about
the U.S. novel. In earlier U.S. novels, as I have tried to demonstrate
throughout *The Illiberal Imagination*, characters that actively desire the
abolition of class are either minor characters that need to be taught that
their feelings and ideas about class are dangerous, or they are villains. In
Stowe's *Dred*, characters that actively desire the abolition of class are now
protagonists—are now heroes, are now a novel's moral center.[45]

Might *Dred* be anticapitalist, then, as well as antislavery? For Jennifer Greeson, Stowe does count as an anticapitalist writer. According to
Greeson, Stowe's *Uncle Tom's Cabin* "fully realizes the Slave South as the
dark satanic field of U.S. industrial modernity." *Uncle Tom's Cabin*, she
argues, "writes the dystopic visions of the modernizing national center
over the imaginative terrain of its Southern other" (172).[46] For Greeson, Simon Legree's plantation should be read, paradoxically enough,
as Stowe's representation of "Western industrialization": "Southern slave
law simply codifies and makes visible the equally despotic, but less trans-
parent, power asymmetry of the industrial capitalist order" (186). By

the same token, though, *Uncle Tom's Cabin* is, for Greeson, "decidedly elitist": Stowe's "description of the enslaved workers on Legree's planta-tion . . . eerily echoes the strong rhetoric of [her] preacher father, Lyman Beecher, on the perils posed to the social order by New England's urban poor" (188). While Greeson suggests that *Uncle Tom's Cabin's* critique of capitalism is limited, she nonetheless reads the novel, especially its final chapter, as a call to its readers to fight "the bad, Legree-style mastery of capitalist modernity, the fallen industrial condition that immediately surrounds them" in the North (189).

I would like to challenge this assessment of Stowe's attitudes toward capitalism, in large measure because *Dred* is anything but an attack on the North's economic system. In fact, *Dred* can be read as a participant in the containment of anticapitalist thought in the 1850s. While *Dred* works to solicit sympathy for poor whites and to paint proslavery as white la-bor's enemy, while the novel draws on, gives voice to, a certain strain of working-class abolitionism, *Dred* portrays class—"white slavery," or economic inequality and exploitation among whites—as fundamentally *southern*. Stowe is thus to be distinguished from the writers and activists in the 1840s and 1850s that combined abolitionism and anticapitalism.

According to Orestes Brownson, for instance, "the system of wages must be supplanted by some other system, or else one half of the human race must forever be the virtual slaves of the other" ("Labouring Classes" 13). John Pickering's 1847 *The Working Man's Political Economy* subsumes slavery under its radical critique of capitalism, railing against both. In the 1840s, George Henry Evans also inveighed against both slavery and capitalism.[47] "Robert Dale, Albert Brisbane, and Horace Greeley," Philip Foner points outs, "opposed not only Negro slavery but all forms of slav-ery."[48] In 1845 the statement of 25,000 New York workingmen signaled their assent to a combination of anticapitalism and abolition:

> To slavery in the abstract, slavery in the concrete, to slavery absolute, slavery feudal, and the slavery of wages; to slavery where it is, and where it is not; from the first Israelite who leaned his ear against the door, and was pierced with his master's awl to the last son of Adam who shall wear the badge to servitude; to Slavery we are utterly op-posed under every phase and modification, and so with firm and sol-emn purpose will remain until our lives end.[49]

Stowe is likewise to be distinguished from a novelist like Lippard, who in his 1844 *The Quaker City; or, The Monks of Monk Hall* had already conjured a dystopian future for the United States defined by "slavery" in both North and South. Again, Devil-Bug dreams of the last days of Philadelphia:

> Then came the slaves of the city, white and black, marching along one mass of rags and sores and misery, huddled together; a goodly tail to the procession of the King. Chains upon each wrist and want upon each brow. Here they were, the slaves of the cotton Lord and the factory Prince; above their heads a loom of iron, rising like a gibbet in the air, and by their sides the grim overseer. . . . So they went trooping by the slaves of the cotton Lord, and the factory Prince. And at their sides, and among their ranks, walked the unseen forms of the shrouded dead.[50]

But for a writer like Stowe in the 1850s, the North needed to be seen as classless; otherwise, the North's superiority was in question, and the United States might be headed toward not just one but two upheavals.

If *Dred* suggests that white workers in the North have reason to league themselves with the cause of abolition, *Dred* refuses to recognize class inequality among whites as a salient feature of the North. Nina's suggestion that the North has escaped class is symptomatic, I would argue, of the deeper ideological worldview given expression by Stowe's novel: here, capitalism is not a system predicated on exploitation and tending toward inequality among whites. Though *Dred* counters anti-Tom novels with its representation of white poverty in the South, *Dred* insinuates that the only true enemy of poor whites in both the South and the North is chattel slavery. This is because the novel suggests that whites in the North are essentially beyond class, imperiled only by the southern elites who would rob them of their supposed freedom and equality. *Dred* quite literally has no space for working-class critiques of class in the U.S. North.

It is worth noting here that protests against white slavery need not have meant anticapitalism. Roediger argues that the very term "*white slavery*" may have been a way of eliding the issue of wage labor—and capitalism—altogether: *white slavery*, Roediger writes, "itself admitted solutions short of an attack on the wage system."[51] "During the 1850s," writes Schocket, "northern political and economic discourse was singularly unable to account for or critique class segmentation in terms of class itself"[52]—which is to say, to explain and take aim at class inequality among whites as a symptom of "free," wage labor relations, of capitalism and the asymmetric accumulation/distribution of resources it may entail. Indeed, some writers who were sympathetic to abolition suggested that "wage slavery" was in fact inescapable. "What of it," Ishmael asks in the first chapter of Herman Melville's *Moby-Dick,* "if some old hunks of a sea-captain orders me to get a broom and sweep down the decks? What does that indignity amount to, weighed, I mean, in the scales of the New Testament? Do you think the archangel Gabriel thinks anything the less of me, because I promptly and respectfully obey that old hunks in that particular instance? Who ain't a slave? Tell me that."[53] Ishmael here simultaneously invokes and neutralizes the figure of the white wage slave. Ishmael may understand himself to be a kind of slave, but he paradoxically signals his consent to his enslavement. He construes slavery as a universal and inescapable condition: "[H]owever the old sea-captains may order me about—however they may thump and punch me about, I have the satisfaction of knowing that it is all right; that everybody else is one way or other served in much the same way—either in a physical or metaphysical point of view, that is; and so the universal thump is passed round, and all hands should rub each other's shoulder-blades, and be content."[54]

Yet, unlike Ishmael, the majority of abolitionists as well as proponents of "free labor ideology" insisted that wage labor should not be construed as slavery.[55] "The *National Anti-Slavery Standard,* official organ of the American Anti-Slavery Society," Philip Foner teaches us, "declared in 1847 that no true Abolitionist could have any sympathy for those who denounced wage slavery as an evil."[56] "One could argue that the antislavery movement," writes Eric Foner, "by glorifying northern society and by isolating slavery as an unacceptable form of labor exploitation, while refusing to condemn the exploitative aspects of 'free' labor relations, served to justify the emerging capitalist order of the North."[57] Indeed, prominent northern economists argued that the North's economy—that capitalism—was fundamentally devoid of and immune to significant class division among whites. According to Henry C. Carey, the prominent economist and ally of abolition, the North was already in the 1850s an essentially classless society. In his 1854 "The North and South" (which first appeared in the *New York Tribune*), Carey writes:

> The great issue of out day is, as we are informed by the Charleston *Evening News,* "the extension or non-extension, of the institution of [slavery] whose foundations are broad and solid in our midst." It is whether free labor shall become slave labor, or slave labor become free labor. At the South, we see a body of great land-owners surrounded by slaves who work for them, while they themselves live upon the profits derived from standing between the men who work to produce cotton, sugar, and tobacco, and those other men who require to consume those commodities. At the North, on the contrary, we see the whole surface of the country divided among a body of small land-owners, unequalled in the world for number, all working for themselves.[58]

Again, Jeffrey Sklansky tells us that according to Carey, the "free development of market relations . . . would transform North and South into a single-class society of independent entrepreneurs."[59]

The representation of northern capitalism as beyond class was something of a reaction formation. It was a defense against attacks on wage labor and northern capitalism by proslavery writers, a defense mounted even from abolitionist figures that in the 1840s were critical of capitalism. "In fact," writes Eric Foner, "it is possible that the growing ideological conflict between the sections had the effect of undermining a tradition of radical criticism within northern society. Men like Horace Greeley, highly critical of certain aspects of their society in the 1840s, became more and more uncritical when faced with the need to defend the North against southern assaults. The choices for America came to be defined as a free society versus a slave society—the idea of alternatives within free society was increasingly lost sight of."[60] Proslavery's takeover of the critique of capitalism in the 1850s may very well have disabled a more robust critical vision of U.S. socioeconomic life, but if Carey is any indication, it also changed the tenor of what bourgeois writers were saying about socioeconomic life in the North. In two decades, we have traveled quite far from James Fenimore Cooper's insistence in *The American Democrat* that class division must exist so long as there is private property. Indeed, with Carey in the 1850s we begin to see quite clearly the disavowal of permanent economic inequality within capitalism, and with this disavowal, an insistence on individual mobility as definitive of socioeconomic life under capitalism.

Dred manifests, as it were, the dialectical process by which class comes to be disavowed in the North under the pressure of southern critiques of northern economic life: Nina Gordon's comments in *Dred* about New Hampshire echo Carey, and they are motivated by slaveholder critiques of the North. By positing the capitalist North as tending toward classlessness, Nina—and Stowe's novel more broadly, I want to argue—suggest that the emancipation of labor in black skin is not merely a *first step* toward the emancipation of labor in white skin. Rather, Stowe's novel supposes that the emancipation of labor in black skin spells the emancipation from class of those with white skin.

PLOTTING CLASSLESSNESS IN *DRED*

That *Dred* figures class inequality among whites as essentially a symptom of southern racial slavery is evident in the subplot of Fanny Cripps, one of *Dred*'s poor southern whites. Fanny's story may seem minor to a novel "about" slavery, but the novel ends with Fanny—and thereby endows her story with extra significance.[61] *Dred* should be read, I want to suggest, as an especially striking example of a novel in which the ending performs an enormous amount of ideological work.

Fanny is the daughter of Sue Peyton and John Cripps. Her mother "had come from a distant branch of one of the most celebrated families in Virginia"—but this branch has descended into poverty (89). Her father was "the son of a small farmer of North Carolina," but because his father had "been so unfortunate as to obtain possession of a few negroes, the whole family became ever after inspired with an intense disgust for all kinds of labor" (89). Nina Gordon is sympathetic to Fanny's plight, and in large measure Fanny motivates Nina's early comments about caring for and elevating poor southern whites. When Fanny's mother dies, Fanny's father marries "one of the lowest of that class of poor whites whose wretched condition is not among the least of the evils of slavery" (400). At this point, Fanny is rescued from her poor white father and stepmother by Tiff, the loyal slave of Fanny's mother. Tiff absconds with Fanny and her brother Teddy to Dred's community in the swamp. In the swamp, Dred "symbolically creates a multiracial—African American, mulatto, white—community with its own laws and religious values as a utopian alternative to the corrupt slavocracy."[62] And this utopian, antislavery community helps to make possible Fanny's escape from poverty: here, radical black abolitionism is very much the ally of the poor southern white.

Yet, wealthy white benefactors are also integral to Fanny's ultimate escape from poverty. Indeed, in *Dred*, poor whites do not emancipate themselves from poverty: instead, they are rescued from poverty by wealthy whites. Edward Clayton bankrolls the trip of Fanny—as well as her brother and a number of slaves—to the North (539). Once in the North, Fanny and Teddy in turn become the heirs of their mother's sister, "a maiden lady of very singular character, who, by habits of great penuriousness, had amassed a large fortune, apparently for no other purpose than that it should, some day, fall into the hands of somebody who would know how to enjoy it" (543). That the northern branch of the Peyton family has not descended into poverty is itself indicative of Stowe's notions about the difference between North and South. Early in *Dred*, Stowe insists that "gradual decay . . . has conducted many an old Virginian family to poverty and ruin. Slave labor, of all others the most worthless and profitless, had exhausted the first vigor of the soil, and the proprietors gradually degenerated from those habits of energy which were called forth by the necessities of the first settlers" (37). According to Stowe's narrator, white fortunes in the South are lost because of slavery; in the North, in contrast, they are made. Having inherited her aunt's wealth and under Clayton's guardianship, Fanny is "placed at one of the best New England schools"; her brother, too, is "placed at school in the same town" (543).

At the end of *Dred*, Fanny and her brother are found living in "a little Gothic cottage, a perfect gem of rural irregularity and fanciful beauty" (547). Teddy is now a college student. Fanny, for her part, is set to marry. According to Amy Schrager Lang, 1850s sentimental novels such as Maria Cummins's *The Lamplighter* are "narratives not of advancement but of recovery, not of mobility but of inheritance."[63] On some level, this narrative grammar organizes Fanny's plot in *Dred*. But though Fanny's plot might be read in terms of "the reconstitution of a lost gentility"[64] (and though Fanny's loyal slave Tiff certainly reads it this way [548]), Fanny moves in the North into the middle class more than she returns to gentility.

In anti-Tom novels, poor whites who travel to the North become exploited wage slaves. In *Dred,* class does remain a salient feature of northern socioeconomic life, but only insofar as it is figured in terms of race. The black slaves who have escaped to the North become wageworkers. Yet these now-free blacks are comfortable and contented in their new roles (542–43), revealing that Stowe, unlike Harriet Wilson in *Our Nig* (1859), is not interested in the potential perils of "free labor" for free blacks in the North.[65] By the same token, *Dred* insists that southern poor whites who escape to the North are no longer subject to economic inequality among whites: Fanny and Teddy appear, in the concluding chapter of the novel, to have escaped altogether from class inequality among whites. Not insignificantly, the "large fortune" Fanny's aunt has bequeathed to Fanny was "amassed" by "great penuriousness"—and not via the exploitation of others' labors (543). All told, Fanny's subplot insinuates that the North is without meaningful class divisions *among whites.* The moment Fanny arrives in the North, class becomes a thing of the past for her. Again, Stowe's *Dred* departs from the cultural logic— the commitment to class—of earlier U.S. novels, but not in the direction of a radical critique of the economy in the U.S. North. In so doing, *Dred* reveals that the illiberal imagination has come to a close, at least for the time being.

Conclusion

*T*he *Illiberal Imagination* has ventured three interrelated arguments. They are, in a nutshell: first, the U.S. novel has from its
beginning been "about" class; second, early U.S. novels "about" class
are to be read as rejoinders to emergent forms of oppositional political
economy; and, third, through the 1840s the U.S. novel does not hide
class—but, rather, works to naturalize it.

In making these arguments, I have been picking a bone with "the
liberal tradition"—with an understanding of American literary history wherein class does not, cannot, matter. As I noted in the introduction, I'm not the first to pick this particular bone. One of my hopes,
though, is that the case I've made for the significance of class to the *early*
nineteenth-century U.S. novel, in addition to being convincing in its
own right—in addition, that is, to helping those of us who work on early
nineteenth-century U.S. literature rethink its defining "issues"—helps
those of us who are interested in the entanglements of class and U.S.
literature to recognize that *early* U.S. literature, too, is our turf, should
be our turf.

But I'd like lay bare now, finally, that my arguments here are also in
conversation with a foundational (and, to me, quite influential) Marxian account of the nineteenth-century *European* novel. And I'd like to
conclude by airing out how the way I have read for class "in" early U.S.
fiction—a way of reading which is (to get a bit ahead of myself here)
made possible by how class is in fact "in" the early U.S. novel—relates
to two activities that have recently (and, once again) caught some flak:
"symptomatic reading" and "critique."

WHICH CLASSES?

If for the "the liberal tradition" the nineteenth-century U.S. novel is about anything but class, according to Marxian thinkers the nineteenth-century European novel is (of course) all about class. In *The Historical Novel*, Georg Lukács argued that the nineteenth-century European historical novel inherited from the Enlightenment a "historical awareness of the decisive role played in human progress by the struggles of classes in history."[1] The nineteenth-century European historical novel itself, Lukács contends, narrates history in terms of class struggle—*as* class struggle. Yet, and this is crucial, for Lukács the classes that really matter before 1848—both to European history and to the European historical novel— are not the bourgeoisie and the proletariat; rather, the struggle that defines European history and gives shape to European fiction (historical and otherwise) before 1848 is the struggle between the bourgeoisie and the aristocracy, largely because the proletariat had yet to develop, according to Lukács, a genuinely radical sense of itself and of its role in history. And, for Lukács, it is only after 1848 that the European novel's function becomes waging a reactionary war against the proletariat.[2] That the classes that matter to early nineteenth-century European fiction are the bourgeoisie and the aristocracy—that the struggle animating early nineteenth-century European literature is the struggle between the bourgeoisie and the aristocracy—is, I think, something of a truism for Marxian studies of European fiction.[3]

Is Lukács right about which classes matter to early nineteenth-century European fiction? Might the early nineteenth-century European novel, just as much as the late nineteenth-century European novel, be conceived of as participating primarily in a conflict between bourgeoisie and proletariat? These are questions that would take me far afield of the literary historical purview of *The Illiberal Imagination*. I invoke Lukács (and the historical narrative of European political and cultural development on which he hangs his analysis of the European novel), however, in order to emphasize that my arguments here are, though clearly influenced by a Marxian tradition, also an attempt to revise Marxian literary historical commonplaces about not just where—but also *when*—class struggle between bourgeoisie and proletariat enters the history of the novel. My revision has required adopting what might be called flexible definitions of "the proletariat" as well as "class consciousness." It has required accepting that William Manning counts—or, that Cornelius Blatchly counts, or Thomas Skidmore does—in the history of "the proletariat" and the history of "class consciousness." But once we grant as much, and once we recognize that these figures and the versions of class politics for which they stand also matter to the history of the early U.S. novel, a new literary historical narrative emerges. Indeed, what we can then see is that the U.S. novel turns on the confrontation between the bourgeoisie and the economically marginal—between the bourgeoisie and hostility "from below" to the bourgeois order of things—as early as, if not earlier than, the European novel begins to do so. The U.S. novel does not lag behind the European novel. Perhaps it's the opposite.

For Critique

The stakes here have thus been in part historiographical. But this book is also, at least implicitly, a book about literary interpretation, insofar as it has made an argument about how to read novels—insofar as it has engaged in reading for a particular "issue" in a particular historical phase of the U.S. novel. By arguing that the early U.S. novel is indeed "about" class, *The Illiberal Imagination* has modeled a practice of reading for class that perhaps parts ways with what gets called "symptomatic reading." Yet, it stands as an argument, nonetheless, for "critique."

As defined by Stephen Best and Sharon Marcus, symptomatic reading "encompasses an interpretative method that argues that the most interesting aspect of a text is what it represses"—a method that, though originating with Freud, Marx, and Althusser, is perhaps best exemplified in the field of literary criticism by Jameson's *The Political Unconscious.*[4] *The Political Unconscious* is indeed a programmatic statement on behalf of reading for "what the text represses."[5] "Interpretation proper," Jameson writes, "always presupposes, if not a conception of the unconscious itself, then at least some mechanism of mystification or repression in terms of which it would make sense to seek a latent meaning behind a manifest one, or to rewrite the surface categories of a text in the stronger language of a more fundamental interpretative code" (60).

Moreover, for Jameson, class struggle is itself part of the "latent meaning" of nineteenth-century realism, an important element of what nineteenth-century realism represses, and thus part of what it is the job of the critic to make manifest—to make visible. "It is detecting the traces of [the] uninterrupted narrative [of class struggle]," Jameson writes, "in restoring to the surface of the text the repressed and buried reality of this fundamental history, that the doctrine of a political unconscious finds its function and its necessity" (20). According to the program of symptomatic reading (granting that this is really the right name for the method Jameson lays out), to read for class in the literary text is to read for how—but also to what end—the literary text *hides* class conflict within itself. It is not only to identify that the literary text does in fact hide class conflict but also to argue that the literary text does its most important ideological work with respect to class—that the literary text participates in class conflict—*precisely by hiding* class conflict, by concealing it, or by displacing it into other categories. We are encouraged to map how the literary text that is not apparently about class conflict nonetheless participates in class conflict. We are primed, in other words, to be on the lookout for how the literary text rejects a social ontology that defines the social in terms of class conflict.

The Illiberal Imagination has argued that we can read early U.S. novels as expressions of—but also attempts to manage—an underlying contradiction (namely, class itself). I have been suggesting, to put it another way, that that what makes certain early U.S. novels "interesting" is what these novels work "to repress"—or, better, work *to suppress:* in a phrase, emergent forms of class consciousness. Thus have I sought, on the one hand, to document (and to describe) forms of oppositional political economy in the early United States and, on the other, to highlight that early U.S. novels go to lengths to argue, as it were, against these forms of oppositional political economy. Here, a central vocation of the early U.S. novel is checking forms of thinking not only according to which class exists in the United States but also according to which the relationship between classes is one of conflict and according to which class is unjust—and, thus, according to which the U.S. socioeconomic order should be fundamentally transformed. And early U.S. novels check oppositional political economy, I have argued, in one of two ways. Either they teach us that disaffection with class inequality breeds dangerous desires and unleashes dangerous behaviors (this is the lesson of Brackenridge's *Modern Chivalry* and of Cooper's Littlepage trilogy, where economic egalitarians would abrogate what these novels calls "liberty"); or, they teach us that class inequality is itself good for individuals, and that classes should not be thought of as fundamentally antagonistic (this is the lesson of Brown's Philadelphia novels and Sedgwick's *The Poor Rich Man* and *Live and Let Live,* novels in which poverty enables individual development and in which there are bonds between poor and rich). All told, early U.S. novels teach their readers not to take oppositional political economy, in a word, seriously.

Yet, I have also thus argued that early U.S. novels are (as the word "teach" above flags) to be read as didactic, especially where class is concerned. I have argued that early U.S. novels do not precisely *hide* oppositional political economy. They allude directly to it. They acknowledge its very existence. In this, they take it quite seriously (albeit in a different sense). Moreover, I've tried to show that early U.S. novels argue against oppositional political economy quite loudly. Another one of my hopes is that this book will help us to acknowledge (if we haven't already) that ideas about class—that arguments against oppositional political economy—are in fact quite pronounced, quite explicit, rather than unspoken or masked, in early U.S. novels. Or, alternatively: I hope to have shown that varieties of bourgeois class ideology are out in the open, so to speak, in early U.S. novels. What is also "interesting" about the early U.S. novels in this study, then, is that class and ideological positions about class are not "latent subtext" so much as "manifest content" in them. We find this stuff on, well, "the surface" of early U.S. novels. I have sought "to unveil" the class politics of the early U.S. novel, and not really "to unmask" them.[6]

Just as symptomatic reading has come under fire, critique in general has been called into question.[7] Symptomatic reading and critique may be one and the same; both may be instantiations of what Paul Ricoeur called "the hermeneutics of suspicion"—or, of the assumption that the text conceals its true meaning, and that interpretation proper (to use Jameson's phrase above) entails the discovery of this occluded, encrypted meaning.[8] But critique is also a mode of reading whose fundamental question is: What is the relationship between the literary text and structures of power (of dominance and exploitation) beyond the literary text? Or, alternatively: To what extent is the literary text complicit in those structures of power? The watchword of critique is Walter Benjamin's oft-quoted hypothesis that there "is no document of civilization which is not at the same time a document of barbarism."[9]

I'll end by acknowledging what should already be clear: though it isn't perhaps fair to describe this book as an exercise in what gets called symptomatic reading, this book has been written (arguing as it does for the complicity of the early U.S. novel in class) with an abiding commitment to critique. The impetus behind critique often is, it seems to me, utopian desire.[10] Perhaps critique helps to keep utopian desire alive.

Notes

Introduction

1. Trilling, *The Liberal Imagination*, 260–61.

2. Ibid., 262; my emphasis.

3. Writes Hartz: "The Americans, though models to all the world of the middle class way of life, lacked the passionate middle class consciousness which saturated the liberal thought of Europe. . . . A triumphant middle class . . . can take itself for granted. This point, curiously enough, is practically never discussed, though the failure of the American working class to become class conscious has been a theme of endless interest. And yet the relationship between the two suggests itself at once. Marx himself used to say that the bourgeoisie was the great teacher of the proletariat" (*The Liberal Tradition*, 51, 52). According to Hartz, "the master assumption of American political thought" is "the reality of atomistic social freedom" (62). Daniel Rodgers aptly summarizes Hartz's theory of American history: "Without a feudal past, the inner dialectical engine of history had no purchase [in the United States]. No Robespierre, no de Maistre, no Marx, no Goebbels, no Stalin, only . . . eternal Locke" ("Exceptionalism," 29).

4. As Andrew Lawson points out, Trilling's book—and the same could be said of Hartz's *The Liberal Tradition*—was exemplary of a "liberal vision of a classless America that was adopted by the founding fathers of American studies in the 1950s, inflected by the Cold War rhetoric of American exceptionalism" (introduction, 2).

5. Writes Amy Schrager Lang: "It has been argued that, however 'real' the structure of class in America, Americans have no 'native discourse' of class in which to render their experience of that structure. Lacking a vocabulary, as it were, in which to express the experience of class—its complacencies, as well as its injuries and its struggles—and deeply committed, moreover, to liberal individualism and the promise of open mobility, Americans displace the reality of class into discourses of race, gender, ethnicity, and other similarly 'locked-in' categories of individual identity" (*The Syntax of Class*, 6).

6. Macpherson, *The Political Theory*, 48.

7. The recent scholarship with ramifications for the question of whether "liberalism" captures what we find in early and antebellum literature is vast. We can, though, identify two major trends in this scholarship. First, scholars have recovered the centrality of residual "republicanism" to early U.S. political thought and literature. Karen Weyler argues, for instance, that the early U.S. novel does not express "wholly liberal ideology"; instead, "the novel as a genre sought ways to accommodate the tenets of liberalism, especially economic individualism, without compromising the individual virtue so esteemed by republicanism" (*Intricate Relations*, 19). Likewise, contending that the opposition of republicanism and liberalism is itself incoherent, Stephen Shapiro tells us that "liberalism is an overly expansive term that does not adequately delimit the leading traits of capitalist activity in the phase between early modern merchant capital and nineteenth-century industrial capitalism"—or, of the ideology we find in early U.S. novels (*The Culture and Commerce*, 14–15, 19). Second, scholars have identified how middle-class fiction in the 1840s and 1850s identifies selfhood not with the market so much as with extramarket locations and activities. Gillian Brown and Lori Merish have demonstrated that antebellum domestic fiction construed not the market but the feminized, sentimental space of the middle-class home as the domain of individual autonomy and freedom—for women as well as men. According to Brown, while for Macpherson "market society's construction of self" aligns the self "with market relations such as exchange value, alienability, circulation, and competition," antebellum domestic fiction instead imagines "the private domain of individuality apart from the marketplace" (Brown, *Domestic Individualism*, 2, 3). Paradoxically enough, "domesticity signifies the feminization of selfhood in service to an individualism available to (white) men" (7). Likewise, Merish contends that domestic sentimental fiction constituted "middle-class subjectivity" in terms of "an intimate emotional engagement with domestic possessions"; the version of the middle-class subject organizing sentimental domestic fiction is not to be confused, Merish argues, with "the prototypical liberal subject," who is "rational and calculating economic man," but instead is to be thought of primarily as "not a producer but a consumer, whose emotional complexity and refinement—her 'inner wealth'—are secured and elaborated through 'object relations,' through caring involvement with a select group of objects" (*Sentimental Materialism*, 116). For Merish, "Liberalism has supplied an emotional and sentimental, as well as a rational and utilitarian, justification for private property, in which the protection of one's economic assets is underwritten not so much by a right to self-interested and rational profit-making as by an imperative to enjoy one's intimate belongings at length with the confidence of secure proprietorship" (117).

8. On the antebellum novel and middle-class identity formation, see, e.g., Brodhead, "Sparing the Rod"; G. Brown, *Domestic Individualism*; and Pfister, *The Production of Personal Life*.

9. As Lang explains, "The novel is generally taken to be the definitive literary

genre of the 'middle class' by virtue of its focus on individual self-making in the fluid social universe generated by a market economy, even in those American narratives where that enterprise is thwarted by the impact of racial and gender inequality" (*The Syntax of Class*, 9).

10. Ibid.

11. No theory of the nineteenth-century U.S. novel more brutally argues for its middle classness than Myra Jehlen's "The Novel and the Middle Class in America." If in Europe "the rise of the . . . insurgent middle class is associated with an attack on . . . static absolutism," Jehlen argues, in the U.S. middle-class culture was always already "dominant," always already "able to co-opt alternative and oppositional forms [of culture and politics] with unusual effectiveness, to the point of appearing to preclude even their possibility" (128, 127). For Jehlen, nineteenth-century U.S. literature is thus always an expression of liberalism and liberal individualism.

12. Class has been crucial to accounts of late eighteenth-century U.S. literature, if by class we mean middle-class values. Stephen Shapiro, for example, has argued that late eighteenth-century U.S. fiction "expresses a particular set of middle-class interests (*The Culture and Commerce*, 4). I am interested, instead, in how the middle-class novel—from its beginning—wages a battle against emergent forms of class protest as opposed to residual forms of feudalist ideology. On the early U.S. novel as antifeudalist, see, e.g., Fliegelman's *Prodigals and Pilgrims*, 36–66. On "emergent" and "dominant" in literary historical analysis, see Williams, *Marxism and Literature*, 121–27.

13. Just over thirty years ago, Michael Gilmore wrote: "Class as a thematic concern or formal consideration [in U.S. literary studies], once the obligatory nod has been made, usually recedes into the background, if it does not vanish altogether" ("Hawthorne," 215). Over the last three decades, however, this tendency has been challenged. Michael Denning's *Mechanic Accents*, Eric Lott's *Love and Theft*, and Shelly Streeby's *American Sensations* probe the vexed politics of working-class antebellum literature and culture. William Dow's *Narrating Class in American Fiction*, Gavin Jones's *American Hungers*, Lang's *The Syntax of Class*, Andrew Lawson's *Walt Whitman* and *Downwardly Mobile*, Lance Newman's *Our Common Dwelling*, and Eric Schocket's *Vanishing Moments* unveil how "classic" as well as now forgotten best-selling nineteenth-century writers negotiated the paradox of economic inequality and the challenges of working-class militancy.

14. Sylvia Jenkins Cook's *Working Women, Literary Ladies* zeroes in on the 1840s. Nicholas K. Bromell's *By the Sweat of the Brow*, Carolyn R. Maibor's *Labor Pains*, and Cindy Weinstein's *The Literature of Labor*—which all unpack the literary representation of work in nineteenth-century American literature— focus on "American Renaissance" writers (and, in the case of Weinstein, postbellum writers). Lawson's *Walt Whitman* and Newman's *Our Common Dwelling* offer in-depth engagements with the class politics of the writings of individual American Renaissance authors. Amal Amireh's *The Factory Girl* reaches back

to the 1820s, but (with the exception of Catharine Maria Sedgwick's *The Poor Rich Man*) Amireh's study treats novels from the 1840s and later. In *American Hungers,* Jones begins his study of the literary representation of economic deprivation in the 1840s. In *Labor's Text,* an encyclopedic study of the representation of workers in American fiction, Laura Hapke also begins her story in the late 1840s. Dow's *Narrating Class* starts in the 1850s (with Walt Whitman's *Leaves of Grass*). Lang's *The Syntax of Class* treats novels only from the 1850s and 1860s. The earliest literary artifact that merits sustained attention in Schocket's superb *Vanishing Moments,* a critique of the politics of cross-class representation in nineteenth- and early twentieth-century U.S. literature, is Rebecca Harding Davis's 1855 *Life in the Iron-Mills.*

15. Blumin, *The Emergence of the Middle Class,* 9–10.

16. Locke's "whole theory of property," writes Macpherson, "is a justification of the natural right not only to unequal property but to unlimited individual appropriation" (*The Political Theory,* 221). According to Macpherson, Locke's notion of "civil society" comes into being "to protect unequal possessions, which have already in the state of nature given rise to unequal rights" (231).

17. Hugh Henry Brackenridge, *Modern Chivalry,* 303; hereafter cited in the text.

18. Catharine Maria Sedgwick, *The Poor Rich Man, and the Rich Poor Man,* 111; hereafter cited in the text.

19. "Mobility changes the experience of class," Schocket has explained, "but it does not make it go away" (*Vanishing Moments,* 16). I return to this cogent formulation in chap. 3.

20. Barthes, *Mythologies,* 129.

21. "According to the best estimates, the share of national wealth held by the richest 10 percent jumped, mainly after 1820, from the 49.6 percent of 1774 to reach 73 percent by 1860. The richest 1 percent more than doubled their share from 12.6 percent to 29 percent. . . . Capitalist development widened inequality in consumption as well as income. While the conveniences and luxuries of the well-to-do became cheaper and better under increasing applications of capital and technology, poor people's labor-intensive necessities of food, clothing, firewood, and shelter became relatively more expensive" (Sellers, *The Market Revolution,* 238).

22. This is not to say the nineteenth-century U.S. novel was constitutionally incapable of protesting class inequality in the United States. We might discover precisely this with Lippard's *The Quaker City* (1844) or a novel such as Herman Melville's *Pierre; or, the Ambiguities* (1852).

23. Franco Moretti: "In every age, different and even mutually conflicting symbolic forms coexist" (*Signs Taken for Wonders,* 16).

24. Again, Moretti: "Formal patterns are what literature uses in order to master historical reality, and to reshape its materials in the chosen ideological key" (*The Way of the World,* xiii).

25. Marx, *Capital,* vol. 1, 273.

26. Ibid., 274.

27. Marx, "Wage Labour and Capital," 204.

28. Marx, *Capital*, vol. 1, 873–940.

29. Ibid., 280.

30. "Workers and bosses are not the only classes under capitalism. There are the chronically destitute—people who live in abject poverty who cannot find steady work, or any work at all, some of whom turn to petty crime to survive. In addition, between labor and capital there is a middle class that consists of professionals, managers, and small businesspeople—sometimes referred to as the petty bourgeoisie" (D'Amato, *The Meaning of Marxism*, 107).

31. Marx, *Capital*, vol. 3, 927.

32. Marx, "Manifesto," 474.

33. "Long before me," Marx wrote to Joseph Weydemeyer in 1852, "bourgeois historians had described the historical development of [the] class struggle and bourgeois economists the economic anatomy of the classes. What I did that was new was to prove: 1) that the *existence of classes* is only bound up with *particular phases in the development of production*, 2) that the class struggle necessarily leads to the *dictatorship of the proletariat*, and 3) that this dictatorship itself only constitutes the transition to the *abolition of all classes* and to *a classless society*" (Marx, "Class Struggle," 220). We also find this narrative of inevitable class polarization, class struggle, and finally the transcendence of capitalism—and thus class—via revolution in chap. 32 of *Capital*, vol. 1, "The Historical Tendency of Capitalist Accumulation" (927–30).

34. Dimock and Gilmore, introduction to *Rethinking Class*, 2.

35. Gibson-Graham, *The End of Capitalism*, 19.

36. Seymour, *Against Austerity*, 172.

37. Schocket, *Vanishing Moments*, 14.

38. Schocket follows Stephen Resnick and Richard Wolff in defining class as a *process* of exploitation. See Schocket, *Vanishing Moments*, 14; and Resnick and Wolff, *Knowledge and Class*, 1–37.

39. Markels, *The Marxian Imagination*, 21. Markels also draws on Resnick and Wolff for his concept of class.

40. Schocket, *Vanishing Moments*, 15. "As long as surplus value is extracted from labor power," Schocket further explains, "class continues to be a relevant phenomenon for both workers and for social and cultural critics" (16).

41. Ibid., 21.

42. I owe the phrase "structural definition of class" to G. A. Cohen: "the structural definition of class," writes Cohen, "defines [a] class with reference to the position of its members in the economic structure, their effective rights and duties within it" (*Karl Marx's Theory of History*, 73).

43. Denning, *Culture in the Age of Three Worlds*, 154.

44. Thompson, *The Making of the English Working Class*, 807.

45. Writes Gavin Jones: "An overwhelming interest in oppressed subject positions [in literary history] has tended to evade the problem of economic in-

equality by centering social marginalization on the cultural identity of the marginalized" (*American Hungers*, 7). Andrew Lawson makes a consonant point:
"questions of economic structure," he writes, "have tended to become blurred
by discussions of class that direct attention to its gendered and racialized man-
ifestations" (*Downwardly Mobile*, 17).

46. For class as subsumed under race and gender, see, for instance, Elizabeth Maddock Dillon, according to whom under early and antebellum U.S.
capitalism we witness a "raced and gendered division of labor that define[s]
the white male as the inviolable property owner of private property and white
women and blacks as producers and species of property" (*The Gender of Freedom*, 21). On class as displaced into race, gender, and ethnicity in both antebellum literature and scholarship on antebellum literature, see Lang, *The Syntax
of Class*, 6–13.

47. Writes Eugene Genovese: "Slavery rested on the principal of property in
man—of one man's appropriation of another's person as well as the fruits of his
labor. By definition and in essence it was a system of class rule, in which some
people lived off the labor of others. American slavery subordinated one race to
another and thereby rendered its fundamental class relationships more complex
and ambiguous; but they remained class relationships" (*Roll, Jordan, Roll*, 3).
"Historians," Jeanne Boydston writes, "have frequently analyzed the working-
class family as a collectivity, run according to a communal ethic. But by law and
custom the family was not an egalitarian society. The husband owned, not only
the value of his own labor time, but the value of his wife's as well. And this was
a prerogative of manhood that working-class males were ill-prepared to give
up" (*Home and Work*, 135).

48. Federici, *Caliban and the Witch*, 17.

49. Ibid., 63–64. Or, as Joan Acker puts it, "Gender and race are built into
capitalism and its class processes through the history of racial and gender seg-
regation of paid labor and through the images and actions of white men who
dominate and lead central capitalist endeavors" (*Class Questions*, 85).

50. Walter Johnson: "If slavery was not capitalist how do we explain its commercial character: the excrescence of money changers and cotton factors in
southern cities who yearly handled millions and millions of pounds of foreign
exchange; the mercantile ambitions of southern slaveholders who wanted to
take over Cuba and Mexico and Nicaragua so as to insure their commercial
dominance and greatness; the thriving slave markets at the centers of their cities
where prices tracked those that were being paid for cotton thousands of miles
away? The standard answer has been to say that slavery was 'in but not of' the
capitalist economy, a beguilingly otiose formulation, which implies some sort
of special unity of process ('in') which it defines only negatively in relation to an
orthodox definition of 'capitalism.' The existing discussion [on the relationship
between slavery and capitalism] . . . has devolved into a set of more-or-less tau-
tological propositions about how you define the categories of historical analysis
(if 'capitalism' is defined as that-mode-of-production-characterized-by-wage-

labor then slavery was, by definition, not 'capitalist'). But doesn't it make more sense to think about the political economy of the eighteenth- and nineteenth-century Atlantic as a single space, its dimensions defined by flows of people, money, and goods, its nested temporalities set by interlocking (though clearly distinct) labor regimes, cyclical rhythms of cultivation and foreign exchange, and shared standards of calculability and measurement?" ("The Pedestal and the Veil," 303–4). On the interrelationship of capitalism and slavery, see Baptist, *The Half Has Never Been Told*; Beckert, *Empire of Cotton*; Johnson, *River of Dark Dreams*; and Schermerhorn, *The Business of Slavery*.

51. Robinson, *Black Marxism*, 200.

52. See esp. Roediger, *The Wages of Whiteness*.

53. Exemplary of this strain of polemic is Walter Benn Michael's *The Trouble with Diversity*. Writes Benn Michaels: "The argument of [this book], in its simplest form, will be that we love race—we love identity—because we don't love class. We love thinking that the differences that divide us are not the differences between those of us who have money and those who don't but are instead the differences between those of us who are black and those who are white or Asian or Latino or whatever. A world where some of us don't have enough money is a world where the differences between us present a problem: the need to get rid of equality or to justify it. A world where some of us are black and some of us are white—or biracial or Native American or transgendered—is a world where the differences between us present a solution: appreciating our diversity. So we like to talk about the differences we can appreciate, and we don't like to talk about the ones we can't" (6).

54. Fraser, "Rethinking Recognition," 110.

55. Writes Eric Lott: "When fighting against exploitative employers or companies, black workers may well present their case as a racial one. Hence the success of black worker campaigns in North Carolina, where University of North Carolina–Chapel Hill housekeepers, or non-union organizing campaigns against black workers in poultry gulags, or strikes at local K-Marts have made labor demands *in the form of antiracist activism*: these were successful to varying degrees because they forwent the left fundamentalism that says only 'class matters.' . . . Such campaigns meet capital-state formations or agglomerations the way they've been greeted: as particularized, super-exploitable wage labor. To whine about this as divisive, self-interested, or marginal 'identity politics' seems insane when the country, at local and state levels, and notwithstanding the destruction of affirmative action, seems less and less able to discredit worker protests fought on the ground in the name of racial justice" (*The Disappearing Liberal Intellectual*, 42).

56. "Marx's and Engel's theory of revolution," Cedric Robinson explains, "was insufficient in scope: the European proletariat and its social allies did not constitute *the revolutionary* subject of history, nor was working-class consciousness necessarily *the* negation of bourgeois culture" (*Black Marxism*, 4).

57. Writes Anne Janowitz: "The criticism of essentialist thought, which is

crucial to structural understandings of social formations, has allowed us to interpret the meanings of gender and race as socially constructed and not inarguably deriving their meanings from biological features. But class is meaningful only *as* a social category, and so to approach it as analogous with the anti-essentialist, structuralist-derived projects of race and gender studies amounts to an analytical confusion. . . . When literary critics make class, race, and gender all interchangeable tokens along an axis of substitution, the subsequent pathologies of capitalism become racism, sexism, and classism. Understood as a set of subjectively experienced *attitudes* (socially constructed though they be), racism, sexism, and classism then appear to be contestable through struggles of representation, ideology, even 'structures of feeling'" ("Class and Literature," 240).

58. As Fraser explains, to the extent that for "identity politics" "maldistribution is merely a secondary effect of misrecognition," "it follows from this view that all maldistribution can be remedied indirectly, by a politics of recognition: to revalue unjustly devalued identities is simultaneously to attack the deep sources of economic inequality; no explicit politics of redistribution is needed" ("Rethinking Recognition," 110).

59. Glickstein, *American Exceptionalism*, 5. "Except for a few reformers and the early labor movement from 1830 to the turn of the century," James Huston argues, "most statements by Americans in the nineteenth century [about class] were smugly self-congratulatory. Europe had pauperized masses ruled over by the opulent, aristocratic few, but in America, equality ruled in politics *and* economics" (*Securing the Fruits*, 84–85).

60. J. Hector St. John de Crèvecoeur, *Letters from an American Farmer*, 67, 70. Letter 9 may unsettle this description of American equality: here, Farmer James recounts happening upon "a Negro, suspended in [a] cage and left there to expire" (178). The sign of the violence that subtends racial slavery in the United States consequently overwhelms James. But Letter 9 does not in fact contradict Letter 3, the message of Letter 3 being that in the United States all men of European ancestry can become property owners and thus achieve "competence" and "ample subsistence."

61. Appleby, *Capitalism and a New Social Order*, 78.

62. Abraham Lincoln, *Speeches and Writings*, 343.

63. Marx, *Capital*, vol. 1, 280.

64. Throughout the early nineteenth century, according to James Huston, prominent American political economists hewed to the republican belief that "wealth inequalities arose from governmental practices—taxes, monopolies, bureaucracies, financial manipulations, an established church, aristocratic laws of entail and primogeniture, and control of politics by an aristocracy"—and not from the subjection of labor to a capitalist market. If the United States fundamentally lacked these practices, then workers were assured of "the full fruits of their labor" and general economic equality among white, male citizens was thus guaranteed (*Securing the Fruits*, 153).

65. See Pessen, *Riches, Class, and Power*; Rockman, *Scraping By*; and Billy G.

Smith, *The "Lower Sort*. Writes Lawson: "Early Americans entered a marketplace where they became profoundly unequal in terms of property and wealth" (introduction, 1).

66. Rockman, "Class," 532. "Capitalism," writes Rockman, "is a system in which a subset of society has the power to set the rules of commercial exchange, to limit communal access to productive resources, to control the terms of their own labor and that of their family, and to obtain the access to the labor of non-family members as a mechanism for acquiring additional productive resources" (531).

67. Orren, *Belated Feudalism*, 8.

68. Tomlins, *Law, Labor, and Ideology*, 34.

69. Burke, *The Conundrum of Class*, 24.

70. James Madison, "The Federalist No. 10," 42.

71. See Wilentz, "Against Exceptionalism"; Wilentz, *Chants Democratic*; and Schultz, *The Republic of Labor*.

72. On class structure and formation as well as working-class radicalism in the early United States, see, e.g., Bronstein, *Land Reform*; Glickstein, *American Exceptionalism*; J. Huston, *Securing the Fruits*; R. Huston, *Land and Freedom*; Lause, *Young America*; Rediker, "'Good Hands, Stout Heart'"; Rockman, "Class" and *Scraping By*; Schultz, *The Republic of Labor*; B. G. Smith, *The "Lower Sort"*; Tomlins, *Law, Labor, and Ideology*; Twomey, *Jacobins and Jeffersonians*; and Wilentz, "American Exceptionalism" and *Chants Democratic*.

73. Martha Meredith Read, *Monima*, 17, 14.

74. Davidson, *Revolution and the Word*, 258.

75. Savage, *The Factory Girl*.

76. Writes Cook of *The Factory Girl*: "It is an account of the endeavors of Mary Burnham, a selfless young woman, to use her experiences in the newly mechanized workplace of the American factory for the good of others. Mary earns vitally needed income for her family, volunteers to teach factory children in her limited spare time, and sets an example to her more self-indulgent workmates of self-control and self-sacrifice. Her reward, after several years of arduous work, is marriage to a widower with two sons, a return to a life of purely domestic service, and, in recognition of her literary proclivities, a gift from her new family of a Bible and writing desk. Mary thus provides a model for the new working woman of unselfishness and dedication to the service of others" (*Working Women*, 4).

77. The authorship of *Equality* is disputed. Though *Equality* is typically attributed to John Reynolds, Michael Durey argues that John Lithgow was its author. See Durey, "John Lithgow's *Lithconia*."

78. Schultz, *The Republic of Labor*, 202.

79. Reynolds, *Equality*, 1; hereafter cited in the text.

80. Indeed, as Jennifer Nedelsky has demonstrated, for the framers of the U.S. Constitution, "the protection of property meant the protection of unequal property and thus the insulation of both property and inequality from demo-

cratic transformation. . . . It also meant that the illegitimacy of redistribution defined the legitimate scope of the state" (*Private Property*, 2).

81. Manning, *The Key of Liberty*, 137; hereafter cited in the text.

82. Luther, *An Address to the Working Men*, 8.

83. Skidmore, *The Rights of Man to Property!*, 357–58; hereafter cited in the text.

84. Dimock, *Empire for Liberty*, 32.

85. John Locke, *Second Treatise of Government*, 29. As Macpherson maintains, Locke's version of possessive individualism justifies unequal property, wage labor, and "unlimited individual appropriation" (*The Political Theory*, 217–21). Or, as Mark Blyth argues, Locke worked to "naturalize income and wealth inequality, legitimate the private ownership of land, explain the emergence of labor markets, and depoliticize the invention of the device called money that made all these things possible" (*Austerity*, 105).

86. Marx, *Capital*, vol. 1, 927, 928.

87. Feuer, "The North American Origins," 66.

88. Marx, *Economic and Philosophic Manuscripts*, 100.

89. Simpson, *The Working Man's Manual*, 36; hereafter cited in the text.

90. Writes Edward Pessen: "Everywhere, according to Simpson, workingmen were degraded, forced to work long hours for low wages, denied the privileges and the opportunities which distinguished a civilized from a barbarian society, and held in undisguised contempt" ("The Ideology of Stephen Simpson," 333).

91. Again, Pessen: "Neither he nor labor desired equality of wealth or a community of property, [Simpson] assured the public" (ibid., 335).

92. Marx, "Manifesto," 479.

93. Pickering, *The Working Man's Political Economy*, 3.

94. Pickering, like other members of the National Reform Association, argued that this division of society was due to an "unnatural" distribution of land—due to "*legalizing private and exclusive property in the elements of nature*" (ibid., 179). He was, then, writing in the vein established by Skidmore.

95. Davis, *Prisoners of the American Dream*, 16.

96. See DuBois, *Black Reconstruction in America*; Saxton, *The Rise and Fall of the White Republic*; Roediger, *The Wages of Whiteness*; and Lott, *Love and Theft*.

97. Roediger, *The Wages of Whiteness*, 16. Likewise, scholarship on bourgeois identity formation in antebellum literature has revealed discourses of race to be central to the processes by which professional men reconciled themselves to their subordination to the market economy—to the insecurities and instabilities of competition and entrepreneurship. For "race" in the making of professional masculinity, see Gilmore, *The Genuine Article*; and Anthony, *Paper Money Men*.

98. Mary Templin summarizes this line of argument: "Many historians consider the rise of the middle class and the ideology of domesticity to be inseparable, since increasing affluence and the shift from home to factory production

made new, noneconomic roles for middle-class women necessary and desirable, while domestic practices of child rearing and conservation of resources helped to maintain and perpetuate middle-class position. . . . [T]he middle-class (and especially upper-middle-class) woman became both a marker and enforcer of class divisions through her own separation from manual labor, her emphasis upon the emotional aspects of domesticity, and her display and expectation of proper manners" (*Panic Fiction,* 66).

99. Stanley, "Home Life," 78.

100. Boydston, *Home and Work,* 152; hereafter cited in the text. "Historians," Boydston writes earlier, "have frequently analyzed the working-class family as a collectivity, run according to a communal ethic. But by law and custom the family was not an egalitarian society. The husband owned, not only the value of his own labor time, but the value of his wife's as well. And this was a prerogative of manhood that working-class males were ill-prepared to give up" (135).

101. Christine Stansell complicates this assessment of the role of gender ideology in white male labor activism. She shows, on the one hand, that male antebellum labor activists—in particular, members of the National Trades' Union—"envisioned a nineteenth-century home not unlike the bourgeois ideal, a repository for women's 'true' nature as well as a refuge from the miseries of wage labor" (*City of Women,* 138). On the other hand, she considers the men of the NTU "radical," highlighting their anticapitalism: "They offered a fiery critique of the entire system of capitalist wage relations. They sought working-class dignity, not bourgeois respectability. True, their formulations at times echoed those of evangelicals and ladies' magazines. Their opposition to women's labor, however, was not a capitulation to bourgeois society but a protest against it" (138). Nonetheless, Stansell explains that while in the early 1830s women tailors and other women workers (in New York and elsewhere) began to organize, male workers could not imagine women either as potential economic equals or equal players in the labor movement. "Women," in the opinion of the NTU, "quite simply lacked the strength of character to sustain themselves in the struggle against tyranny in the workplace" (139). For the NTU, women were to be rescued by male workers. "The republic to which the workingmen were committed," writes Stansell, "was, in the end, a republic of men" (140). The NTU was blind to "the alternative possibility: that women might organize along with men" (141).

102. Tomlins, "Afterword," 215–16.

103. Jameson, *The Political Unconscious,* 19–20.

104. My notion of speech-space is inspired by Alex Woloch's notion of character-space in *The One vs. the Many.*

105. Bakhtin, *The Dialogic Imagination,* 262; hereafter cited in the text.

106. Bakhtin: "All languages of heteroglossia, whatever the principle underlying and making each unique, are specific points of view on the world, forms for conceptualizing the world in words, specific world views, each characterized by its own objects, meaning and values. As such they all may be juxtaposed to one another, mutually supplement one another, contradict one another and be

interrelated dialogically. As such they encounter one another and co-exist in the consciousness of real people—first and foremost, in the creative consciousness of people who write novels. As such, these languages live a real life, they struggle and evolve in an environment of heteroglossia. Therefore they are all able to enter into the unitary plane of the novel" (*The Dialogic Imagination*, 292). Likewise, writes Bakhtin, the "speaking person in the novel is always, to one degree or another, an *ideologue,* and his words are always *ideologemes.* A particular language in a novel is always a particular way of viewing the world, one that strives for a social significance" (333).

107. Jameson, *The Political Unconscious,* 85.

108. "Rhetoric," writes Moretti, "has a social, emotive, partisan character, in short, an *evaluative* character. To persuade is the opposite of to convince. The aim is not to ascertain an intersubjective truth but to enlist support for a *particular* system of values" (*Signs,* 3).

109. Writes Bakhtin: "The social and historical voices populating language . . . are organized in the novel into a structured stylistic system that expresses the differentiated socio-ideological position of the author amid the heteroglossia of his epoch" (*The Dialogic Imagination,* 300). Barbara Foley reminds us that while Bakhtin sometimes "spoke of the novel as 'a genre that is both critical and self-critical . . . in all its openendedness' . . . Bakhtin also polemically distinguished what he viewed as Dostoievsky's attainment of a 'pluralvocal' novel from the 'monologism' that he saw characterizing all modes of the novel before—and most after—the novelist's time. For Bakhtin, 'heteroglossia' did not signify protopoststructuralist subversion and free play, but the contradictory coexistence of different social discourses within a single text" (*Radical Representations,* 256).

110. Culler, *The Pursuit of Signs,* 169–70.

111. Chatman, *Story and Discourse,* 146.

112. For Chatman, both "covert" and "overt" narrators exist on the level of discourse (ibid., 182).

113. Writes Shirley Samuels: "Certainly, the emergence of the middling classes accompanied an increase in the production and consumption of novels in the early United States" (*Reading the American Novel,* 12). Of course, as Michael Denning in *Mechanic Accents* and Shelley Streeby in *American Sensations* have documented, beginning in the 1840s novels were increasingly written *for* the working class.

114. For Jay Fliegelman, the eighteenth-century English novel, to which the late eighteenth-century U.S. novel was indebted, was a vehicle for the dissemination of "the new rationalist pedagogy": "The new rationalist pedagogy (and its moral sense and Rousseauistic variations) may be said to have contributed immeasurably to the form of the novel's development. It is no accident that the rise of the English novel coincided with a new social emphasis on the moral and cultural significance of education; for it was only as a form of pedagogy that much of eighteenth-century fiction was considered acceptable by a large portion of

the English reading public" (*Prodigals and Pilgrims,* 36). Fliegelman argues that the novel's dissemination of "the new rationalist pedagogy" helped pave the way for "the American revolution against patriarchal authority" (36–66). For Cathy Davidson, the late eighteenth-century U.S. novel "served as a major locus of republican education" (*Revolution and the Word,* 70). She argues that early U.S. novelists "encouraged individualistic striving toward self-improvement and self-education" (66), and thus that the early U.S. novel's brand of pedagogy—or the version of pedagogy to which it was committed—was democratic, egalitarian (69). As should be clear, I am offering a different take on the politics of the early U.S. novel. My view is more consonant with Matthew Garrett's. According to Garrett, early U.S. episodic novels, for example, *Constantius and Pulchera* and *Trials of the Human Heart,* "meld adventure and didacticism" (*Episodic Poetics,* 91). Garrett frames *Constantius* and *Trials* with Hannah More's *Cheap Repository,* whose "counter-revolutionary morsels," he notes, were "first printed in London between 1795 and 1798, became quite popular, were reprinted in Philadelphia in 1800, and soon gave rise to an American variety of tract literature." "More herself," writes Garrett, "designed the *Repository* to be an antidote to anything, printed or otherwise, that would lull the masses into less-than-industrious pleasure or inspire them to carry the banner of universal *fraternité*"; "didactic" novels like *Constantius* and *Trials,* were "consonant, in terms of both narrative form and evident sociopolitical ambition, with the tract enterprise" (95). On antebellum fiction as a form of pedagogy for middle-class readers, see esp. Baym, *Novels, Readers, and Reviewers;* and Brodhead, "Sparing the Rod."

115. Tompkins, *Sensational Designs,* 126.

116. Davidson, on the divergent way in which critics have characterized Mervyn: "Most of the debate centers on the character of Arthur Mervyn. He is a 'hero whose virtue . . . stands in need of no riches.' He is an inconstant scoundrel who betrays the love of a good woman for the lucre of a wealthy widow. He is a model of 'enlightened self interest' and 'rigid morality' but also a 'young American on the make' and a 'meddlesome, self-righteous bungler who comes close to destroying himself and everyone in his path.' He is a man of 'constancy' and 'virtuous impulses' or a 'modern bourgeois teenage Tartuffe,' a 'chameleon of convenient virtue'—and a 'chameleon of convenient vice.' He is an 'innocent,' 'an American Adam,' who has, however, a 'tendency toward casuistry and rather indiscreet curiosity.' He is 'a mama's boy, pampered and spoiled,' an 'imp of the perverse.' Or, 'neither a hero nor a villain,' Mervyn 'lacks the force of will to be either.' He is, symbolically and structurally, Maravegli, the self-sacrificing gentleman and the type of saintly benevolence. He is, figuratively and even literally, Clavering, the consummate con man posing as a country bumpkin for his own nefarious purposes. 'Pierce Arthur Mervyn,' yet another critic writes, 'and all you find is Arthur Mervyn'" (*Revolution and the Word,* 240).

117. On the distinction between "listening" and "suspicion" in interpretation, see Ricoeur, *Freud and Philosophy.*

118. Barthes, *S/Z,* 3.

119. Eagleton, "Ideology, Fiction, Narrative," 78.

120. Likewise invoking Louis Althusser's notion of ideology (from "Ideology and Ideological State Apparatuses"), Hayden White posits that "narrative is . . . a particularly effective system of discursive meaning production by which individuals can be taught to live a distinctively 'imaginary relation to their real conditions of existence,' that is to say, an unreal but meaningful relation to the social formations in which they are indentured to live out their lives and realize their destinies as social subjects" (*The Content of the Form,* x). Or, writes Ramón Saldívar: "Ideology . . . involves the essentially narrative, or fabulous, attempt of the subject to inscribe a place for itself in a collective and historical process that excludes the subject and that is basically nonnarratable" ("Narrative, Ideology," 15).

121. That ideology is narrative in form is likewise one of the great hypotheses of that ur-text of contemporary Marxian literary theory, Jameson's *The Political Unconscious.* Writes Jameson: "The aesthetic act is itself ideological, and the production of aesthetic or narrative form is to be seen as an ideological act in its own right, with the function of inventing imaginary or formal 'solutions' to unresolvable social contradictions" (79). According to Jameson, "All literature must be read as a symbolic meditation on the destiny of a community" (70).

122. According to Marx, capitalist political economy conceives of the seller and buyer of labor as equals: the seller of labor "and the owner of money meet in the market, and enter into relations with each other on a footing of equality as owners of commodities, with the sole difference that one is a buyer, the other a seller; both are therefore equal in the eyes of the law" (*Capital,* vol. 1, 271).

123. Fitzhugh, *Sociology for the South,* 18; hereafter cited in the text.

124. Sklansky, *The Soul's Economy,* 80.

1. Charles Brockden Brown, Poverty, and the Bildungsroman

1. Shapiro, *The Culture and Commerce,* 165.

2. Justus, "Arthur Mervyn, American," 315.

3. Goddu, *Gothic America,* 32. "The ascendancy of 'liberal capitalism,'" writes Steven Watts, "entangled growing numbers of citizens in complex webs of commodification and profit seeking that enshrined the competing individual as a social ideal" (*The Romance of Real Life,* 2). "The sacrifice of personal advantage to the commonwealth, a long-standing republican ideal," Watts continues, "slowly receded before the notion that personal enterprise created productivity and prosperity and thereby *produced* the public good" (6–7). Walter Licht argues that the crucial transformation was not from republicanism to liberalism, but from mercantilism to nonmercantilism: "Scholarly debates concerned with the nature of American society at the turn of the nineteenth-century are mired because attention normally focuses on individual attitudes and behaviors. Establishing whether the majority of Americans were traditional or in-

dividualistic, market- or nonmarket-driven is an impossible task. Usually the statements of elites are invoked to back one interpretation or another; whether those pronouncements actually represent the views of different Americans, be they men or women, old stock or newcomers, whites or blacks, rich or poor, is not known. Diversity of activity and experience is known . . . yet the notion that American society was transforming from a mercantile order dissolves such alternative perspectives as premodern/modern or nonmarket/market" (*Industrializing America*, 19).

4. For some eighteenth-century writers, Philip Gould writes, "commercial exchange refines human passions and socializes human behavior" ("Race, Commerce," 160).

5. Of eighteenth-century transatlantic anxiety about "commerce" and the merchant, J. G. A. Pocock writes: "The landed man, successor to the master of the classical *oikos*, was permitted the leisure and autonomy to consider what was to others' good as well as his own; but the individual engaged in exchange could discern only particular values—that of the commodity which was his, that of the commodity for which he exchanged it. His activity did not oblige or even permit him to contemplate the universal good as he acted upon it, and he consequently continued to lack classical rationality. It followed that he was not the conscious master of himself, and that in the last analysis he must be thought of as activated by nonrational forces" (*The Machiavellian Moment*, 464).

6. Writes Carl Ostrowski: "The economic liberalism pursued by speculators and embodied by the title character [Arthur Mervyn] would have been judged wanting by Brown's original audience when viewed in light of the still influential ideology of classical republicanism and the restraints and duties it imposed on the civic-minded individual" ("'Fated to Perish,'" 4). For *Arthur Mervyn* as a critique of forms of economic individualism as corrupting and corrupt, see, in addition to Ostrowski, Goddu, *Gothic America*, 31–51; Weyler, *Intricate Relations*, 140–82; Doolen, *Fugitive Empire*, 75–109; Shapiro, *The Culture and Commerce*, 259–301; and Smith-Rosenberg, *This Violent Empire*, 413–64.

For *Arthur Mervyn* as a defense of forms of economic self-interestedness as beneficial to the U.S. polity, see, e.g., Tompkins, *Sensational Designs*, 62–93; Hinds, *Private Property*, 68–98; and Baker, *Securing the Commonwealth*, 119–36. Baker argues that Brown's *Arthur Mervyn* imagines the commercial ethos of self-interest as the cause, paradoxically, of sympathetic bonds between individuals and a kind of disinterestedness, precisely because commercial self-interest leads to situations of mutual economic dependence: "In Arthur Mervyn the corruption that comes with indebtedness and economic insecurity promotes communal union precisely because it encourages a process by which readers and auditors of narratives come to sympathize with others. . . . Corruption mitigates disinterestedness, and it is when Mervyn is most susceptible to the influence of his own interests that he is also most capable of imagining the distresses of a 'brother in calamity.' For this reason the commercial-minded are uniquely positioned to investigate with and identify the misfortunes of others, and this positioning governs how they process narratives as well" (*Securing the Commonwealth*, 120, 132).

7. There are notable exceptions to this neglect of Brown's representation of economic subalternity. Ed White suggests that Brown's novel *Wieland* represents a "fairly sophisticated engagement with the rural subaltern" ("Carwin the Peasant Rebel," 44). Stephen Shapiro, who also attends to Brown's representation of economic subalternity, argues that Brown's fiction works to critique class inequality in the new nation (*The Culture and Commerce*, 259–301). Mark Decker also reads *Arthur Mervyn* as a novel about class division, suggesting that it stages upper-class anxieties about who should be admitted to the "better sort" ("A Bumpkin before the Bar."). My approach, in contrast to Decker's, illuminates *Arthur Mervyn*'s construction and affirmation of poverty itself. Matthew Pethers has recently called attention to the centrality of poverty in *Ormond*, arguing that *Ormond*, as a version of "the parabolic social mobility narrative," "remedies the problem of poverty through the rhetoric of moral virtue" ("Poverty, Providence," 707). I return to Pethers's arguments about *Ormond* below.

8. Smith-Rosenberg, *This Violent Empire*, 417.

9. If we think about class as a process (as opposed to fixed identity positions), then poverty—even temporary poverty—is a symptom of class to the extent that it is made possible by the asymmetric extraction of surplus value from labor. In other words, that some can become poor temporarily while others are wealthy is owing to the ways capitalism distributes wealth.

10. In her seminal reading of *Arthur Mervyn*, Cathy Davidson argues that *Arthur Mervyn* can be read as telling two antithetical stories about America as it moves into capitalist modernity. The novel may be a story of "cultural diversity, feminism, and class mobility," according to which America is figured as a "vital, dynamic society that flourishes in heterogeneity and originality" (*Revolution and the Word*, 252). Or, the novel may present America as a place of "egomania and alienation" (252). "Take your pick," Davidson writes of *Arthur Mervyn*, "America the corrupt or America the beautiful" (251). Davidson's way of reading *Arthur Mervyn* is recapitulated by later critics of Brown, for whom Brown's novels represent either endorsements of America as a break with the European past or as exposés of the ways in which European-style inequalities still haunt America and must be expunged if America is to move forward on its world-historical mission. Yet, to ask whether Brown confirms or criticizes America's fantasies about itself—to ask whether he imagines America as a new and virtuous community or not, on the way to being a new and virtuous community or not—is to miss the import of *Ormond* and *Arthur Mervyn*. Here, the United States is—but should remain—a class society.

11. Jones, *American Hungers*, 3.

12. Bakhtin, *Speech Genres*, 21.

13. Moretti, *The Way of the World*, 15.

14. "For Althusser, a modern society depends for coherence on the educa-

tion of individuals to locate them within sociocultural categories and to induce them to observe—without threat of force—the constraints defining their respective positions. Thus the modern state creates a contradiction within the subject between the ideology of free subjectivity and the fact of social subjection" (Armstrong, *How Novels Think*, 29).

15. As David Montgomery reminds us, late eighteenth- and early nineteenth-century "Americans associated liberty with the ownership of productive property. Its opposite—lack of property—was thus a form of slavery" (*Beyond Equality*, 30).

16. Whereas republicanism associates freedom with land, Elizabeth Maddock Dillon points out, liberalism associates it with "mobile property"; nonetheless, freedom was linked to property ownership in both traditions (*The Gender of Freedom*, 148–52).

17. Stanley, "Home Life," 84–85.

18. Sánchez-Eppler, *Dependent States*, 151.

19. For Pethers, the "parabolic social mobility narrative" "privileges the spiritual value of industriousness over its material benefit through a recursion to Providence," but also works to align "wealth and virtue" ("Poverty, Providence," 712). The parabolic social mobility narrative does not suggest that the ability to make money is itself the sign of "virtue"; rather, parabolic social mobility narratives are narratives about individuals who are rewarded by "divine approval" and return to wealth because of "their forbearance of poverty and not their facility with riches" (724).

20. Marin, *Utopics*, xxiv.

21. B. G. Smith, *The "Lower Sort,"* 84; hereafter cited in text.

22. Kant, *Political Writings*, 54.

23. Adam Smith, *An Inquiry into the Nature and Causes*, 2:781, 782; hereafter cited in the text.

24. Godwin, *An Enquiry Concerning Political Justice*, 292; hereafter cited in the text.

25. Scholars debate Brown's relationship to Godwin and Godwinian radicalism. For Brown as antagonistic to Godwinian radicalism, see, e.g., Clemit, *The Godwinian Novel*; for Brown as a proponent of and modernizer of Godwinian radicalism, see, e.g., Shapiro, *The Culture and Commerce*. Wil Verhoeven suggests that Brown's relationship to transatlantic radicalism was ambivalent: "Brown combined," he writes, "eighteenth-century European radicalism with homegrown, conservative American political instincts" ("'This Blissful Period,'" 11). Dorothy Hale corroborates this reading of Brown's relationship to Godwin in her comparative reading of Brown's *Arthur Mervyn* and Godwin's novel *Caleb Williams*. In *Arthur Mervyn*, Hale writes, "the rebellion against tyranny—specifically, the English tyranny Godwin excoriates [in *Caleb Williams*]—has already been accomplished" ("Profits of Altruism," 57). "The vicious British power relations of master and servant are replaced in America," Hale continues, "by the equality afforded by the free enterprise system. We are made to see that,

because America has no systemic evil, it needs no systemic and hence no systematic reforms." I agree with Hale's assessment that *Arthur Mervyn* calls for no systematic reforms, but my reading of the novel diverges from Hale's insofar as I call attention to its celebration of poverty. That is, for Hale, *Arthur Mervyn* denies systemic inequality in the United States, whereas I argue that what *Arthur Mervyn* does is invite its readers not to lament the very existence of class in the United States.

26. Charles Brockden Brown, "Walstein's School of History," 338.

27. Charles Brockden Brown, *Wieland and Memoirs of Carwin the Biloquist*, 315.

28. *Ibid.*, 316.

29. Propp, *Morphology of the Folktale*, 29.

30. Trilling, *Sincerity and Authenticity*, 16.

31. Julia Stern, on Craig: "Craig personifies the monstrous implications of ascendant liberalism unrestrained" (*The Plight of Feeling*, 211). Teresa Goddu, on Welbeck: "The gothic villain of this apparitional world is Welbeck, the economic man. . . . Representing in his aristocratic Englishness the vices of a fully developed commercial society—rampant individualism, speculative wealth, indolence, sensual excess—Welbeck embodies both the degenerate past that the nation has fled and the corruption that haunts its future" (*Gothic America*, 35). Scholars that interpret Brown's Philadelphia novels as indictments of "commerce" often do so by calling attention to the themes of economic dissimulation and fraud in these novels. Writes Carroll Smith-Rosenberg: "Concern for the general good, ethical business practices, morality, and honesty had no place within the world of commerce as Brown portrayed that world in *Arthur Mervyn*. Fraud and deception characterize every commercial venture. In the darkness of night, merchants plot to defraud one another; fraudulent bills of exchange are presented as real—or perhaps real ones are represented as forgeries (one never truly knows). Heiresses are seduced and abandoned, fortunes stolen, friendships betrayed, murders committed, bodies buried in crypts under imposing Philadelphia mansions. Self-interest reigns supreme" (*This Violent Empire*, 418).

32. "Several of Brown's novels," writes Robert Levine, "portray Americans generally as self-promoting plotters seeking to take advantage of their competitors in the marketplace. Brown's villains, however, tend to be at an even greater remove from the community, far more skilled in the arts of duplicity, and acutely self-conscious about the philosophical, psychological, and political implications of their actions. In addition, his principal villains, even those born in America, seem more European than American" (*Conspiracy and Romance*, 16). As Luke Gibbons points out, Brown's *Wieland* (1798) and *Edgar Huntly* (1799) both feature "destructive Irish interlopers on American soil" and "coincided with the moral panic over foreign subversion by French and Irish revolutionaries" ("Ireland, America," 30).

33. Weber, *The Protestant Ethic*, 57; hereafter cited in the text.

34. Charles Brockden Brown, *Ormond*, 10; hereafter cited in the text.

35. For a consonant reading of Craig as disaffected worker, see Drexler and White, "Secret Witness," 338–41.

36. Charles Brockden Brown, *Arthur Mervyn*, 355; hereafter cited in the text.

37. Charles Brockden Brown, *Edgar Huntly*, 38; hereafter cited in the text.

38. Armstrong, *How Novels Think*, 29.

39. See, for instance, J. Stern, *The Plight of Feeling*, 153–258. Hana Layson argues that *Ormond* criticizes Wollstonecraftian feminism's reliance on masculine ideals of rationality and revolutionary violence ("Rape and Revolution").

40. The fever, as many critics have argued, can function as a metaphor—for commercial corruption or political revolution (especially the French Revolution). For the fever as metaphor of commercial corruption, see esp. Ostrowski, "'Fated to Perish'"; for the fever as a metaphor for political revolution in the context of the French Revolution, see Levine, "Arthur Mervyn's Revolutions"; and Samuels, *Romances of the Republic*, 23–43. For critiques of the interpretative metaphorization of the fever, see Waterman, *Republic of the Intellect*, 189–230; and also Shapiro, who writes: "For *Arthur Mervyn*, [treating Brown as a writer of allegory] has resulted in an obsession with revealing its description of the yellow fever plague as a message about commerce, the national imaginary, and so on. Despite its sensationalism, Brown uses the plotting of the plague just as 'Walstein's School' suggests: as a nonallegorical mechanism for staging and amplifying already existing social dynamics regarding property (class) and sex (gender) and their intersection in race" (*The Culture and Commerce*, 270).

41. For feminist appraisals of Constantia's rejection of Balfour, see Cowell, "Class, Gender, and Genre," 133; and Layson, "Rape and Revolution," 166–67.

42. Cowell, "Class, Gender, and Genre," 132.

43. Verhoeven, "Displacing the Discontinuous," 216.

44. Lewis, "Attaining Masculinity," 38.

45. Verhoeven suggests that Constantia represents Lockean as well as Wollstonecraftian ideals: she embodies, he writes, "the Lockean ideal of a being whose passions are kept under control by the 'determination of the mind,' and whose life is spent in the optimistic Godwinian belief that 'every day contribut[es] to rectify some error or confirm some truth'"; but, "Constantia is not only the child of Lockean principles, she is also the product of Wollstonecraft's ideas on the modern woman" ("Displacing the Discontinuous," 216).

46. Lewis, "Attaining Masculinity," 38.

47. Ibid.

48. Essays and chapters on *Arthur Mervyn* often begin with this question: is the novel's eponymous protagonist a disinterested citizen or a self-interested confidence man? For a number of scholars, the ambiguity of Arthur's character on the spectrum of disinterestedness and interestedness signals Brown's deconstruction of the very opposition on which the republican-liberalism paradigm depends: according to one way of reading the novel, the rise of "commerce" makes it impossible to tell, on the one hand, who is and who is not a "good citizen" and, on the other hand, if "commerce" is good or bad for the early

United States. Davidson's reading of *Arthur Mervyn* remains the model of this type of deconstructive reading: "It did not, in short, take the twentieth century to invent Derrida or Bakhtin. *Arthur Mervyn,* I would finally suggest might be seen as an early American version of Bakhtin's 'dialogical' text, a carnivalesque performance in which the author resolutely refuses to delimit his intentions while also allowing his characters their own ambiguities and even a spirit of 'revolt' against any constraining properties the text might threaten to impose. . . . *Arthur Mervyn* can, of course, accommodate the pieties of its time or ours, but only through a provisional and partial reading that is both asserted and questioned within the text" (*Revolution and the Word,* 253). Likewise, Goddu writes: "Arthur, as America, is either healthy or unhealthy. The critical debate, however, depends on a dichotomy that the novels proposes then subverts" (*Gothic America,* 40).

49. Though Elizabeth Hinds observes that both *Ormond* and *Arthur Mervyn* share concerns with political economy, on Hinds's reading *Ormond* and *Arthur Mervyn* differ because they are overdetermined by emerging bourgeois gender ideology: *Arthur Mervyn's* male protagonist projects us into the realm of market relations, while *Ormond's* female protagonist sets off questions about female labor in the private property that is domestic space (*Private Property,* 22). But in both novels, poverty becomes synonymous with freedom and individual growth.

50. Moretti, *The Way of the World,* 15.

51. Spangler, "Charles Brockden Brown's *Arthur Mervyn,*" 588.

52. Arthur is "the consummate capitalist male," Hinds writes, "because he combines a desire for wealth with a desire for fame and distinction" (*Private Property,* 76). Mine is a different reading of Arthur.

53. Writes Ostrowski, for example: "Mervyn hovers around the city and speculates in men, women, and documents, not working but trading his way up from poverty to affluence" ("'Fated to Perish,'" 7–8).

54. According to Jane Tompkins's reading of *Arthur Mervyn,* a passage like the one in which Arthur formulates his ideal apprenticeship should be read as one of the novel's "abstract propositions" on the benefits of the city over the country, dynamism over stasis, and thus commerce over agriculture (*Sensational Designs,* 67).

55. Rediker, "'Good Hands, Stout Heart,'" 139.

56. As Moretti observes, "capitalist rationality cannot generate *Bildung*" because "capital, due to its purely quantitative nature, and the competition it is subject to, can be a fortune only in so far as *it keeps growing*": capital can "never stop," but the protagonist of the bildungsroman must, because "*Bildung* is truly such only if, at a certain point, it can be seen as concluded" (*The Way of the World,* 26).

57. One way of ideologically managing "the gradual transition to wage labor from 1800 to 1860" was, writes David Roediger, to construe it as "a rite of passage on the road to economic independence of free farming or of self-employed

craft labor" (*The Wages of Whiteness,* 45). What is crucial about Arthur's plan is precisely how it dissociates this "rite of passage" from accumulation via work.

58. "A host of Americans at the time of the Revolution," writes James Huston, "agreed that wage labor was a sign of dependence and of individuals not receiving the fruits of their labor . . . some American conceived of wage labor as a power relationship between people. To work for another individual meant that the employer controlled the worker's remuneration and thus had the capacity to reward the laborer less than the laborer's efforts merited. For most eighteenth-century Americans, therefore, wages carried a stigma of dependence" (*Securing the Fruits,* 26).

59. For corresponding observations on this reversal of power, see Hale, "Profits of Altruism," 66; and Levine, "Arthur Mervyn's Revolutions," 152–53.

60. Rockman, *Scraping By,* 8.

61. Shapiro, *The Culture and Commerce,* 275.

62. For Arthur as republican citizen, see, e.g., Warner, *Letters of the Republic,* 151–76.

63. Goddu, *Gothic America,* 31–51.

64. Marx, *Grundrisse,* 83.

65. On Sean X. Goudie's reading, Arthur's reward from the Maurices "signifies the complicity of the United States in West Indian slavery. . . . It also represents U.S. involvement in a parallel U.S. plantation economy, which Mervyn's narrative romanticizes by depicting the domestic sphere of a Southern white mercantile family transported from Charleston to Baltimore, rather than the domestic scene of a Southern plantation in South Carolina" (*Creole America,* 197).

66. For Hale, this episode is exemplary of what she calls Arthur's "moral profiteerism" ("Profits of Altruism," 61). For Ostrowski, "Mervyn's actions in this scene bear an uncanny resemblance to those of a currency speculator as described by Dr. Stevens early in the novel: Mervyn receives documents from one party and carries them to another, receiving a thousand dollar profit for no more labor than was required to deliver them" ("'Fated to Perish,'"12).

67. As Hale observes, Arthur makes the case for philanthropy but does not develop a critique of "the capitalist system"; because Arthur does not have "power to shelter or otherwise aid those, like Clemenza, whom he wishes to help," he can be only a "moral middleman" who can "show the prosperous . . . their individual duty" ("Profits of Altruism," 63).

68. Hale: "With every virtuous deed, [Arthur] becomes more sanguine about material wealth" (ibid., 62).

69. Hegel, *Aesthetics,* vol. 1, 593.

70. Eleanor Sickels records P. B. Shelley's dissatisfaction with *Arthur Mervyn's* conclusion: "The transfer of the hero's affections from a simple peasant-girl to a rich Jewess displeased Shelley extremely, and he could only account for it on the ground that it was the only way in which Brown could bring his story to an uncomfortable conclusion" ("Shelley and Charles Brockden Brown," 1116).

71. Some critics describe *Arthur Mervyn* as essentially divided between its

first and second halves; these critics are prone to voicing dissatisfaction with the novel's end. Book 1, Norman Grabo writes, is a "book of masculine cunning, deceit, and sickness," while book 2 documents Arthur's "exposure to forces of healing and wholeness" (*The Coincidental Art*, 117). Hinds offers a similar description: for her, the novel is split between a male-dominated "risk-driven market" and a "familiar, female-dominated economy of security" (*Private Property*, 96). Robert Ferguson tells us that Arthur is one of Brown's "outsiders on the brink of rebellion," who in marrying an older, wealthy woman travels an "oedipal pattern" and ultimately gives up his rebellion in an attempt to accommodate to society (*Law and Letters*, 148). Michael Warner likewise suggests that in the final chapters of *Arthur Mervyn* Brown forsakes his mission of dramatizing the search for public-oriented knowledge to focus instead on a desire "for intersubjective recognition and mutual esteem" that can only be obtained in "the intimate recognition of romantic love" (*Letters of the Republic*, 170). Such assessments of *Arthur Mervyn*'s ending see it as kind of regression from radicalism to conservatism in the novel: for Steven Watts, to give one more example, the novel ends with Arthur's "return—both personally and culturally—to the womb" (*Romance of Real Life*, 114). Other critics, however, have suggested that *Arthur Mervyn*'s ending continues what they suggest is the novel's antagonistic relationship to dominant ideologies of self and society. Sian Silyn Roberts, for example, argues that *Arthur Mervyn* "breaks the Lockean rule of one mind per body and introduces the possibility that one mind may exist across two bodies" ("Gothic Enlightenment," 318). The marriage of Achsa and Arthur, Roberts concludes, is a marriage between two individuals "whose excesses render them less than human in the Enlightenment sense," and thus this marriage "replaces the static sentimental model" of a community of self-enclosed, self-governing individuals "with a civil society predicated on the mutually constitutive potential of radical difference" (325). For Stephen Shapiro, the marriage between Achsa and Arthur continues *Arthur Mervyn*'s critique of ideologies of racial difference: "As *Arthur Mervyn* ends with the romantic pairing of a plebeian native (white, Christian) male and an exotic wealthy female, Brown proposes egalitarian miscegenation, rather than recolonizing the slaves back to Africa, as the best vehicle for overcoming racism in postslavery society" (*The Culture and Commerce*, 264–65).

72. Schocket, *Vanishing Moments*, 16.

2. *Modern Chivalry*'s Defense of "the Few"

1. Chase, *The American Novel*, 1.

2. *Modern Chivalry* has been characterized as a picaresque novel (esp. by Davidson in *Revolution and the Word*, 173–78). It has also been read as a riff on the quixotic novel; see, e.g., Sarah Wood, *Quixotic Fictions*, 75–106. Yet, the protagonist whose adventures organize—bind together—*Modern Chivalry* is not a picaro in the traditional sense (he is not poor, etc.); moreover, on more than one occasion this protagonist makes a point of insisting that he is not to

be confused with the protagonist of *Don Quixote*. In calling *Modern Chivalry* an episodic travel novel, I follow Matthew Garrett's conceptualization of the episodic novel, because *Modern Chivalry*'s plot can be grasped as a repetition of episodes that rehearse over and over again a set of didactic claims; see Garrett, *Episodic Poetics*, 92–95.

3. Ellis, *After the Revolution*, 101.

4. Ibid., 102.

5. Looby, *Voicing America*, 204.

6. S. Wood, *Quixotic Fictions*, 99.

7. Battistini, "Federalist Decline and Despair," 163. "Though the contentiousness of early America has been well established," Battistini continues, "few other early American authors struggled so long and inventively to represent this discord" (163).

8. J. Ellis, *After the Revolution*, 100.

9. Looby, *Voicing America*, 243.

10. Gordon Wood, *The Radicalism of the American Revolution*, 258.

11. Davidson, *Revolution and the Word*, 152, 153; hereafter cited in text.

12. Looby, *Voicing America*, 243.

13. Cotlar, *Tom Paine's America*, 158; hereafter cited in the text.

14. Writes William H. Hoffa of Brackenridge's narrator: "But while it is generally true that the narrative voice which dominates *Modern Chivalry* assumes the characteristics of detached, expansive omniscience, interpreting and judging the immediate and broader social, political, and philosophical significance of the adventures of Farrago and Teague, its ultimate seriousness is continually, though unpredictably, undercut by degrees of doubt, self-consciousness, ludicrousness, and even nonsense" ("The Language of Rogues," 294.) Brackenridge's narrator, writes S. Wood, "swing[s] unpredictably between sense and nonsense, insight and stupidity" (*Quixotic Fictions*, 99). On her reading, "locating any stable or authoritative voice proves impossible in *Modern Chivalry*, an encyclopaedia of contradictory public opinions, distinguished by a polemical tone and a shifting ironic stance" (99).

15. Jordan, *Second Stories*, 59. Farrago, writes Cathy Davidson, "views his fellow citizens with a mechanical misanthropy and never considers the possibility that an illiterate man might be wise or a poor man prudent. His attitude toward others is unremittingly patronizing. Lawmakers in Philadelphia, he would insist, have only the best interests of the populace at heart, even though that populace consists mostly of 'uppity' provincials who do not even merit their betters' concern. His views are too simplistic, too 'reactionary,' to be taken seriously" (*Revolution and the Word*, 175). Hoffa makes a similar observation about Farrago: "Much of what he says contains sound principles and rational counsel, but he also is guilty of hyperbolic, ineffectual, loaded, deceitful, and misleading language, especially in his 'advice' to Teague and to the others whom he feels himself superior" ("The Language of Rogues," 292). Farrago's "many lectures to various assemblages of the American citizenry," Hoffa continues, "are frequently

so arch and pompous in tone, manner, and presumption that he succeeds only in making a fool of himself. While he tries to be witty and parade his superior erudition or experience, his auditors often react with understandably mute incomprehension, disdain, and even anger and violence" (293).

16. My reading of *Modern Chivalry* is consonant with Cynthia Jordan's. Jordan, too, contends that *Modern Chivalry* "speaks . . . of the need for a social hierarchy based on education" and "of the need for class manipulation at the hands of a paternalistic leadership drawn from the educated elite" (*Second Stories*, 59). Moreover, she also points out that throughout the second half of *Modern Chivalry* "the authorial voice intrudes with increasing preachiness to promote the mode of authority the Captain represents" (70).

17. Woloch, *The One vs. the Many*, 25.

18. Bakhtin, *The Dialogic Imagination*, 91. "This most abstract of all chronotopes," Bakhtin explains, "is also the most static. In such a chronotope the world and the individual are finished items, absolutely immobile. In it there is no potential for evolution, for growth, for change. As a result of the action described in the novel, nothing in its world is destroyed, remade, changed, or created anew. What we get is a mere affirmation of the identity between what had been at the beginning and what is at the end. Adventure-time leaves no trace" (110).

19. Lukács, *History and Class Consciousness*, 48.

20. According to Dana Nelson, *Modern Chivalry* "offers readers something different from a simple 'either/or' choice between Hamilton and Washington's federalism and the westerners' democratic economic localism. Rather, Brackenridge's vision is unapologetically 'both/and.' . . . Acknowledging the perils, messiness, and mistakes that result from local practices, Brackenridge insists that this end—the people's end—of the democratic spectrum is nevertheless an important balancing against the excesses, tyranny, and mistakes of formal, representative institutions" (*Commons Democracy*, 67). "*Modern Chivalry*," Nelson continues, "offers a range of ideas about what democratic practices might include. And it frames as productive and even crucial the tensions produced between direct democratic local traditions and the federal representative order" (68). On Nelson's celebratory reading of *Modern Chivalry*, "true democracy" for Brackenridge entails a balancing act: "In the end, for Brackenridge, true democracy is not about getting the right answers or settling questions. It's about what happens in the middle: between the governed and the governing, between the representatives and represented, between the vernacular and the institutional, between freedom and despotism, between either and or. It's about having the patience to linger with riddling political questions, as well as the wisdom to appreciate human diversity and division, fallibility and foibles, as a fundamental part of making political community together" (83). My argument, in contrast, is that *Modern Chivalry* works against plebeian notions of what constitutes "true democracy" by construing elites as necessary to the political and economic health of the early United States.

21. Bakhtin, *Speech Genres*, 21; hereafter cited in text.

22. Adam Smith, *The Wealth of Nations*, 1:330; hereafter cited in text.

23. Quoted in Twomey, *Jacobins and Jeffersonians*, 185–86.

24. Manning, *The Key of Liberty*, 125; hereafter cited in text.

25. Manning gives voice, writes Christopher Tomlins, to a "distinguishably plebeian standpoint" (*Law, Labor, and Ideology*, 8).

26. According to Merrill and Wilentz's notes to *The Key of Liberty*, "A Free Republican" is Benjamin Lincoln Jr., and the "numbers" to which Manning refers appeared in *The Independent Chronicle* between November 24, 1785, and February 24, 1785 (221).

27. There was, writes Stuart Blumin, "a fundamental, unresolved contradiction in the social standing of the majority of middling folk": "The social degradation of manual work circumscribed the status of all artisans, but the independence of many, and the prosperity of a few, strained the very idea of a clearly differentiated set of social levels" (*The Emergence of the Middle Class*, 36). As Eric Foner explains, "Philadelphia's artisan culture . . . was pervaded by ambiguities and tensions, beginning with the inherent dualism of the artisan's role, on the one hand, as a small entrepreneur and employer and, on the other hand, as a laborer and craftsman" (quoted in ibid., 36).

28. On the 1806 cordwainer strike, see Tomlins, *Law, Labor, and Ideology*, 128–38.

29. Merrill and Wilentz, "Introduction," 60.

30. Gordon Wood, *Empire of Liberty*, 352–53.

31. Rediker, review of *The Key of Liberty*, 149.

32. Lukács, *History and Class Consciousness*, 52.

33. Marx, "Manifesto," 484.

34. Thompson, *The Making of the English Working Class*, 9.

35. Ibid., 807.

36. Wilentz, *Chants Democratic*, 95.

37. Ibid., 102.

38. Davidson, *Revolution and the Word*, 237.

39. Gordon Wood, "Interests and Disinterestedness," 95.

40. Ibid., 96.

41. Cornell, *The Other Founders*, 181–84.

42. Bouton, *Taming Democracy*, 106, 107.

43. Shankman, *Crucible of American Democracy*, 5; hereafter cited in the text.

44. Ed White, introduction to *Modern Chivalry*, xi.

45. J. Ellis, *After the Revolution*, 102.

46. Ibid., 103.

47. For example, writes Thomas Slaughter, "self-styled friends of order denounced the rebels' 'total subversion of government.' . . . The 'Jacobin' or 'insurgent' clubs, as their detractors now termed the democratic societies, were portrayed as advocates for renaming Washington County 'La Vendee.' . . . With the French Revolution as their context and seminal cause for the Rebellion, friends

of order had only to explain how Jacobin ideals had come to infect the 'sans culottes of Pittsburgh'" (*The Whiskey Rebellion*, 194–95). According to J. Ellis, "Radical clubs, calling themselves Democratic-Republican Societies, appeared in western Pennsylvania. . . . Members claimed to be ideological descendants of the Sons of Liberty; they set up liberty poles, terrorized tax collectors and expressed kinship with the Jacobins in the French Revolution" (*After the Revolution*, 103).

48. Slaughter, *The Whiskey Rebellion*, 195.

49. Quoted in Thompson, *The Making of the English Working Class*, 92.

50. Elliott, *Revolutionary Writers*, 202.

51. Rice, *The Transformation of Authorship*, 139.

52. Jordan, *Second Stories*, 70.

53. Richard Ellis, *The Jeffersonian Crisis*, 277.

54. Cotlar, "Joseph Gales," 355.

55. Bouton, *Taming Democracy*, 262.

56. Tomlins, *Law, Labor, and Ideology*, 15.

57. Nedelsky, *Private Property*, 1, 2.

58. Cotlar, *Tom Paine's America*, 171.

59. Madison, "The Federalist No. 10," 42, 46.

60. Sellers, *The Market Revolution*, 47, 51.

61. Tomlins, *Law, Labor, and Ideology*, 34.

62. Marx, "Manifesto," 489.

63. Ferguson, *Law and Letters*, 121.

64. Ed White arrives at a similar conclusion: Part 2 of *Modern Chivalry*, he observes, "increasingly focuses on what were called 'the liberal professions'—lawyers and judges, but also doctors, apothecaries, clerics, teachers, and writers—as the emerging ruling class"; the "the liberal professions" are endowed by the novel, he argues, "with more abstract knowledge and concepts, and are therefore to be trusted as experts in the management of people, values, and tradition." According to White, *Modern Chivalry* suggests that because the law "concerns economic and political relations among people, . . . accordingly lawyers and judges should be trusted as a kind of gifted managerial class" (introduction, xxiii).

65. Rancière, *Aesthetics and Its Discontents*, 24.

66. G. Wood, *Empire of Liberty*, 218.

67. "No person who is a friend to liberty will be against a large expense in learning, but it ought to be promoted in the cheapest and best manner possible," Manning wrote. He called for "every state to maintain as many colleges in convenient parts thereof"; he called for "every county to keep as many grammar schools or academies in convenient parts thereof" in which "[n]o student or scholar would pay anything for tuition"; and he called for "every town to be obliged to keep as much as six weeks of writing school in the winter and twelve weeks of a woman school in the summer in every part of the town—so that none should be thronged with too many scholars, and no scholar should have

too far to travel." "Every person," he contended, is "to be obliged to send his children to school—for the public is as much interested in the learning of one child as another" (*Key of Liberty*, 182).

68. Nelson, "Indications of the Public Will," 31.

69. Rice, *The Transformation of Authorship*, 139.

70. Robbins, "On the Rentier," 907.

71. For Cynthia Jordan, *Modern Chivalry* is about Farrago's increasing lack of control over the polity (*Second Stories*, 71–77). Yet, the novel in fact concludes with Farrago successfully reasserting his control over the polity and containing radical plebeian political desire.

3. The Providence of Class

1. Gura, *Truth's Ragged Edge*, 61. As Lucinda Damon-Bach and Victoria Clements remind us in their introduction to a recent collection of essays on Sedgwick, she "enjoyed a popularity equivalent to, if not greater than, that of Cooper, Irving, Melville, or Poe." *The Poor Rich Man* and *Live and Let Live*, they point out, were—with *Home* (1835)—"Sedgwick's most widely read works" (introduction, xxix, xxv).

2. For influential readings of *Hope Leslie* along these lines, see Fetterly, "'My Sister! My Sister!'"; Gould, *Covenant and Republic*, 61–90; and Nelson, *The Word in Black and White*, 65–89.

3. I am not the first to call attention to what Sarah Robbins calls the "class-inflected agenda" of Sedgwick's 1830s novels ("Periodizing Authorship," 2). I depart, however, from a critical predilection (or desire, perhaps) to read these novels as reformist in orientation and effect.

4. Lang, *The Syntax of Class*, 17.

5. Gates, "Sedgwick's American Poor," 180.

6. Ousley, "The Business of Housekeeping," 136. Ousley characterizes *Live and Let Live* as "a diatribe, grounded in the ethos of sentimentalism, against the cruel exploitation of the 'domestics' who labor in American homes" (137). Mary Templin has argued that Sedgwick, along with Hannah Farnham Saywer Lee and Eliza Lee Cabot Follen, sketched out "a blueprint for a domesticated economy" ("'Dedicated to the Works of Beneficence,'" 102).

7. Winthrop, "A Model of Christian Charity," 79.

8. Lazerow, *Religion and the Working Class*, 181.

9. Joseph Fichtelberg makes a complementary argument. On his account, sentimental fiction "works to humanize economic crisis and make it more manageable" by imagining heroines flexible enough to thrive amid the economic crises that punctuate the nineteenth century, and thus it should be read as seeking to "legitimate the market" (*Critical Fictions*, 14).

10. The "commercial construction of liberal political subjectivities," Merish writes, "reinforced the political and national hegemony of the middle class"; it did so, she suggests, by inscribing "class as a voluntary (and *malleable*) identification, one expressed and shaped by taste and domestic consumption—a

configuration of class(lessness) central to the logic of the 'American Dream'" (*Sentimental Materialism*, 47–48). I return to "classlessness" in Gillian Brown's account of sentimentalism near the close of this chapter.

11. Halttunen, *Confidence Men and Painted Women*, 194.

12. Lang, *The Syntax of Class*, 18.

13. Like novels centered on the bootstrapping success of male protagonists, these sentimental novels can be read as participating in the "fantasy of absolute social fluidity in America" (Gould, "Class," 70).

14. Lang, *The Syntax of Class*, 2.

15. Wright, "The People at War," 178.

16. Burke, *The Conundrum of Class*, 75.

17. Ibid., 54.

18. Burnap, "The Social Influence of Trade," 419.

19. James Fenimore Cooper, *The American Democrat*, 135; hereafter cited in text.

20. Quoted in Glickstein, *American Exceptionalism*, 138.

21. While the paradigm of "classlessness" may help to explain Sedgwick's *Home* (1835) or later sentimental novels, it does not do justice, I am arguing, to *The Poor Rich Man* and *Live and Let Live*. For *Home* as a novel that trades in fantasies of working-class mobility into the middle class, see Merish, *Sentimental Materialism*, 120; and Rucavado, *Class Difference*, 73–80.

22. On increasing economic inequality in the antebellum period, see, e.g., Pessen, *Riches, Class, and Power*.

23. Dimock and Gilmore, introduction, 6.

24. Schocket, *Vanishing Moments*, 22.

25. Mary Templin has also recognized the importance of economic paternalism to Sedgwick's vision of class relations. Paternalistic relationships in Sedgwick's novels, Templin writes, "bind the classes together in love rather them separating them with antagonism" (*Panic Fictions*, 99). Yet, Templin argues that Sedgwick imagines economically paternalistic relationships between middle-class and working-class characters in order to carve out a "middle ground" for the middle class between rich and poor (65–105). I emphasize, in contrast, how Sedgwick's paternalism is part and parcel of an argument for a binary division of society into rich and poor. Templin is too quick to fold Sedgwick's fiction into the story of a middle class that defines itself as "in the middle."

26. See Fliegelman, *Prodigals and Pilgrims*, and *Declaring Independence*. Writes Looby of "republicanism" in late eighteenth- and early nineteenth-century America: "A liberal market society formed and developed fairly quickly after the Revolution, and this fact effectively consigns the reactionary discourse of classical republicanism to the role of ideology in the strong sense of false consciousness. If republican ideas survived into the nineteenth century, they do so as a mystification of real social processes" (*Voicing America*, 241).

27. Appleby, *Capitalism and a New Social Order*, 78.

28. Ellen Meiksins Wood, *The Pristine Culture of Capitalism*, 138.

29. Ibid., 138–39.

30. Pocock, *The Machiavellian Moment*, 517, 516. "Classical republicanism," Wai-Chee Dimock writes, "celebrated hierarchy as . . . the operative condition for a civic order" (*Residues of Justice*, 42).

31. For characterizations of "republicanism" and "liberalism" in these terms, see Appleby, *Capitalism and a New Social Order;* and Looby, *Voicing America*, 241. Jeffersonian liberals, writes Appleby, "endowed American capitalism with the moral force of their vision of a social order for free and independent men" (104). "Republicanism" and "liberalism" were not, a number of scholars have argued, mutually exclusive, but rather were fundamentally entangled through-out the late eighteenth and early nineteenth centuries. See Dillon, *The Gender of Freedom;* Kloppenberg, "The Virtues of Liberalism"; and Smith-Rosenberg, "Domesticating Virtue." Nina Baym contends that many antebellum women's novels combined "liberal individualism" with "conservative communitarianism" (*Women's Fiction*, xxviii).

32. Dobson, "Reclaiming Sentimental Literature," 267.

33. Pearson, *The Rights of the Defenseless*, 130. Or, as Susan Ryan writes of the antebellum culture of benevolence, the "simultaneous erasure and persistence of difference facilitates both the sentimental bond that creates the desire to give and the maintenance of hierarchy that suggests such giving is safe, that it does not threaten the identity or status of the giver, that it does not, ultimately, make helper and helped the same" (*The Grammar of Good Intentions*, 19).

34. As Susan Ryan argues, antebellum writing about benevolence often held that "benevolent individuals . . . should work to soften the effects of poverty but should not attempt to eradicate inequality itself, for in so doing they would eliminate their own *'means of moral improvement'*" (*The Grammar of Good Intentions*, 10). Schocket makes a similar point. On his reading, the nineteenth- and early twentieth-century "American labor narrative"—the bourgeois story told about white workers—is "formulated around a set of . . . conventions that together comprise a cycle of class unveiling and remediation" (*Vanishing Moments*, 3). Thus, "the American labor narrative" has a sentimental structure: it solicits sympathy for the class Other. But, as Schocket argues, because "sympathy as a representational mode lies within the social relations of capitalism," "one cannot assume that sympathy is always or even usually a progressive step toward the amelioration of suffering" (5, 6). In fact, "sympathetic investment" in the class Other can forestall inquiry into "the structural causes for inequity" (32).

35. Tocqueville, *Democracy in America*, 3.

36. On labor unrest, see Newman, *Our Common Dwelling*, 25–34; and Wilentz, *Chants Democratic*.

37. Fisk, *Capital against Labor*, 3.

38. Newman, *Our Common Dwelling*, 31.

39. Wilentz argues that in the 1820s and 1830s "labor spokesman and spokes-woman" "formulated their own conception of the labor theory of value" which

"clashed directly with capitalist conceptions of wage-labor as commodity" ("Against Exceptionalism," 10).

40. Blatchly, *An Essay on Common Wealth*, 86–87; hereafter cited in text.

41. Lazerow, *Religion and the Working Class*, 9.

42. Quoted ibid., 179.

43. Linnebaugh and Rediker, *The Many-Headed Hydra*, 41–42. The phrase was introduced into English translations of the Old Testament by William Tyndale in 1530 (ibid., 42).

44. Fisk, *Capital against Labor*, 5.

45. Brownson, "Review of *An Essay*," 361.

46. Brownson, "The Laboring Classes," 438; hereafter cited in text.

47. "The crux of Blatchly's radicalism," notes Wilentz, "lay in his combination of Christian ethics, republican politics, and the labor theory of value." "Blatchly's Christian republican jeremiad," Wilentz continues, "blamed economic inequality not on political corruption alone but on private property and usury. So long as private property existed, all laws and privileges would favor the propertied" (*Chants Democratic*, 161).

48. Despite drawing primary inspiration from the ideas of Charles Fourier, 1840s U.S. utopian socialist projects were also indebted to American Christian economic egalitarians like Blatchly and Brownson. Blatchly was an early proponent of the communitarianism of Robert Owen, whose planned communities (like New Harmony) were precursors of U.S. Fourierism (Harris, *Socialist Origins*, 10). Blatchly's *Essay on Common Wealth* includes pages from Owen's *New Views of Society*, recommending Owen's ideas as one solution to economic inequality in the United States. George Ripley, founder of Brook Farm, perhaps the most well-known Fourierist experiment in the United States, recognized Fourierism's similarity to Owen's ideas but additionally "credited Brownson with the inspiration for Brook Farm" (Guarneri, *The Utopian Alternative*, 83, 45).

49. Harris, *Socialist Origins*, 10.

50. George Ripley et al., "Brook Farm's First (Published) Constitution (1844)."

51. Even in John Nichols's *The "S" Word*, socialism does not take the field in the United States until the 1850s.

52. Jones, *American Hungers*, 31. This assessment begins with Herman Melville's 1854 diptych "Poor Man's Pudding and Rich Man's Crumbs," which is in part a satire of *The Poor Rich Man*. When *The Poor Rich Man* is mentioned in literary history, it is often as a foil for Melville's sketch. Paul Lewis, for example, writes: "Sedgwick's unnuanced treatment of the benefits of poverty and the disadvantages of wealth eventually succumbed to Melville's 'blistering satire'" ("'Lectures or a Little Charity,'" 263).

53. Blackmar, *Manhattan for Rent*, 104.

54. Fisk, *Capital against Labor*, 7.

55. "The Aikins may not be wealthy and may need to labor to survive," Amal Amireh writes, "yet in their contentment and in their possession of certain

manners and virtues they are an example of a poor family with middle-class values" (*The Factory Girl,* 55).

56. According to Templin, Sedgwick's novel suggests through the example of Beckwith's housing investment that "the marketplace ought to be an expansion of the household, operated according to domestic values of trust and humility" ("'Dedicated to the Works of Beneficence,'" 93). In Beckwith's housing investment, she continues, "Sedgwick unites the economic and the domestic—making money by building homes—through a project that is centered on the welfare of others" (95). This is an important point: while critics have suggested that midcentury domestic fiction produces an image of the middle-class home as somehow beyond the marketplace, in Sedgwick's novel homes are always inside the market; they are commodities in their own right. Equally important is Templin's observation that men are just as likely as women to be the dispersers of market-based benevolence that produces ideal homes (95–96).

57. Theodore Sedgwick, *Public and Private Economy,* vol. 1; hereafter cited in text.

58. Hofstadter, *The American Political Tradition,* 79.

59. On the link between "possessive individualism" and justifications for economic inequality, see Macpherson, *The Political Theory,* 194–238.

60. The conflict between narrator and character is at the center of D. A. Miller's analysis of the politics of Jane Austen's "style" (*Jane Austen*).

61. "In myriad ways," writes Amy Dru Stanley, "the deepening intrusion of market relations into family economies involved all sorts of different women in selling commodities, making commodities, buying commodities, turning parts of their homes into commodities, disposing of their time and skill as commodities. Even for the middle class, the idea is no longer tenable that the world of most women was remote from the market, that their labor had no cash value, that their homes were not also places of work, both paid and unpaid" ("Home Life," 78).

62. Stansell, *City of Women,* 12. This was the case, Stansell observes, even as "the manufacturing system extended its reach" (155).

63. Catharine Maria Sedgwick, *Live and Let Live,* 44; hereafter cited in the text.

64. Ousley, "The Business of Housekeeping," 133.

65. Ibid., 136.

66. Brownson, "Review," 361.

67. Sedgwick tells us that she refers to Wordsworth's *The Excursion.*

68. Boydston convincingly argues that unpaid women's housework—whether working- or middle-class—was, as a source of economic value, essential to capital accumulation in the early nineteenth-century United States. Unpaid working-class housework enabled employers to pay their male workers less; unpaid housework in middle-class households thus made possible capital accumulation in the form of savings (*Home and Work,* 140).

69. Barbara Ryan, *Love, Wages, Slavery,* 1.

70. Ibid., 42.

71. Of course, as Harry Braverman explains, "the capitalist who hires a servant is not making profits but spending them" (*Labor and Monopoly,* 285).

72. The reader of *Live and Let Live,* Ousley observes of this passage, is thus "left with both a validation of the social hierarchy and its economic foundation" ("The Business of Housekeeping," 142).

73. Writes Gillian Brown: "To equalize labor and eliminate the 'laboring class' in America's emergent republic society, Stowe advocates the 'dignity of labor,' the dignity of 'the lady who does her own work.' Stowe's endorsement of self-reliant labor correlates with 'the doctrine of universal equality' in American society" (*Domestic Individualism,* 54).

74. Gould, "Class," 71.

75. Schocket, *Vanishing Moments,* 16.

76. Fisk, *Capital against Labor,* 6.

77. Rebecca Harding Davis, *Life in the Iron-Mills,* 45; hereafter cited in the text.

4. No Apologies for the Anti-Renters

1. Fisher, *Hard Facts,* 53.

2. Fiedler, *Love and Death,* 184.

3. Zinn, *A People's History,* 211–52.

4. Chase, *The American Novel,* 51.

5. Bewley, *The Eccentric Design,* 65, 66.

6. Writes Nelson: "Readers habitually assume that in writing [these novels], Cooper exercised only partisan advocacy for the political outcome he preferred from the Anti-rent Wars, not the skills of a novelist. Few who have studied these novels treat them as serious literature, scanning them instead biographically" (*Commons Democracy,* 133–34); hereafter cited in the text.

7. Chase, *The American Novel,* 47. Alexander Saxton argues that even though Cooper's "politics were, in the formal sense, Jacksonian, his social values were Old Federalist" (*The Rise and Fall,* 193). For Granville Hicks, the Littlepage novels are essentially a defense of the Hudson Valley landlords: "Try as he might to convince himself and others that he was defending the rights of private property in the abstract it was a particular kind of property that interested him." Cooper was, writes Hicks, "specifically defending the class to which he belonged, the class of large landlords, which he regarded as a bulwark not only against the masses but also against the commercial aristocracy" ("Landlord Cooper," 98). For John P. McWilliams, the Littlepage novels are less an endorsement of a specific class than a defense of constitutional law and liberty: the way anti-renters "exerted pressure violated Cooper's standards for honorable civil conduct" and "rendered the due processes of political change and law enforcement impossible for nearly a decade" (*Political Justice,* 308, 307). If for Hicks the Littlepage novels are an archly conservative defense of the "gentleman" against the "ruffian" (108), for McWilliams, in contrast, they are a further expression

of Cooper's "republican political faith" (301). If for Hicks the Littlepage novels stage an anachronistic defense of the dying class to which Cooper belonged, and if for McWilliams they carry out Cooper's lifelong goal of defending constitutional legal processes, I argue that the ideological function of the Littlepage novels is to legitimate not the landlord class as such or an abstract notion of civil law but rather the asymmetrical ownership of property in general.

8. Bewley, *The Eccentric Design*, 65.

9. Egan Jr., *The Riven Home*, 32–60.

10. Schachterle, "The Themes of Land."

11. McGann, "Fenimore Cooper's Anti-Aesthetic," 150.

12. Ibid., 153.

13. "*The Redskins*," observes Nelson, "gives the last word to the Onondaga character Susquesus. . . . Cooper has the antiquated Susquesus condemn the property lust of all the novels' white characters. . . . In this way, Cooper leaves readers today with the option of writing all three novels off as a simple tale of white greed" (*Commons Democracy*, 135). For Nelson, Cooper's trilogy deserves attention because it "helps us track historically the substantive, if diminishing threat that the power of commons democracy posed to the growing economic power of liberalism in the early United States. . . . The novel helps us see how the universal suffrage that seems like a democratic advance covers over the more complicated capitalist constraining and harnessing of 'democracy' in this period" (137). I agree that in attending to Cooper's trilogy we cannot help being reminded of oppositional political economy in the antebellum United States; yet, I highlight how Cooper's novels helped the U.S. bourgeoisie in the 1840s to consolidate itself ideologically against economic egalitarianism.

14. As Reeve Huston explains, Whig and Democrat politicians hijacked the anti-rent movement and "placed the anti-renters' vision of free labor on the narrowest possible foundation"; in effect, mainstream politicians "transformed the anti-renters' conception of freedom as land, security, equality, and exchange into the freedom to compete and prosper in a buoyant capitalist economy. In their vision, nothing was guaranteed but the freedom then being endorsed by the courts and by economic elites" ("Land and Freedom," 33).

15. "James Fenimore Cooper," 67.

16. Nelson explains why this struggle is difficult to remember: "The nation's commitment to developing capitalist power at the direct expense of democratic power hardened in this era, and it did so in ways that are difficult to conceptualize—let alone historically remember—with precision. It's hard to remember alternatives because the casting of [the] formal separation of property from political status through universal suffrage is historically understood as an already accomplished and *democratic good*. This casting occludes from view those arguments that depended on this prior link, and which held out a far more substantive notion of democratic equality (access) than simple equality before the law (opportunity)" (*Commons Democracy*, 171).

17. James Fenimore Cooper, *The Redskins*, xvi; hereafter cited in the text.

18. Lawson-Peebles, "Property, Marriage, and Women," 52.

19. Cooper, *The American Democrat*, 137.

20. Ibid., 138.

21. McWilliams, *Political Justice*, 307.

22. Fliegelman, *Prodigal and Pilgrims*, 126.

23. Catharine Beecher, *A Treatise on Domestic Economy*, 3.

24. Watt, *The Rise of the Novel*, 138.

25. Skidmore, *The Rights of Man to Property!*, 3–4.

26. Harris, *Socialist Origins*, 98.

27. Wilentz, *Chants Democratic*, 184.

28. Ibid., 336.

29. Tuchinsky, *Horace Greeley's* New-York Tribune, 137.

30. Glickstein, *American Exceptionalism*, 131.

31. Bronstein, *Land Reform*, 23.

32. Sklansky, *The Soul's Economy*, 30. For the influence of Paine on Skidmore and other land reformers, see Kaye, *Thomas Paine*, 134–39.

33. Thomas Jefferson, *The Essential Jefferson*, 154.

34. Skidmore, *The Rights of Man to Property!*, 32.

35. James Huston summarizes the basic tenets of the labor theory of wealth at the heart of land reformers' arguments: "When a person bestowed his labor on an object, the value thus created and added to the object morally belonged only to that person and to no other because of the act of individual labor. . . . The labor theory of property/value became the standard by which to judge the righteousness of property distribution. When the laborer obtained full remuneration for the values he created, the resulting distribution of wealth (or income) was natural and just. Unjust wealth distributions occurred when by one means or another the fruits of labor were transferred from the laborer to a non-laborer. In colonial eighteenth-century parlance, the key phrase indicating the operation of the principle of the labor theory of property/value was 'the fruits of labor'" (*Securing the Fruits*, 8).

36. Quoted in Foley, "From Wall Street to Astor Place," 94.

37. Again, Dimock contends "Skidmore's militancy is not only compatible with the established order but in some sense generated by it, for his militancy is above all the militancy of an imperial self" (*Empire for Liberty*, 32).

38. Marx, *Capital*, vol. 1, 927, 928.

39. Ibid., 927.

40. "Everyone," writes Macpherson, "sees that Locke's assertion and justification of a natural individual right to property is central to his theory of civil society and government" (*The Political Theory*, 197). But if Locke argued that every individual has a right to the "*Labour* of his Body, and the *Work* of his Hands," he simultaneously made the case for "an unlimited natural right of appropriation" (200, 203). In fact, according to Macpherson, Locke read the "inequality of possession of land" back into the "state of nature," and thereby legitimated it as an expression of natural rights (209). From here, Locke was

"concerned to show that the right to unequal property is a right men bring with them into civil society" (218). Writes Cotlar: "Painites in the late eighteenth century took the natural rights tradition in very different direction [from Locke], arguing that since the right to property was universal, every person should by right have enough to sustain himself" (*Tom Paine's America*, 122).

41. Tuchinsky, *Horace Greeley's New-York Tribune*, 127.

42. Ibid., 128.

43. Lause, *Young America*, 56–57.

44. On Skidmore's indirect impact on Marx, see Feuer's *Marx and the Intellectuals*, 210–15.

45. Masquerier, "Declaration," 66; hereafter cited in the text.

46. R. Huston, "Land and Freedom," 21–23.

47. Fitzhugh, *Sociology for the South*, 71.

48. R. Huston, "Land and Freedom," 24.

49. Tuchinsky, *Horace Greeley's* New-York Tribune, 132, 133.

50. James Fenimore Cooper, *Satanstoe*, 3; hereafter cited in the text.

51. Godden, "Pioneer Properties," 125–26.

52. Dekker, *The American Historical*, 90.

53. Cooper, *The American Democrat*, 135; hereafter cited in text.

54. James Fenimore Cooper, *The Chainbearer*, 123; hereafter cited in the text.

55. Cooper distinguishes, in good liberal fashion, between two types of equality: "equality of condition" and "equality of rights." For Cooper, "equality of rights" is "a peculiar feature of democracies." Cooper further subdivides "rights" into "political" and "civil." Equality of political rights entails universal (white, adult, male) "suffrage" as well as "eligibility to office." Equality of civil rights, in turn, means "all men are equal before the law . . . all classes of the community being liable equally to taxation, military service, jury duties, and to the other impositions attendant on civilization." That is, "an equality of civil rights may be briefly defined to be an absence of privileges" (*The American Democrat*, 43).

56. Tawil, *The Making of Racial Sentiment*, 90–91.

57. Fiedler, *Love and Death*, 26.

58. Ibid., 211.

59. Tawil, *The Making of Racial Sentiment*, 92.

60. Tawil: "Cooper's fictions, no less than those of his female counterparts, tend to find their resolutions in marriage and the formation of a middle-class household around an Anglo-American heterosexual couple" (*ibid.*, 129). Signe O. Wegner makes a similar point: Cooper, she observes, "took from the popular books of his day" and "presented himself as a writer of domestic, i.e., women's fiction" (*James Fenimore Cooper*, 3). "Like many other nineteenth-century writers of domestic fiction," Wegner explains, "Cooper often closes his novels with a marriage prospect, a wedding, or an epilogue detailing the characters' future"; he thus participates in what Wegner calls the "feminized genre" of domestic fiction (5).

61. Henry Nash Smith, *Virgin Land*, 51.

62. Romero, *Home Fronts*, 48–49.

63. Baym, "The Women," 698.

64. Ibid., 709. Likewise, Dimock shows that in *The Deerslayer* Cooper's commitment to social "equality" between partners as a "marital ideal" "foregrounds class" (*Residues of Justice*, 37). On Cooper's unwillingness to imagine interracial marriages, see also Tawil, *The Making of Racial Sentiment*, 69–151.

65. Nathaniel Hawthorne, *The House of the Seven Gables*, 137.

66. Ibid., 149.

67. Mary P. Ryan, *The Empire of the Mother*, 26.

68. Welter, "The Cult of True Womanhood," 152.

69. M. P. Ryan, *The Empire of the Mother*, 37.

70. For inflections of this argument, see G. Brown, *Domestic Individualism*; Pfister, *The Production of Personal Life*; and M. P. Ryan, *The Empire of the Mother*.

71. Again, the dichotomy of home and market was itself a kind of fiction, especially for working-class women.

72. As Christine Stansell and Stuart Blumin have argued, the economic struggles of antebellum workers prohibited the acquisition of the kind of wealth on which middle-class domesticity and its attendant ideal of "woman" was predicated.

73. Lang, *Syntax of Class*, 38.

74. *Ibid.*, 38.

75. Pfister, *The Production of Personal Life*, 130.

76. According to Alexander Saxton, the marriage plots of Cooper's Leatherstocking novels must be read in the context of the "the Fee Soil Movement:" "What the Free Soil Movement, as a class-alliance-in-the-making, required for its operating myth was the story of a man of yeoman or artisan background who would win the love of an upper-class young lady and claim her, not by force or stealth, but by convincing her he had the power and right to do so." For Saxton, Cooper's "Old Federalist mentality could hardly have endorsed either the Free Soil alliance or cross-class marriage" (*The Rise and Fall*, 197). Cooper does not in either *The Chainbearer* or *The Redskins* endorse the marriage of "a man of yeoman or artisan background" to "an upper-class lady"; yet, *The Chainbearer* and *The Redskins* do end with cross-class marriages, insofar as the poor Dus marries the wealthy Mordaunt, and the poor Mary marries the wealthy Hugh.

77. Slotkin, *The Fatal Environment*, 103.

78. Ibid.

79. James Fenimore Cooper, *The Prairie*, 61.

80. "If we compare Thousandacres to Ishmael Bush and to Natty," McWilliams points outs, "we see how Cooper attributed squatter's arguments to increasingly less sympathetic characters as he grew older" (*Political Justice*, 321).

81. R. Huston, *Land and Freedom*; hereafter cited in text.

82. Nelson, too, cites this passage from *Land and Freedom*, reminding us also that "indigenous political leaders of the late-eighteenth- and nineteenth-

century increasingly [took] for granted predictable behavioral divides between" Native Americans and whites (*Commons Democracy*, 166).

83. Mark Rifkin, *Settler Common Sense*, xvi. Rifkin explains how both land reform and anti-rent intersect with "settler common sense" in his magisterial reading of the complex relationship between, on the one hand, Herman Melville's *Pierre* and, on the other, the arguments of land reformers and anti-renters about economic inequality, labor, and property rights in land (141–94).

84. With respect to Cooper's representation of the anti-rent "Indians," Philip J. Deloria writes: "Cooper responded by characterizing them as unreasonable savages who had corrupted new national ideals of political stability and economic continuity. For Cooper . . . , the injins' rebellious proclivity for murder, arson, cowardice, and bad manners . . . placed them outside the borders of American society" (*Playing Indian*, 39).

85. Lause, *Young America*, 78; cited hereafter in text.

86. Writes McWilliams: "The savage's new respect for civil laws of property has led the Indian to ally himself with the gentry and their faithful black against the gentry's own tenants. The Indian finally serves as a standard of principled fidelity against which whites are judged" (*Political Justice*, 327).

87. Deloria, *Playing Indian*, 40.

5. Working-Class Abolitionism and Antislavery Fiction

1. Lott, *Love and Theft*, 219; hereafter cited in text.

2. Tawil, *The Making of Racial Sentiment*, 154.

3. S. Ryan, *The Grammar of Good Intentions*, 153.

4. Rowe, "Stowe's Rainbow Sign," 39.

5. Levine, introduction to *Dred*, xvii.

6. David S. Reynolds, *Mightier than the Sword*, 163.

7. Meer, *Uncle Tom Mania*, 239.

8. Harriet Beecher Stowe, *A Key*, 184.

9. Harriet Beecher Stowe, *Dred*, 107; hereafter cited in the text.

10. Meer has also pointed out the consonance between the chapter "Poor White Trash" in *A Key* and this speech by Clayton in *Dred* (*Uncle Tom Mania*, 239).

11. Hurst, "Beyond the Pale," 637.

12. Ibid., 636.

13. Rowe, "Stowe's Rainbow Sign," 46.

14. Marx, *Capital*, vol. 1, 414.

15. Quoted in Mandel, *Labor, Free and Slave*, 79.

16. Eric Foner, *Free Soil*, xix.

17. Roediger, *The Wages of Whiteness*, 68, 74.

18. Schocket, *Vanishing Moments*, 47.

19. Quoted in Roediger, *The Wages of Whiteness*, 77.

20. See ibid., 74–76; and Gourevitch, *From Slavery*, 37.

21. Helwig, "Denying the Wages of Whiteness," 87.

22. Roediger, *The Wages of Whiteness*, 86.

23. Douglass, *My Bondage*, 226.

24. Lippard, *The Quaker City*, 389.

25. On Lippard's use of "white slaves" to imagine interracial working-class solidarity, see Helwig, "Denying the Wages of Whiteness."

26. Walt Whitman, "American Workingmen," 199.

27. Nordhoff, *America for Free Working Men!*, 3.

28. Ibid., 9.

29. Eric Foner, *Politics and Ideology*, 57.

30. Fitzhugh, *Sociology for the South*, 18; hereafter cited in text.

31. Fitzhugh, *Cannibals All!*, 13.

32. Peterson, *The Cabin and the Parlor*, 186–87.

33. Hentz, *The Planter's Northern Bride*, 31–32.

34. Rush, *The North and the South*, 129–30.

35. See esp. Meer, *Uncle Tom Mania*, 232–52.

36. Mandel, *Labor, Free and Slave*, 123.

37. Quoted ibid., 125.

38. Quoted ibid., 128–29.

39. Ibid., 129.

40. S. Ryan, *The Grammar of Good Intentions*, 156.

41. Rowe, "Stowe's Rainbow Sign," 46.

42. Stowe, *A Key*, 185–86.

43. Douglass, *My Bondage*, 226.

44. Writes Meers: "Stowe asks her readers to sympathize with what she portrays as an oppressed class but not to identify with it" (*Uncle Tom Mania*, 242).

45. That characters who actively desire political change are *heroes* in *Dred* also indicates *Dred's* morphological and ideological distance from the "classic" nineteenth-century realist novel. In *The Antinomies of Realism*, Jameson returns to what he calls "the usual point about the structural and inherent conservatism and anti-politicality of the realist novel as such" (215). According to Jameson, the "classic" realist novel—the nineteenth-century realist novel—articulates what he calls "ontological realism," or a thoroughgoing commitment to "the density and solidity of what is" (215). That the realist novel "absolutely resists and repudiates" a future that is different from the present, he contends, "can be judged from its conventional treatment of political characters" (213). Jameson observes that as a rule the realist novel *satirizes* "figures of the political" and thus of "the anti-ontological"; the nineteenth-century realist novel, in other words, satirizes characters that desire and strive to bring into being a future that differs from the status quo.

46. Greeson, *Our South*, 172; hereafter cited in text.

47. See Mandel, *Labor, Free and Slave*, 84–85.

48. Philip Foner, *History of the Labor Movement*, 272.

49. Quoted ibid., 272.

50. Lippard, *The Quaker City*, 389–90.

51. Roediger, *The Wages of Whiteness*, 73.

52. Schocket, *Vanishing Moments*, 38.

53. Herman Melville, *Moby-Dick*, 21.

54. Ibid. On the significance of Ishmael's embrace of wage labor in the context of "free labor ideology," see McGuire, "'Who Ain't a Slave?'"

55. On "free labor ideology," see E. Foner, *Free Soil;* and Glickstein, *American Exceptionalism.*

56. P. Foner, *History of the Labor Movement*, 270.

57. E. Foner, *Politics and Ideology*, 24.

58. Carey, *The North and the South*, 21.

59. Sklansky, *The Soul's Economy*, 87.

60. E. Foner, *Politics and Ideology*, 24.

61. Peter Brooks: "The sense of a beginning, then, must in some important way be determined by the sense of an ending. We might say that we are able to read present moments—in literature and, by extension, in life—as endowed with narrative meaning only because we read them in anticipation of the structuring power of those endings that will retrospectively give them the order and significance of a plot" (*Reading for the Plot*, 94).

62. Rowe, "Stowe's Rainbow Sign," 45.

63. Lang, *The Syntax of Class*, 28.

64. Ibid.

65. On *Our Nig*'s critique of "free labor" for free blacks in the North, see Dowling, *Capital Letters*, 27–43.

Conclusion

1. Lukács, *The Historical Novel*, 27.

2. Writes Lukács: "For the countries of Western and Central Europe the Revolution of 1848 means a decisive alteration in class groupings and in class attitudes to all important questions of social life, to the perspectives of social development. The June battle of the Paris proletariat in 1848 constitutes a turning-point in history on an international scale. Despite Chartism, despite sporadic uprisings in France during the 'bourgeois monarchy,' despite the rising of the German weavers in 1844, here for the first time a decisive battle is carried out by force of arms between proletariat and bourgeoisie, here for the first time the proletariat enters upon the world-historical stage as an armed mass, resolved upon the final struggle; during these days the bourgeoisie for the first time fights for the naked continuance of its economic and political rule" (*The Historical Novel*, 171). Lukács argues that before 1848 the bourgeoisie and its fiction are "progressive" (even revolutionary); after 1848, the bourgeoisie and its fiction become "reactionary." Writes Nancy Armstrong: "George Lukács identifies 1848 or thereabouts as the moment when the novel abandoned its attempts to imagine a more flexible and inclusive social order" (*How Novels Think*, 142).

3. In his study of the nineteenth-century European bildungsroman, Moretti argues, for example, that this genre turns on the "encounter" between

the bourgeoisie and the aristocracy—and, moreover, that the early (and late) nineteenth-century bildungsroman seeks to generate a "compromise" between these two classes (*The Way of the World,* viii).

4. Best and Marcus, "Surface Reading," 3.

5. Jameson, *The Political Unconscious,* 48; hereafter cited in text.

6. Riffing on Ricoeur's *Freud and Philosophy,* Rita Felski writes: "The difference between a hermeneutics of restoration and a hermeneutics of suspicion, we might say, lies in the difference between unveiling and unmasking" (*The Limits of Critique,* 32).

7. For Felski, the "key elements" of critique are "a spirit of skeptical questioning or outright condemnation, an emphasis on [critique's] precarious position vis-à-vis overbearing and oppressive social forces, the claim to be engaged in some kind of radical intellectual and/or political work, and the assumption that whatever is *not* critical must be *uncritical*" (*The Limits of Critique,* 2). "Why is it," she asks, "that critics are so quick off the mark to interrogate, unmask, expose, subvert, unravel, demystify, destabilize, take issue, and take umbrage? What sustains their assurance that a text is withholding something of vital importance, that their task is to ferret out what lies concealed in its recesses and margins?" (5).

8. On the relationships between "critique," "symptomatic reading," and "the hermeneutics of suspicion," see ibid., 30–84. "Reading is imagined," Felski says of symptomatic reading as suspicious reading (and vice versa), "as an act of digging down to arrive at a repressed or otherwise obscured reality. Like a valiant archaeologist, the critic excavates a rocky and resistant terrain in order to retrieve, after arduous effort, a highly valued object. The text is envisaged as possessing qualities of interiority, concealment, penetrability, and depth; it is an object to be plundered, a puzzle to be solved, a hieroglyph to be deciphered. . . . Real meaning is at odds with apparent meaning and must be painstakingly exhumed by the critic" (*ibid.,* 53, 56). Critique is often "shorthand," writes Christopher Castiglia, "for the righteous digging around in a text for hidden displacements of the social struggles that evade all but the politically savvy and serious critic" ("Twists and Turns," 61).

9. Benjamin, *Illuminations,* 256. As Pfister notes, section 7 of Benjamin's "Theses on the Philosophy of History"—where Benjamin contends that the historical materialist critic's task is to identify the links between "documents of civilization" and "barbarism" and thus to "brush history against the grain"—is "the *locus classicus* that exemplifies seminal aspects of some well-known complicity critiques, a passage whose significance reverberates throughout the work of such critics as Raymond Williams, Terry Eagleton, Fredric Jameson, and Alan Sinfield" (*Critique for What?,* 123–24).

10. Castiglia finds something similar: "I would argue that *true* (as opposed to rote) critique is deeply hopeful. Without an ideal of how the world *could* look, what social visions are possible, an imaginative speculation that shows the current state of affairs to be sadly lacking, we would not be motivated to

suspect what postures as the real and the inevitable. Theodor Adorno insists that every utopian statement is a 'determined negation,' a critique of the present in the act of articulating a more desirable future. But the opposite is also true: through critique, we imply ideals as the metric by which we measure the present and the past. Every critique, in other words, is a determined idealism" ("Twists and Turns," 62).

Bibliography

Acker, Joan. *Class Questions: Feminist Answers*. New York: Rowman & Littlefield, 2006.

Amireh, Amal. *The Factory Girl and the Seamstress: Imagining Gender and Class in Nineteenth-Century American Fiction*. New York: Garland, 2000.

Anthony, David. *Paper Money Men: Commerce, Manhood, and the Sensational Public Sphere in Antebellum America*. Columbus: Ohio State University Press, 2009.

Appleby, Joyce. *Capitalism and a New Social Order: The Republican Vision of the 1790s*. New York: New York University Press, 1984.

Armstrong, Nancy. *How Novels Think: The Limits of Individuals, 1719–1900*. New York: Columbia University Press, 2005.

Baker, Jennifer Jordan. *Securing the Commonwealth: Debt, Speculation, and Writing in the Making of Early America*. Baltimore: Johns Hopkins University Press, 2005.

Bakhtin, Mikhail. *The Dialogic Imagination: Four Essays*. Ed. Michael Holquist, trans. Caryl Emerson and Michael Holquist. Austin: University of Texas Press, 1981.

———. *Speech Genres and Other Late Essays*. Trans. W. McGee. Austin: University of Texas Press, 1986.

Baptist, Edward. *The Half Has Never Been Told: Slavery and the Making of American Capitalism*. New York: Basic Books, 2014.

Barthes, Roland. *Mythologies*. Trans. Annette Lavers. New York: Hill and Wang, 2001.

———. *S/Z: An Essay*. Trans. Richard Miller. New York: Hill and Wang, 1970.

Battistini, Robert. "Federalist Decline and Despair on the Pennsylvania Frontier: Hugh Henry Brackenridge's *Modern Chivalry*." *Pennsylvania Magazine of History and Biography* 133.2 (2009): 149–66.

Baym, Nina. *Novels, Readers, and Reviewers: Responses to Fiction in Antebellum America*. Ithaca: Cornell University Press, 1984.

————. "The Women of Cooper's Leatherstocking Tales." *American Quarterly* 23.5 (1971): 696–709.

————. *Women's Fiction: A Guide to Novels by and about Women in America, 1820–1870.* Urbana: University of Illinois Press, 1993.

Beckert, Sven. *Empire of Cotton: A Global History.* New York: Knopf, 2014.

Beecher, Catharine. *A Treatise on Domestic Economy, For the Use of Young Ladies at Home, and at School.* Boston: Marsh, Capen, Lyon, and Webb, 1841.

Benjamin, Walter. *Illuminations: Essays and Reflections.* Trans. Harry Zohn. New York: Schocken Books, 1969.

Best, Stephen, and Sharon Marcus. "Surface Reading: An Introduction." *Representations* 108.1 (2009): 1–21.

Bewley, Marius. *The Eccentric Design: Form in the Classic American Novel.* New York: Columbia University Press, 1963.

Blackmar, Elizabeth. *Manhattan for Rent, 1785–1850.* Ithaca: Cornell University Press, 1989.

Blatchly, Cornelius. *An Essay on Common Wealth.* In *Socialism in America: From the Shakers to the Third International: A Documentary History,* comp. Albert Fried. New York: Columbia University Press, 1992.

Blumin, Stuart. *The Emergence of the Middle Class: Social Experience in the American City, 1760–1900.* New York: Cambridge University Press, 1989.

Blyth, Mark. *Austerity: The History of a Dangerous Idea.* New York: Oxford University Press, 2013.

Bouton, Terry. *Taming Democracy: "The People," the Founders, and the Troubled Ending of the American Revolution.* New York: Oxford University Press, 2007.

Boydston, Jeanne. *Home and Work: Housework, Wages, and the Ideology of Labor in the Early Republic.* New York: Oxford University Press, 1990.

Brackenridge, Hugh Henry. *Modern Chivalry.* Ed. Ed White. Indianapolis: Hackett, 2009.

Braverman, Harry. *Labor and Monopoly: The Degradation of Work in the Twentieth Century.* New York: Monthly Review Press, 1974.

Brodhead, Richard. "Sparing the Rod: Discipline and Fiction in Antebellum America." *Representations* 21 (1988): 67–96.

Bromell, Nicholas K. *By the Sweat of the Brow: Literature and Labor in Antebellum America.* Chicago: University of Chicago Press, 1993.

Bronstein, Jamie L. *Land Reform and Working-Class Experience in Britain and the United States, 1800–1862.* Stanford: Stanford University Press, 1999.

Brooks, Peter. *Reading for the Plot: Design and Intention in Narrative.* Cambridge, MA: Harvard University Press, 1984.

Brown, Charles Brockden. *Arthur Mervyn; or, Memoirs of the Year 1793.* Ed. Sydney J. Krause and S. W. Reid. Rev. ed. Kent, OH: Kent State University Press, 2002.

————. *Edgar Huntly; or Memoirs of a Sleep-Walker, with Related Texts.* Ed. Philip Barnard and Stephen Shapiro. Indianapolis: Hackett, 2006.

———. *Ormond; or, the Secret Witness.* Ed. Sydney J. Krause, S. W. Reid, and Russel B. Nye. Kent, OH: Kent State University Press, 1982.

———. "Walstein's School of History." In *Arthur Mervyn; or, Memoirs of the Year 1793, with Related Texts,* ed. Philip Barnard and Stephen Shapiro. Indianapolis: Hackett, 2008.

———. *Wieland and Memoirs of Carwin the Biloquist.* Ed. Jay Fliegelman. New York: Penguin, 1991.

Brown, Gillian. *Domestic Individualism: Imagining Self in Nineteenth-Century America.* Berkeley: University of California Press, 1990.

Brownson, Orestes. "The Laboring Classes." In *The Transcendentalists: An Anthology,* ed. Perry Miller. Cambridge, MA: Harvard University Press, 1950.

———. "Review of *An Essay on the Moral Constitution and History of Man.*" *Christian Examiner and General Review* 18.3 (1835): 345–68.

Burke, Martin J. *The Conundrum of Class: Public Discourse on the Social Order in America.* Chicago: University of Chicago Press, 1995.

Burnap, Rev. G.W. "The Social Influence of Trade, and the Dangers and Duties of the Mercantile Classes." In *The Merchant's Magazine and Commercial Review,* vol. 4. New York, 1841.

Carey, Henry C. *The North and the South.* New York: Printed at the Office of the Tribune, 1854.

Castiglia, Christopher. "Twists and Turns." In *Turns of Events: Nineteenth-Century American Literary Studies in Motion,* ed. Hester Blum. Philadelphia: University of Pennsylvania Press, 2016.

Chase, Richard. *The American Novel and Its Tradition.* Garden City, NY: Doubleday, 1957.

Chatman, Seymour. *Story and Discourse: Narrative Structure in Fiction and Film.* Ithaca: Cornell University Press, 1978.

Clemit, Pamela. *The Godwinian Novel: The Rational Fictions of Godwin, Brockden Brown, and Mary Shelley.* Oxford: Clarendon Press, 1993.

Cohen, G. A. *Karl Marx's Theory of History: A Defence.* New York: Oxford University Press, 2000.

Cook, Sylvia Jenkins. *Working Women, Literary Ladies: The Industrial Revolution and Female Aspiration.* New York: Oxford University Press, 2008.

Cooper, James Fenimore. *The American Democrat.* Cooperstown, NY: E. H. Phinney, 1838.

———. *The Chainbearer; or, The Littlepage Manuscripts.* New York: W. A. Townsend and Company, 1860.

———. *The Prairie.* New York: Penguin Classics, 1987.

———. *The Redskins; or, Indian and Injin: Being the Conclusion of the Littlepage Manuscripts.* New York: W. A. Townsend and Company, 1860.

———. *Satanstoe, or, the Littlepage Manuscripts: A Tale of the Colony.* Albany: State University of New York Press, 1990.

Cornell, Saul. *The Other Founders: Anti-Federalism and the Dissenting Tradition in America, 1788–1828.* Chapel Hill: University of North Carolina Press, 1999.

Cotlar, Seth. "Joseph Gales and the Making of the Jeffersonian Middle Class." In *The Revolution of 1800: Democracy, Race, and the New Republic,* ed. James Horn, Jan Ellen Lewis, and Peter S. Onuf. Charlottesville: University of Virginia Press, 2002.

———. *Tom Paine's America: The Rise and Fall of Transatlantic Radicalism in the Early Republic.* Charlottesville: University of Virginia Press, 2011.

Cowell, Pattie. "Class, Gender, and Genre: Deconstructing Social Formulas on the Gothic Frontier." In *Frontier Gothic: Terror and Wonder at the Frontier in American Literature,* ed. David Morgen, Scott P. Sanders, and Joanne B. Karpinski. Rutherford, NJ: Farleigh Dickinson University Press, 1993.

Crèvecoeur, J. Hector St. John de. *Letters from an American Farmer and Sketches of Eighteenth-Century America.* Ed. Albert Stone. New York: Penguin Books, 1986.

Culler, Jonathan. *The Pursuit of Signs: Semiotics, Literature, Deconstruction.* Ithaca: Cornell University Press, 2001.

D'Amato, Paul. *The Meaning of Marxism.* Chicago: Haymarket Books, 2006.

Damon-Bach, Lucinda L., and Victoria Clements. Introduction to *Catharine Maria Sedgwick: Critical Perspectives,* ed. Damon-Bach and Clements. Boston: Northeastern University Press, 2003.

Davidson, Cathy. *Revolution and the Word: The Rise of the Novel in America.* New York: Oxford University Press, 1986.

Davis, Mike. *Prisoners of the American Dream: Politics and Economy in the History of the U.S. Working Class.* New York: Verso, 1986.

Davis, Rebecca Harding. *Life in the Iron-Mills.* Ed. Tillie Olsen. New York: Feminist Press at the City University of New York, 1985.

Decker, Mark. "A Bumpkin before the Bar: Charles Brockden Brown's *Arthur Mervyn* and Class Anxiety in Postrevolutionary Philadelphia." *Pennsylvania Magazine of History and Biography* 124.4 (2000): 469–88.

Dekker, George. *The American Historical Romance.* New York: Cambridge University Press, 1987.

Deloria, Philip J. *Playing Indian.* New Haven: Yale University Press, 1998.

Denning, Michael. *Culture in the Age of Three Worlds.* New York: Verso, 2004.

———. *Mechanic Accents: Dime Novels and Working-Class Culture in America.* New York: Verso, 1987.

Dillon, Elizabeth Maddock. *The Gender of Freedom: Fictions of Liberalism and the Literary Public Sphere.* Stanford: Stanford University Press, 2004.

Dimock, Wai Chee. *Empire for Liberty: Melville and the Poetics of Individualism.* Princeton: Princeton University Press, 1989.

———. *Residues of Justice: Literature, Law, Philosophy.* Berkeley: University of California Press, 1996.

Dimock, Wai Chee, and Michael T. Gilmore. Introduction to *Rethinking Class: Literary Studies and Social Formations.* New York: Columbia University Press, 1994.

Dobson, Joanne. "Reclaiming Sentimental Literature." *American Literary History* 69.2 (1997): 263–88.

Doolen, Andy. *Fugitive Empire: Locating Early American Imperialism.* Minneapolis: University of Minnesota Press, 2005.

Douglass, Frederick. *My Bondage and My Freedom.* New York: Penguin Classics, 2003.

Dow, William. *Narrating Class in American Fiction.* New York: Palgrave, 2009.

Dowling, David. *Capital Letters: Authorship in the Antebellum Literary Market.* Iowa City: University of Iowa Press, 2009.

Drexler, Michael, and Ed White. "Secret Witness; or, the Fantasy Structure of Republicanism." *Early American Literature* 44.2 (2009): 333–63.

DuBois, W. E. B. *Black Reconstruction in America.* New York: Free Press, 1998.

Durey, Michael. "John Lithgow's *Lithconia:* The Making and Meaning of America's First 'Utopian Socialist' Tract." *William and Mary Quarterly* 49.4 (1992): 675–94.

Eagleton, Terry. "Ideology, Fiction, Narrative." *Social Text* 2 (1979): 62–80.

Egan, Ken, Jr. *The Riven Home: Narrative Rivalry in the American Renaissance.* Selingsgrove, PA: Susquehanna University Press, 1997.

Elliott, Emory. *Revolutionary Writers: Literature and Authority in the New Republic, 1725–1810.* New York: Oxford University Press, 1982.

Ellis, Joseph J. *After the Revolution: Profiles of Early American Culture.* New York: Norton, 1981.

Ellis, Richard. *The Jeffersonian Crisis: Courts and Politics in the Young Republic.* New York: Oxford University Press, 1971.

Federici, Silvia. *Caliban and the Witch: Women, the Body, and Primitive Accumulation.* New York: Autonomedia, 2004.

Felski, Rita. *The Limits of Critique.* Chicago: University of Chicago Press, 2015.

Ferguson, Robert. *Law and Letters in American Culture.* Cambridge, MA: Harvard University Press, 1984.

Fetterly, Judith. "'My Sister! My Sister!': The Rhetoric of Catharine Maria Sedgwick's *Hope Leslie.*" *American Literature* 70.3 (1998): 491–516.

Feuer, Lewis. *Marx and the Intellectuals: A Set of Post-Ideological Essays.* Garden City, N.Y.: Anchor Books, 1969.

———. "The North American Origins of Marx's Socialism." *Western Political Quarterly* 16.1 (1963): 53–67.

Fichtelberg, Joseph. *Critical Fictions: Sentiment and the American Market, 1780–1870.* Athens: University of Georgia Press, 2003.

Fiedler, Leslie. *Love and Death in the American Novel.* Normal, IL: Dalkey Archive Press, 1997.

Fisher, Philip. *Hard Facts: Setting and Form in the American Novel.* New York: Oxford University Press, 1985.

Fisk, Theophilus. *Capital against Labor: An Address Delivered at Julien Hall before the Mechanics of Boston, on Wednesday Evening, May 20.* Boston: The Daily Reformer, 1835.

Fitzhugh, George. *Cannibals All! Or, Slaves Without Masters.* Ed. C. Vann Woodward. Cambridge, MA: Belknap Press of Harvard University Press, 1960.

———. *Sociology for the South; or, The Failure of Free Society.* Richmond, VA: A. Morris, 1854.

Fliegelman, Jay. *Declaring Independence: Jefferson, Natural Language, and the Culture of Performance.* Stanford: Stanford University Press, 1993.

———. *Prodigals and Pilgrims: The American Revolution against Patriarchal Authority.* New York: Cambridge University Press, 1982.

Foley, Barbara. "From Wall Street to Astor Place: Historicizing Melville's 'Bartleby.'" *American Literature* 72.1 (2000): 87–116.

———. *Radical Representations: Politics and Form in U.S. Proletarian Fiction, 1921–1941.* Durham: Duke University Press, 1993.

Foner, Eric. *Free Soil, Free Labor, Free Men: The Ideology of the Republican Party before the Civil War.* New York: Oxford University Press, 1995.

———. *Politics and Ideology in the Age of the Civil War.* New York: Oxford University Press, 1980.

Foner, Philip. *History of the Labor Movement in the United States, from Colonial Times to the Founding of the American Federation of Labor.* New York: International Publishers, 1947.

Fraser, Nancy. "Rethinking Recognition." *New Left Review* 3 (2000): 107–20.

Garrett, Matthew. *Episodic Poetics: Politics and Literary Form after the Constitution.* New York: Oxford University Press, 2014.

Gates, Sondra Smith. "Sedgwick's American Poor." In *Catharine Maria Sedgwick: Critical Perspectives,* ed. Lucinda L. Damon-Bach and Victoria Clements. Boston: Northeastern University Press, 2003.

Genovese, Eugene. *Roll, Jordan, Roll: The World the Slaves Made.* New York: Vintage Books, 1976.

Gibbons, Luke. "Ireland, America, and Gothic Memory: Transatlantic Terror in the Early Republic." *boundary 2* 31.1 (2004): 25–47.

Gibson-Graham, J. K. *The End of Capitalism (As We Knew It): A Feminist Critique of Political Economy.* Minneapolis: University of Minnesota Press, 2006.

Gilmore, Michael T. "Hawthorne and the Making of the Middle Class." In *Rethinking Class: Literary Studies and Social Formations,* ed. Wai Chee Dimock and Gilmore. New York: Columbia University Press, 1984.

Gilmore, Paul. *The Genuine Article: Race, Mass Culture, and Literary Manhood.* Durham, NC: Duke University Press, 2001.

Glickstein, Jonathan A. *American Exceptionalism, American Anxiety: Wages, Competition, and Degraded Labor in the Antebellum United States.* Charlottesville: University of Virginia Press, 2002.

Godden, Richard. "Pioneer Properties, or 'What's in a Hut?'" In *James Fenimore Cooper: New Critical Essays,* ed. Robert Clark. Totowa, NJ: Barnes & Noble, 1985.

Goddu, Teresa. *Gothic America: Narrative, History, and Nation.* New York: Columbia University Press, 1997.

Godwin, William. *An Enquiry Concerning Political Justice.* Ed. Mark Philp. London: William Pickering, 1993.

Goudie, Sean X. *Creole America: The West Indies and the Formation of Literature and Culture in the New Republic.* Philadelphia: University of Pennsylvania Press, 2006.

Gould, Philip. "Class." In *A Companion to American Fiction, 1780–1865,* ed. Shirley Samuels. Malden, MA: Blackwell Publishing, 2004.

———. *Covenant and Republic: Historical Romance and the Politics of Puritanism.* New York: Cambridge University Press, 1996.

———. "Race, Commerce, and the Literature of Yellow Fever in Early National Philadelphia." *Early American Literature* 35.2 (2000): 157–86.

Gourevitch, Alex. *From Slavery to the Cooperative Commonwealth: Labor and Republican Liberty in the Nineteenth Century.* New York: Cambridge University Press, 2015.

Grabo, Norman. *The Coincidental Art of Charles Brockden Brown.* Chapel Hill: University of North Carolina Press, 1981.

Greeson, Jennifer. *Our South: Geographic Fantasy and the Rise of National Literature.* Cambridge, MA: Harvard University Press, 2010.

Guarneri, Carl J. *The Utopian Alternative: Fourierism in Nineteenth-Century America.* Ithaca: Cornell University Press, 1991.

Gura, Philip. *Truth's Ragged Edge: The Rise of the American Novel.* New York: Farrar, Straus and Giroux, 2013.

Hale, Dorothy. "Profits of Altruism: *Caleb Williams* and *Arthur Mervyn.*" *Eighteenth-Century Studies* 22 (1988): 47–69.

Halttunen, Karen. *Confidence Men and Painted Women: A Study of Middle-Class Culture in America, 1830–1870.* New Haven: Yale University Press, 1982.

Hapke, Laura. *Labor's Text: The Worker in American Fiction.* New Brunswick: Rutgers University Press, 2001.

Harris, David. *Socialist Origins in the United States: American Forerunners of Marx, 1817–1832.* N.p.: Assen, Van Corcum & Company, 1996.

Hartz, Louis. *The Liberal Tradition in America: An Interpretation of American Political Thought since the Revolution.* San Diego: Harcourt Brace, 1991.

Hawthorne, Nathaniel. *The House of the Seven Gables.* Ed. Robert S. Levine. New York: W. W. Norton, 2006.

Hegel, G. W. F. *Aesthetics: Lectures on Fine Art.* Vol. 1, trans. T. M. Knox. New York: Oxford University Press, 1988.

Helwig, Timothy. "Denying the Wages of Whiteness: The Racial Politics of George Lippard's Working-Class Protest." *American Studies* 47.3/4 (2006): 87–111.

Hentz, Caroline Lee. *The Planter's Northern Bride.* Philadelphia: T. B. Peterson and Brothers, 1854.

Hicks, Granville. "Landlord Cooper and the Anti-Renters." *Antioch Review* 5.1 (1945): 95–109.

Hinds, Jane Wall. *Private Property: Charles Brockden Brown's Gendered Economics of Virtue*. Newark: University of Delaware Press, 1997.

Hoffa, William H. "The Language of Rogues and Fools in Brackenridge's *Modern Chivalry*." *Studies in the Novel* 12.4 (1980): 289–300.

Hofstadter, Richard. *The American Political Tradition*. New York: Vintage, 1989.

Hurst, Allison. "Beyond the Pale": Poor Whites as Uncontrolled Social Contagion in Harriet Beecher Stowe's *Dred: A Tale of the Dismal Swamp*." *Mississippi Quarterly* 63.4 (2010): 635–53.

Huston, James L. *Securing the Fruits of Labor: The American Concept of Wealth Distribution, 1765–1900*. Baton Rouge: Louisiana State University Press, 1998.

Huston, Reeve. *Land and Freedom: Rural Society, Popular Protest, and Party Politics in Antebellum New York*. New York: Oxford University Press, 2000.

———. "Land and Freedom: The New York Anti-Rent Wars and the Construction of Free Labor in the Antebellum North." In *Labor Histories: Class, Politics, and Working-Class Experience*, ed. Eric Arnesen, Julie Green, and Bruce Laurie. Urbana: University of Illinois Press, 1998.

"James Fenimore Cooper." *Atlantic Monthly* 9 (January 1862): 52–68.

Jameson, Fredric. *The Antinomies of Realism*. New York: Verso, 2013.

———. *The Political Unconscious: Narrative as a Socially Symbolic Act*. Ithaca: Cornell University Press, 1981.

Janowitz, Anne. "Class and Literature: The Case of Romantic Chartism." In *Rethinking Class*, ed. Wai Chee Dimock and Michael T. Gilmore, 239–66. New York: Columbia University Press, 1994.

Jefferson, Thomas. *The Essential Jefferson*. Ed. Jean Yarbrough. Indianapolis: Hackett, 2006.

Jehlen, Myra. "The Novel and the Middle Class in America." In *Ideology and Classic American Literature*, ed. Sacvan Bercovitch and Jehlen. New York: Cambridge University Press, 1986.

Johnson, Walter. "The Pedestal and the Veil: Rethinking the Slavery/Capitalism Question." *Journal of the Early Republic* 24.2 (2002): 299–308.

———. *River of Dark Dreams: Slavery and Empire in the Cotton Kingdom*. Cambridge, MA: Harvard University Press, 2013.

Jones, Gavin. *American Hungers: The Problem of Poverty in U.S. Literature, 1840–1945*. Princeton: Princeton University Press, 2008.

Jordan, Cynthia. *Second Stories: The Politics of Language, Form, and Gender in Early American Fiction*. Chapel Hill: University of North Carolina Press, 1989.

Justus, James. "Arthur Mervyn, American." *American Literature* 42 (1970): 304–24.

Kant, Immanuel. *Political Writings*. Ed. Hans Reiss. 2nd enl. ed. New York: Cambridge University Press, 1991.

Kaye, Harvey J. *Thomas Paine and the Promise of America*. New York: Hill and Wang, 2005.

Kloppenberg, James T. "The Virtues of Liberalism: Christianity, Republicanism, and Ethics in Early American Political Discourse." *Journal of American History* 74.1 (1987): 9–33.

Lang, Amy Schrager. *The Syntax of Class: Writing Inequality in Nineteenth-Century America.* Princeton: Princeton University Press, 2003.

Lause, Mark. *Young America: Land, Labor, and the Republican Community.* Urbana: University of Illinois Press, 2005.

Lawson, Andrew. *Downwardly Mobile: The Changing Fortunes of American Realism.* New York: Oxford University Press, 2012.

———. Introduction to *Class and the Making of American Literature: Created Unequal,* ed. Lawson. New York: Routledge, 2014.

———. *Walt Whitman and the Class Struggle.* Iowa City: University of Iowa Press, 2006.

Lawson-Peebles, Robert. "Property, Marriage, and Women in Fenimore Cooper's First Fictions." In *James Fenimore Cooper: New Historical and Literary Contexts,* ed. W. M. Verhoeven. Atlanta: Rodopi, 1993.

Layson, Hana. "Rape and Revolution: Feminism, Antijacobinism, and the Politics of Injured Innocence in Brockden Brown's *Ormond." Early American Studies: An Interdisciplinary Journal* 2.1 (2004): 160–91.

Lazerow, Jama. *Religion and the Working Class in Antebellum America.* Washington, DC: Smithsonian Institution Press, 1995.

Levine, Robert. "Arthur Mervyn's Revolutions." *Studies in American Fiction* 12.2 (1984): 145–60.

———. *Conspiracy and Romance: Studies in Brockden Brown, Cooper, Hawthorne, and Melville.* New York: Cambridge University Press, 1989.

———. Introduction to *Dred: A Tale of the Great Dismal Swamp, by Harriet Beecher Stowe.* Ed. Levine. Chapel Hill: University of North Carolina Press, 2000.

Lewis, Paul. "Attaining Masculinity: Charles Brockden Brown and Woman Warriors of the 1790s." *Early American Literature* 40.1 (2005): 37–55.

———. "'Lectures or a Little Charity': Poor Visits in Antebellum Literature and Culture." *New England Quarterly* 73.2 (2000): 246–73.

Licht, Walter. *Industrializing America: The Nineteenth Century.* Baltimore: Johns Hopkins University Press, 1995.

Lincoln, Abraham. *Abraham Lincoln: His Speeches and Writings.* Ed. Roy P. Basler. New York: Da Capo, 2008.

Linnebaugh, Peter, and Marcus Rediker. *The Many-Headed Hydra: Sailors, Slaves, Commoners and the Hidden History of the Revolutionary Atlantic.* Boston: Beacon Press, 2000.

Lippard, George. *The Quaker City; or, The Monks of Monk Hall.* Ed. David S. Reynolds. Amherst: University of Massachusetts Press, 1995.

Locke, John. *Second Treatise of Government.* Ed. C. B. Macpherson. Indianapolis: Hackett, 1980.

Looby, Christopher. *Voicing America: Language, Literary Form, and the Origins of the United States.* Chicago: University of Chicago Press, 1996.

Lott, Eric. *The Disappearing Liberal Intellectual.* New York: Basic Books, 2006.

———. *Love and Theft: Blackface Minstrelsy and the American Working Class.* New York: Oxford University Press, 1993.

Lukács, Georg. *The Historical Novel.* Trans. Hannah and Stanley Mitchell. Lincoln: University of Nebraska Press, 1983.

———. *History and Class Consciousness: Studies in Marxist Dialectics.* Trans. Rodney Livingstone. Cambridge, MA: MIT Press, 1971.

Luther, Seth. *An Address to the Working Men of New England.* 2nd ed. New York: Published at the Office of *The Working Man's Advocate* by George H. Evans, 1833.

Macpherson, C. B. *The Political Theory of Possessive Individualism: Hobbes to Locke.* New York: Oxford University Press, 1962.

Madison, James. "The Federalist No. 10." In *The Federalist,* ed. Terence Ball. New York: Cambridge University Press, 2003.

Maibor, Carolyn R. *Labor Pains: Emerson, Hawthorne, and Alcott on Work and the Woman Question.* New York: Routledge, 2004.

Mandel, Bernard. *Labor, Free and Slave: Workingmen and the Anti-Slavery Movement in the United States.* Urbana: University of Illinois Press, 2007.

Manning, William. *The Key of Liberty: The Life and Democratic Writings of William Manning, "A Laborer," 1747–1814.* Ed. Michael Merrill and Sean Wilentz. Cambridge, MA: Harvard University Press, 1993.

Marin, Louis. *Utopics: The Semiological Play of Textual Spaces.* Trans. Robert A. Vollrath. Amherst, NY: Humanity Books, 1984.

Markels, Julian. *The Marxian Imagination: Representing Class in Literature.* New York: Monthly Review Press, 2003.

Marx, Karl *Capital.* Vol. 1, trans. Ben Fowkes. New York: Vintage, 1977.

———. *Capital.* Vol. 3, trans. David Fernbach. New York: Penguin, 1981.

———. "Class Struggle and the Mode of Production." In *The Marx-Engels Reader,* ed. Robert Tucker. New York: W. W. Norton, 1978.

———. *Economic and Philosophic Manuscripts of 1844.* Trans. Martin Milligan. Buffalo, NY: Prometheus Books, 1988.

———. *Grundrisse: Foundations of the Critique of Political Economy (Rough Draft).* Trans. Martin Nicolaus. New York: Penguin, 1993.

———. "Manifesto of the Communist Party." In *The Marx-Engels Reader,* ed. Robert Tucker. New York: W. W. Norton, 1978.

———. "Wage Labour and Capital." In *The Marx-Engels Reader,* ed. Robert Tucker. New York: W. W. Norton, 1978.

Masquerier, Lewis. "Declaration of the Producing from the Non-Producing Class." In *We, the Other People: Alternative Declarations of Independence by Labor Groups, Farmers, Woman's Rights Advocates, Socialists, and Blacks, 1829–1875,* ed. Philip S. Foner. Urbana: University of Illinois Press, 1976.

McGann, Jerome. "Fenimore Cooper's Anti-Aesthetic and the Representation of Conflicted History." *MLQ* 73.2 (2012): 123–55.

McGuire, Ian. "'Who Ain't a Slave?': *Moby-Dick* and the Ideology of Free Labor." *Journal of American Studies* 37.2 (2003): 287–305.

McWilliams, John P. *Political Justice in a Republic: James Fenimore Cooper's America.* Berkeley: University of California Press, 1972.

Meer, Sarah. *Uncle Tom Mania: Slavery, Minstrelsy, and Transatlantic Culture in the 1850s.* Athens: University of Georgia Press, 2005.

Melville, Herman. *Moby-Dick.* Ed. Hershel Parker and Harrison Hayford. New York: W. W. Norton, 2002.

Merish, Lori. *Sentimental Materialism: Gender, Commodity Culture, and Nineteenth-Century American Literature.* Durham, NC: Duke University Press, 2000.

Merrill, Michael, and Sean Wilentz. "Introduction: William Manning and the Invention of American Politics." In *The Key of Liberty: The Life and Democratic Writings of William Manning, "A Laborer," 1747–1814,* ed. Merrill and Wilentz. Cambridge, MA: Harvard University Press, 1993.

Michaels, Walter Benn. *The Trouble with Diversity: How We Learned to Love Identity and Ignore Inequality.* New York: Picador, 2016.

Miller, D. A. *Jane Austen, or the Secret of Style.* Princeton: Princeton University Press, 2003.

Montgomery, David. *Beyond Equality: Labor and the Radical Republicans, 1862–1872.* Urbana: University of Illinois Press, 1981.

Moretti, Franco. *Signs Taken for Wonders: On the Sociology of Literary Forms.* New York: Verso, 2005.

———. *The Way of the World: The* Bildungsroman *in European Culture.* New York: Verso, 2000.

Nedelsky, Jennifer. *Private Property and the Limits of American Constitutionalism: The Madisonian Framework and Its Legacy.* Chicago: University of Chicago Press, 1990.

Nelson, Dana. *Commons Democracy: Reading the Politics of Participation in the Early United States.* New York: Fordham University Press, 2016.

———. "Indications of the Public Will: *Modern Chivalry*'s Theory of Democratic Representation." *ANQ: A Quarterly Journal of Short Articles, Notes, and Reviews* 15.1 (2002): 23–39.

———. *The Word in Black and White: Reading "Race" in American Literature, 1638–1867.* New York: Oxford University Press, 1993.

Newman, Lance. *Our Common Dwelling: Henry Thoreau, Transcendentalism, and the Class Politics of Nature.* New York: Palgrave, 2005.

Nichols, John. *The "S" Word: A Short History of an American Tradition—Socialism.* New York: Verso, 2011.

Nordhoff, Christopher. *America for Free Working Men! Mechanics, Farmers and Laborers Read! How Slavery Injures the Free Working Man. The Slave-labor*

System the Free Working-man's Worst Enemy. New York: Harper & Brothers, 1865.

Orren, Karen. *Belated Feudalism: Labor, the Law, and Liberal Development in the United States.* New York: Cambridge University Press, 1991.

Ostrowski, Carl. "'Fated to Perish by Consumption': The Political Economy of *Arthur Mervyn.*" *Studies in American Fiction* 32.1 (2004): 3–20.

Ousley, Laurie. "The Business of Housekeeping: The Mistress, the Domestic Worker, and the Construction of Class." *Legacy: A Journal of American Women Writers* 23.2 (2006): 132–47.

Pearson, Susan. *The Rights of the Defenseless: Protecting Animals and Children in Gilded Age America.* Chicago: University of Chicago Press, 2011.

Pessen, Edward. "The Ideology of Stephen Simpson, Upperclass Champion of the Early Philadelphia Workingmen's Movement." *Pennsylvania History: A Journal of Mid-Atlantic Studies* 22.4 (1955): 328–40.

———. *Jacksonian America: Society, Personality, and Politics.* Rev. ed. Urbana: University of Illinois Press, 1985.

———. *Riches, Class, and Power: America before the Civil War.* New Brunswick, NJ: Transaction Publishers, 1990.

Peterson, Charles Jacobs. *The Cabin and the Parlor; or, Slaves and Masters.* Philadelphia: T. B. Peterson, 1852.

Pethers, Matthew. "Poverty, Providence, and the State of Welfare: Plotting Parabolic Social Mobility in the Early Nineteenth-Century American Novel." *Early American Literature* 49.3 (2014): 707–40.

Pfister, Joel. *Critique for What? Cultural Studies, American Studies, Left Studies.* Boulder, CO: Paradigm Publishers, 2006.

———. *The Production of Personal Life: Class, Gender, and the Psychological in Hawthorne's Fiction.* Stanford: Stanford University Press, 1991.

Pickering, John. *The Working Man's Political Economy.* Cincinnati: Thomas Varney, 1847.

Pocock, J. G. A. *The Machiavellian Moment: Florentine Political Thought and the Atlantic Republic Tradition.* 2nd ed. Princeton: Princeton University Press, 2003.

Propp, Vladímir. *Morphology of the Folktale.* Trans. Laurence Scott. Austin: University of Texas Press, 2003.

Rancière, Jacques. *Aesthetics and Its Discontents.* Trans. Steven Corcoran. Malden, MA: Polity, 2009.

Read, Martha Meredith. *Monima; or, the Beggar Girl.* New York: Printed by P. R. Johnson, for I. N. Ralston, 1802.

Rediker, Marcus. "'Good Hands, Stout Heart, and Fast Feet': The History and Culture of Working People in Early America." *Labour/Le Travail* 10 (1982): 123–44.

———. Review of *The Key of Liberty: The Life and Democratic Writings of William Manning, "A Laborer," 1747–1814,* ed. Michael Merrill and Sean Wilentz. *International Labor and Working-Class History* 47 (1995): 147–49.

Resnick, Stephen, and Richard Wolff. *Knowledge and Class: A Marxian Critique of Political Economy.* Chicago: University of Chicago Press, 1987.

Reynolds, David S. *Mightier than the Sword: Uncle Tom's Cabin and the Battle for America.* New York: W. W. Norton, 2012.

Reynolds, James. *Equality; A History of Lithconia.* Philadelphia: Prime Press, 1947.

Rice, Grantland. *The Transformation of Authorship in America.* Chicago: University of Chicago Press, 1997.

Ricoeur, Paul. *Freud and Philosophy: An Essay in Interpretation.* New Haven: Yale University Press, 1970.

Rifkin, Mark. *Settler Common Sense: Queerness and Everyday Colonialism in the American Renaissance.* Minneapolis: University of Minnesota Press, 2014.

Ripley, George. "Brook Farm's First (Published) Constitution (1844)." In *The American Transcendentalists,* ed. Lawrence Buell, 239. New York: Modern Library, 2006.

Robbins, Bruce. "On the Rentier." *PMLA* 127.4 (2012): 905–11.

Robbins, Sarah. "Periodizing Authorship, Characterizing Genre: Catharine Maria Sedgwick's Benevolent Literacy Narratives." *American Literature* 76.1 (2004): 1–29.

Roberts, Sian Silyn. "Gothic Enlightenment: Contagion and Community in Charles Brockden Brown's *Arthur Mervyn.*" *Early American Literature* 44.2 (2009): 307–32.

Robinson, Cedric J. *Black Marxism: The Making of the Black Radical Tradition.* Chapel Hill: University of North Carolina Press, 2000.

Rockman, Seth. "Class and the History of Working People in the Early Republic." *Journal of the Early Republic* 25.4 (2005): 527–35.

———. *Scraping By: Wage Labor, Slavery, and Survival in Early Baltimore.* Baltimore: Johns Hopkins University Press, 2009.

Rodgers, Daniel T. "Exceptionalism." In *Imagined Histories: American Historians Interpret the Past,* ed. Anthony Molho and Gordon Wood. Princeton: Princeton University Press, 1998.

Roediger, David. *The Wages of Whiteness: Race and the Making of the American Working Class.* New York: Verso, 2007.

Romero, Lora. *Home Fronts: Domesticity and Its Critics in the Antebellum United States.* Durham, NC: Duke University Press, 1997.

Rowe, John Carlos. "Stowe's Rainbow Sign: Violence and Community in *Dred: A Tale of the Great Dismal Swamp* (1856)." *Arizona Quarterly* 58.1 (2002): 37–55.

Rucavado, Gina. *Class Difference and the Struggle for Cultural Authority: Rereadings of Sedgwick, Emerson, Whitman, and Hemingway.* PhD diss., Brown University, 2010. Ann Arbor: UMI, 2010. AAT 3470489.

Rush, Caroline E. *The North and the South, or, Slavery and Its Contrasts.* Philadelphia: Published for the Author by Crissy and Markley, 1852.

Ryan, Barbara. *Love, Wages, Slavery: The Literature of Servitude in the United States.* Urbana: University of Illinois Press, 2006.

Ryan, Mary P. *The Empire of the Mother: American Writing about Domesticity, 1830–1860*. New York: Haworth Press, 1982.

Ryan, Susan. *The Grammar of Good Intentions: Race and the Antebellum Culture of Benevolence*. Ithaca: Cornell University Press, 2004.

Saldívar, Ramón. "Narrative, Ideology, and the Reconstruction of American Literary History." In *Criticism in the Borderlands: Studies in Chicano Literature, Culture, and Ideology*, ed. Héctor Calderón and José David Saldívar. Durham, NC: Duke University Press, 1991.

Samuels, Shirley. *Reading the American Novel, 1780–1865*. Malden, MA: Wiley-Blackwell, 2012.

———. *Romances of the Republic: Women, the Family, and Violence in the Literature of the Early American Nation*. New York: Oxford University Press, 1996.

Sánchez-Eppler, Karen. *Dependent States: The Child's Part in Nineteenth-Century American Culture*. Chicago: University of Chicago Press, 2005.

Savage, Sarah. *The Factory Girl*. Boston: Monroe, Francis & Parker, 1814.

Saxton, Alexander. *The Rise and Fall of the White Republic: Class Politics and Mass Culture in Nineteenth-Century America*. New York: Verso, 2003.

Schachterle, Lance. "The Themes of Land and Leadership in 'The Littlepage Manuscripts.'" *Literature in the Early American Republic: Annual Studies on Cooper and His Contemporaries* 1 (2009): 89–131.

Schermerhorn, Jack. *The Business of Slavery and the Rise of American Capitalism, 1815–1860*. New Haven: Yale University Press, 2015.

Schocket, Eric. *Vanishing Moments: Class and American Literature*. Ann Arbor: University of Michigan Press, 2006.

Schultz, Ronald. *The Republic of Labor: Philadelphia Artisans and the Politics of Class, 1720–1830*. New York: Oxford University Press, 1993.

Sedgwick, Catharine Maria. *Live and Let Live; or, Domestic Service Illustrated*. New York: Harper and Brothers, 1837.

———. *The Poor Rich Man, and the Rich Poor Man*. New York: Harper and Brothers, 1836.

Sedgwick, Theodore. *Public and Private Economy*. Vol. 1. New York: Harper and Brothers, 1836.

Sellers, Charles. *The Market Revolution: Jacksonian America, 1815–1846*. New York: Oxford University Press, 1991.

Seymour, Richard. *Against Austerity: How We Can Fix the Crisis They Made*. New York: Pluto Books, 2014.

Shankman, Andrew. *Crucible of American Democracy: The Struggle to Fuse Egalitarianism and Capitalism in Jeffersonian Pennsylvania*. Lawrence: University Press of Kansas, 2004.

Shapiro, Stephen. *The Culture and Commerce of the Early American Novel: Reading the Atlantic World-System*. University Park: Pennsylvania State University Press, 2008.

Sickels, Eleanor. "Shelley and Charles Brockden Brown." *PMLA* 45 (1930): 1116–28.

Simpson, Stephen. *The Working Man's Manual.* Philadelphia: Thomas L. Bonsal, 1831.

Skidmore, Thomas. *The Rights of Man to Property!* New York: Printed for the Author by Alexander Ming, Jr., 1829.

Sklansky, Jeffrey P. *The Soul's Economy: Market Society and Selfhood in American Thought, 1820–1860.* Chapel Hill: University of North Carolina Press, 2002.

Slaughter, Thomas. *The Whiskey Rebellion: Frontier Epilogue to the American Revolution.* New York: Oxford University Press, 1986.

Slotkin, Richard. *The Fatal Environment: The Myth of the Frontier in the Age of Industrialization, 1800–1890.* Norman: University of Oklahoma Press, 1980.

Smith, Adam. *An Inquiry into the Nature and Causes of the Wealth of Nations.* Ed. R. H. Campbell and A. S. Skinner. 2 vols. Indianapolis: Liberty Fund, 1981.

Smith, Billy G. *The "Lower Sort": Philadelphia's Laboring People, 1750–1800.* Ithaca: Cornell University Press, 1990.

Smith, Henry Nash. *Virgin Land: The American West as Symbol and Myth.* Cambridge, MA: Harvard University Press, 1978.

Smith-Rosenberg, Carroll. "Domesticating Virtue: Coquettes and Revolutionaries in Young America." In *American Literary Studies: A Methodological Reader,* ed. Michael Elliott and Claudia Stokes. New York: New York University Press, 2003.

———. *This Violent Empire: The Birth of an American National Identity.* Chapel Hill: University of North Carolina Press, 2010.

Spangler, George. "Charles Brockden Brown's *Arthur Mervyn:* A Portrait of the Young American Artist." *American Literature* 52 (1981): 578–92.

Stanley, Amy Dru. "Home Life and the Morality of the Market." In *The Market Revolution in America: Social, Political, and Religious Expressions, 1800–1880,* ed. Melvyn Stokes and Stephen Conway. Charlottesville: University Press of Virginia, 1996.

Stansell, Christine. *City of Women: Sex and Class in New York, 1789–1860.* New York: Knopf, 1986.

Stern, Julia. *The Plight of Feeling: Sympathy and Dissent in the Early American Novel.* Chicago: University of Chicago Press, 1997.

Stowe, Harriet Beecher. *Dred: A Tale of the Great Dismal Swamp.* Ed. Robert S. Levine. Chapel Hill: University of North Carolina Press, 2000.

———. *A Key to Uncle Tom's Cabin.* New York: Dover, 2015.

Streeby, Shelley. *American Sensations: Class, Empire, and the Production of Popular Culture.* Berkeley: University of California Press, 2002.

Tawil, Ezra. *The Making of Racial Sentiment: Slavery and the Birth of the Frontier Romance.* New York: Cambridge University Press, 2006.

Templin, Mary. "'Dedicated to the Works of Beneficence': Charity as Model for a Domesticated Economy in Antebellum Women's Panic Fiction." In *Our Sisters' Keepers: Nineteenth-Century Benevolence Literature by American*

Women, ed. Jill Bergman and Debra Bernardi. Tuscaloosa: University of Alabama Press, 2005.

―――. *Panic Fiction: Women and Antebellum Economic Crisis*. Tuscaloosa: University of Alabama Press, 2014.

Thompson, E. P. *The Making of the English Working Class*. New York: Vintage, 1966.

Tocqueville, Alexis de. *Democracy in America*. Trans. and ed. Harvey C. Mansfield and Delba Winthrop. Chicago: University of Chicago Press, 2002.

Tomlins, Christopher. "Afterword: Constellations of Class in Early North America and the Atlantic World." In *Class Matters: Early North America and the Atlantic World*, ed. Simon Middleton and Billy G. Smith. Philadelphia: University of Pennsylvania Press, 2008.

―――. *Law, Labor, and Ideology in the Early American Republic*. New York: Cambridge University Press, 1993.

Tompkins, Jane. *Sensational Designs: The Cultural Work of American Fiction, 1790–1860*. New York: Oxford University Press, 1985.

Trilling, Lionel. *The Liberal Imagination: Essays on Literature and Society*. Garden City, NY: Doubleday, 1950.

―――. *Sincerity and Authenticity*. Cambridge, MA: Harvard University Press, 1971.

Tuchinsky, Adam. *Horace Greeley's* New-York Tribune: *Civil War–Era Socialism and the Crisis of Free Labor*. Ithaca: Cornell University Press, 2009.

Twomey, Richard J. *Jacobins and Jeffersonians: Anglo-American Radicalism in the United States, 1790–1820*. New York: Garland, 1989.

Verhoeven, Wil. "Displacing the Discontinuous; or, the Labyrinths of Reason: Fictional Design and Eighteenth-Century Thought in Charles Brockden Brown's *Ormond*." In *Rewriting the Dream: Reflections on the Changing American Literary Canon*, ed. Verhoeven. Atlanta: Rodopi, 1992.

―――. "'This Blissful Period of Intellectual Liberty': Transatlantic Radicalism and Enlightened Conservatism in Brown's Early Writings." In *Revising Charles Brockden Brown: Culture, Politics, and Sexuality in the Early Republic*, ed. Philip Barnard, Mark Kamrath, and Stephen Shapiro. Knoxville: University of Tennessee Press, 2004.

Warner, Michael. *Letters of the Republic: Publication and the Public Sphere in Eighteenth-Century America*. Cambridge, MA: Harvard University Press, 1990.

Waterman, Bryan. *Republic of the Intellect: The Friendly Club of New York City and the Making of American Literature*. Baltimore: Johns Hopkins University Press, 2007.

Watt, Ian. *The Rise of the Novel: Studies in Defoe, Richardson, and Fielding*. London: Chatto & Windus, 1957.

Watts, Steven. *The Romance of Real Life: Charles Brockden Brown and the Origins of American Culture*. Baltimore: Johns Hopkins University Press, 1994.

Weber, Max. *The Protestant Ethic and the Spirit of Capitalism*. Trans. Talcott Parsons. New York: Routledge, 1992.

Wegner, Signe O. *James Fenimore Cooper versus the Cult of Domesticity: Progressive Themes of Femininity and Family in the Novels.* Jefferson, NC: McFarland, 2005.

Weinstein, Cindy. *The Literature of Labor and the Labors of Literature: Allegory in Nineteenth-Century American Fiction.* New York: Cambridge University Press, 1994.

Welter, Barbara. "The Cult of True Womanhood: 1820–1860." *American Quarterly* 18.2 (1966): 151–74.

Weyler, Karen. *Intricate Relations: Sexual and Economic Desire in American Fiction, 1789–1814.* Iowa City: University of Iowa Press, 2004.

White, Ed. "Carwin the Peasant Rebel." In *Revising Charles Brockden Brown,* ed. Philip Barnard, Mark Kamrath, and Stephen Shapiro. Knoxville: University of Tennessee Press, 2004.

———. Introduction to *Modern Chivalry,* by Hugh Henry Brackenridge. Ed. White. Indianapolis: Hackett, 2009.

White, Hayden. *The Content of the Form: Narrative Discourse and Historical Representation.* Baltimore: Johns Hopkins University Press, 1987.

Whitman, Walt. "American Workingmen, Versus Slavery." In *A House Divided: The Antebellum Slavery Debates in America, 1776–1865,* ed. Mason I. Lowance Jr. Princeton: Princeton UP, 2003.

Wilentz, Sean. "Against Exceptionalism: Class Consciousness and the American Labor Movement, 1790–1920." *International Labor and Working-Class History* 26 (1984): 1–24.

———. *Chants Democratic: New York City and the Rise of the American Working Class, 1788–1850.* Twentieth Anniversary Ed. New York: Oxford University Press, 2004.

Williams, Raymond. *Marxism and Literature.* New York: Oxford University Press, 1977.

Winthrop, John. "A Model of Christian Charity." In *The American Puritans: Their Prose and Poetry,* ed. Perry Miller. New York: Anchor Doubleday, 1956.

Woloch, Alex. *The One vs. the Many: Minor Characters and the Space of the Protagonist in the Novel.* Princeton: Princeton University Press, 2003.

Wood, Ellen Meiksins. *The Pristine Culture of Capitalism: A Historical Essay on Old Regimes and Modern States.* New York: Verso, 1991.

Wood, Gordon. *Empire of Liberty: A History of the Early Republic, 1789–1815.* New York: Oxford University Press, 2009.

———. "Interests and Disinterestedness in the Making of the Constitution." In *Beyond Confederation: Origins of the Constitution and American National Identity,* ed. Richard Beeman, Stephen Botein, and Edward C. Carter II. Chapel Hill: University of North Carolina Press, 1987.

———. *The Radicalism of the American Revolution.* New York: Vintage Books, 1993.

Wood, Sarah. *Quixotic Fictions of the U.S.A., 1792–1815.* New York: Oxford University Press, 2005.

Wright, Frances. "The People at War." In *A Documentary History of American Industrial Society,* ed. John R. Commons et al. Vol. 5. Cleveland: Arthur H. Clark Co., 1910.

Zinn, Howard. *A People's History of the United States.* New York: Harper Perennial, 2010.

INDEX